IMAGES
of America

AFRICAN AMERICANS OF NEW ORLEANS

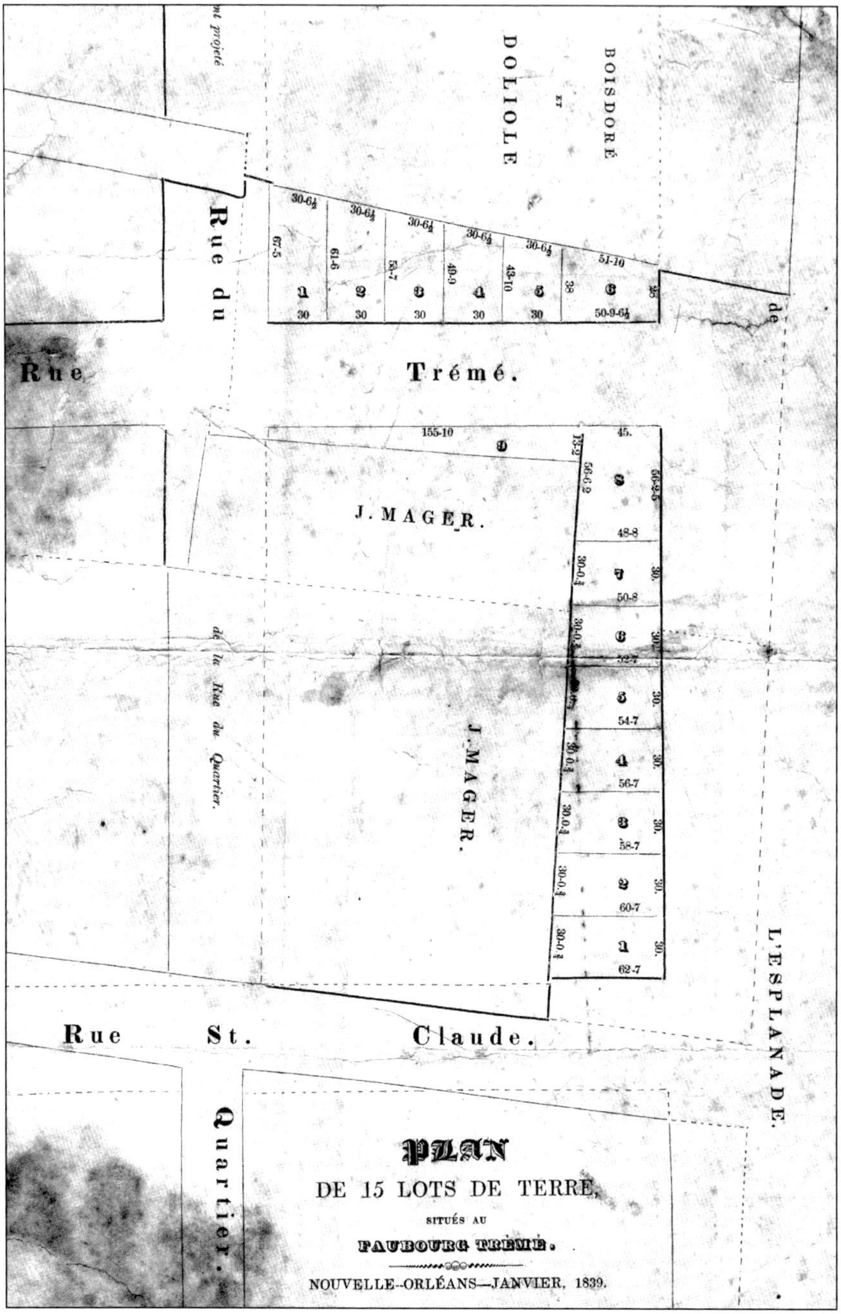

FAUBOURG TREME. Faubourg Treme is considered one of the oldest neighborhoods in New Orleans, as well as one of the oldest continuously occupied African American neighborhoods in the United States. (Courtesy of the Louisiana State Museum.)

ON THE COVER: This image taken by photographer A. P. Bedou shows students at St. Mary's Academy posing in costumes after a dramatic performance. Extracurricular activities such as theater and sports were an integral part of life at St. Mary's Academy. (Courtesy of the Sisters of the Holy Family.)

IMAGES
of America

AFRICAN AMERICANS OF NEW ORLEANS

Turry Flucker and Phoenix Savage

ARCADIA
PUBLISHING

ISBN 978-0-7385-6645-0

Published by Arcadia Publishing
Charleston, South Carolina

Printed in the United States of America

Library of Congress Control Number: 2009929827

For all general information contact Arcadia Publishing at:
Telephone 843-853-2070
Fax 843-853-0044
E-mail sales@arcadiapublishing.com
For customer service and orders:
Toll-Free 1-888-313-2665

Visit us on the Internet at www.arcadiapublishing.com

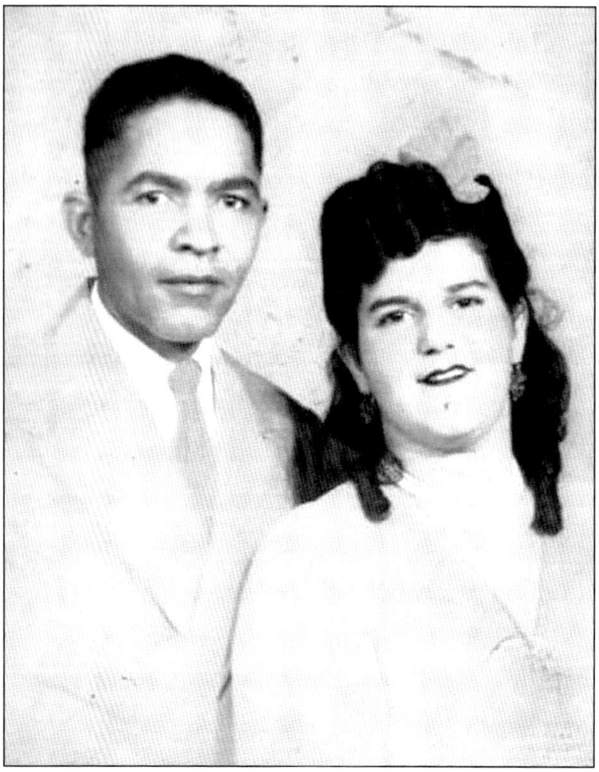

Louis Jude and Aurelia Walker De Pland. This project is dedicated to Aurelia Walker De Pland, who inspired my love for New Orleans. She taught me to have a life filled with family, food, and friends—the New Orleans way. Love, Turry. (Courtesy of S. J. De Pland.)

Contents

ACKNOWLEDGMENTS

This book would not have been possible without the love and support of Austin J. Sonnier. We thank you for your delicious Louisiana Creole specialties, which fed our bodies and our souls.

We also wish to thank the following family and friends for their constant encouragement and good will: Kirby and Yolanda Flucker, Austin M. and Nellie Sonnier, the Savage family, S. J. De Pland, Rhonda Richmond, Oyekundle Oyegbemi, Sister Goddess Circle, Gail D. Hughes, Leah Lewis, Carolyn Bercier, Sarah Dave, Christopher Vignaud, and Michelle Hudson.

A project like this requires the assistance of archivists, historians, and museum professionals. We would like to thank each of them for their assistance during this process: Greg Lambousy (director of collections, Louisiana State Museum); Jeanne Biddiscombe (registrar, Louisiana State Museum); Elizabeth Sherwood (assistant registrar/image requests, Louisiana State Museum); Wayne Phillips (curator of textiles and costumes, Louisiana State Museum); Irene Wainwright (archivist, New Orleans Public Library); Charlene Bonnette (archivist, State Library of Louisiana); Mamie Sterkz Gasperecz (executive director, Hermann-Grima/Gallier Historic Houses); Christopher Harter (director of the library, Amistad Research Center at Tulane University); Lee Hampton (executive director, Amistad Research Center at Tulane University); Michael Campbell (archivist/cataloger, Dillard University Library and Archives); Karen Watkins (executive assistant to the president, Xavier University of Louisiana); and Andrea Jackson (interim archivist, Robert Woodruff Library at Atlanta University).

We would like to give a special thanks to the following individuals who provided us with images from their family archives: Austin M. Sonnier Jr.; Barbara Trevigne; Justice Bernette Joshua Johnson; Keith Weldon Medley; A. P. Tureaud Jr.; Okyeame Haley, J.D.; Lolis Eric Elie; Sybil Haydel Morial; Ron Bechet; Sheleen Jones-Adenle; and Dr. Laura V. Rouzan. The following institutions provided us with invaluable information: the Historic New Orleans Collection, the Special Collections and Archives at the University of New Orleans, Wisconsin Historical Society, Howard University, and the University of Delaware. A very special thanks to the Sisters of the Holy Family and Sr. Carol Leslie.

INTRODUCTION

Intent on controlling the mouth of the Mississippi, France began its rule over the Mississippi Valley in 1699. France would eventually make New Orleans the territory's seat of authority by 1717, and it remained so until 1849, when the state capital changed to Baton Rouge under American rule. With two treaties, Roman Catholic France and Spain played political ping-pong with the Louisiana Territory in their attempt to prevent British (and later American) Protestant rule over lands formerly held by their crowns. France ceded the territory to Spain with the Treaty of Paris in 1763, and Spain governed the Louisiana Territory until 1800, when it signed the Treaty of San Ildelfonso, returning the land to France.

Three years later, under financial duress (due in great part to Napoleon's defeat in present-day Haiti), France sold its entire land interest in North America to the U.S. Government for approximately $15 million. Pres. Thomas Jefferson had originally been interested in buying only "the island of New Orleans" but could not resist the opportunity: the 1803 Louisiana Purchase doubled the landmass of the United States.

The years between 1719 and 1739 saw the largest influx of Africans from the Senegambia region of Africa into the Louisiana colony. As noted by scholars Midlo Hall and Raphael Cassimere, the city's lexicon contained words and phrases from such West African languages as Bambara, Fulbe, and Wolof.

During Spain's 37-year rule, the population of Louisiana grew exponentially, including a large influx of both enslaved and free people of color, as well as French immigrants from the Caribbean and Canada. By 1803, of New Orleans's 8,050 residents, 1,335 were free blacks and 2,775 were enslaved—a marked contrast to 1769 when the white population of New Orleans was just 1,803, with 99 free blacks, and an enslaved population of 1,227.

According to Midlo Hall, Latin-European religious ethics, an unbalanced sex ratio, and a shortage of skilled laborers laid the foundation for the road to freedom. By the 1720s, the French colonial government began systematically apprenticing enslaved males to experienced tradesmen. During its rule of the territory, Spain continued this practice, creating occupational and personal relationships between blacks and whites in urban areas. In addition, many freedmen gained manumission through military service.

Not every person in Louisiana of African descent was or had ever been enslaved. Nonetheless, because slavery was the most common condition of African Americans in early Louisiana, it is worthwhile to look at the processes a person could use to move from enslavement to freedom. This process was unique to those areas governed by France and Spain. Midlo Hall suggests that when a person held in bondage went free in colonial Louisiana, it was likely due to at least one of three factors: the Roman Catholicism of the white population, the high ratio of men to women, or the occupational development of enslaved men.

Being both a good Catholic and the owner of other human beings was not seen as a contradiction in early New Orleans. Roman Catholic slave owners, however, generally differed from their

Protestant counterparts in their approach to slavery. Catholicism in colonial Louisiana was generally inclusionary.

African women were the first to benefit from Catholicism's inclusive nature. The church's official stance held that sexual relations were only permissible within the context of a Catholic marriage, but there were simply not enough European and European-American women to go around. Thus many white men sought out and maintained intimate relations with African women, most of them enslaved and therefore relatively powerless to reject their advances. Some of these women, no doubt, saw these relations as personally advantageous, in many cases helping them economically and increasing their chances of being set free. The result of this racial confluence came to be known as *plaçage*.

The plaçage system that developed over the centuries provided a form of legitimacy to interracial relationships that resulted in offspring, treating these unions very much in the same manner as if they were legal marriages. There was no formal legal standing for the plaçage system, but the system nonetheless continued and created an entire society of persons known as *gens de couleur libre*—free people of color. Importantly, the children of such relationships followed the status of the mother, meaning that those born of a freed woman were in turn born free. Successive generations of racially mixed children (eventually known as Creoles of Color) became a distinctive class in New Orleans and other parts of the original Louisiana territory, forming a middle ground between European Creoles—Louisiana-born people with Spanish or French ancestry—and those Africans and African Americans who were still in bondage and legally defined as human property.

As Midlo Hall has noted, within the colony existed a shortage of the skilled laborers needed to accomplish the economic goals of the Spanish and French. The answer to this dilemma came in the form of trade apprenticeships. Enslaved African and African American men (as well as indentured Europeans) were paired with skilled European blacksmiths, tanners, and other craftsmen to learn a trade. The success of this system not only led to increased revenue for slave-owners, who often rented their workers to other businessmen and allowed these skilled slaves to keep a portion of the wages they earned while "hired out." This in turn allowed enslaved men to save and apply their wages towards their freedom, and afterwards, to their family's manumission. While the number of these free Negroes (the term applied prior to the Civil War) was proportionally small, they did constitute a distinct subgroup within New Orleans's non-white population.

A salient difference between free Negroes and Creoles of Color had to do with parentage. A free Negro did not enjoy the benefit of the plaçage system. Children of the plaçage system were often socially cared for by their mother and their mother's family and economically cared for by their father and his. Many received the benefit of overseas education, inherited large sums of money and land, received a monthly stipend, or were made partners in their fathers' businesses. Most importantly, these children received the benefit of belonging to an elaborate social network. Prior to the Civil War, free Negroes in the South rarely enjoyed the important cultural and social interconnectedness common among Creoles of Color.

Originally, the term *Creole* simply implied that a person was born in the territory of Louisiana. However, in the ensuing years, the children of plaçage arrangements began adopting the term with the caveat "of color" to denote themselves from European Creoles. In fact, under the original definition of the word Creole, a person born into slavery within the Louisiana territory would also be a Creole. In Louisiana today, the term has come to refer to persons of mixed ancestry of French, African, Spanish, Native American, Chinese, and other ethnic backgrounds. Hence the terms *Creole* and *Creole of Color* are still in use today and should be viewed as a cultural and not a racial identification. Throughout this book, the term *African American* is employed, and though some may claim that it does not accurately describe Creoles of Color, it is the intent of the authors to be mindful of this understanding while furthering a unification of identity between all persons of African descent, our ancestral African mothers. The authors recognize that within the American experience there are unique and defining characteristics that have their place within the individual cultural makeup of both African Americans and Creoles of Color, however, we feel that the concept of *E Pluribus Unum* aptly applies in this situation.

The demographics of New Orleans free persons of African descent increased with the influx of Haitians escaping their war-torn nation and eventually with the emancipation of the enslaved. These demographic increases led to political and economic shifts as well as cultural alliances in unexpected ways. For example, the neighborhood today known as Faubourg Maringy developed as an enclave of free black property owners, when the former owner of the lands, Bernard Xavier Philippe de Maringy de Mandeville, selectively sold only to French-speaking persons in the early 1800s. This meant that in many cases, French-speaking free women of color and their offspring were in a position to take advantage of this opportunity, as were free Negroes who spoke French, and the incoming French-speaking Haitians.

New Orleans has traditionally been a city with a strong African American population that has contributed to the infrastructures of the city. There was no building in pre-Katrina New Orleans that did not contain within its bricks and mortar the DNA of a person of African descent. African Americans of New Orleans have over the years blended their unique style, cuisine, and music into the fabric of America. While the population density of African Americans has declined in the aftermath of Hurricane Katrina, the city remains decidedly a blend of historical cultures to which the contributions of African Americans is indelible. While this book illuminates many of these contributions, it in no manner can account for all of them: from the drumbeat of Noble Jordan to the lost lives of the Louisiana Native Guard, from the works of Marie Couvent to Fannie Williams and on to the unnamed free and enslaved women of African descent who brought forth the men and women who so proudly call New Orleans home. To these, these pages respectfully pay tribute. *Adupe.*

One

Twenty Dollars Worth of Work

Pay Me 10 Dollars and I'll give you 20 Dollars of Work.

—Allison "Tootie" Montana (1922–2005)

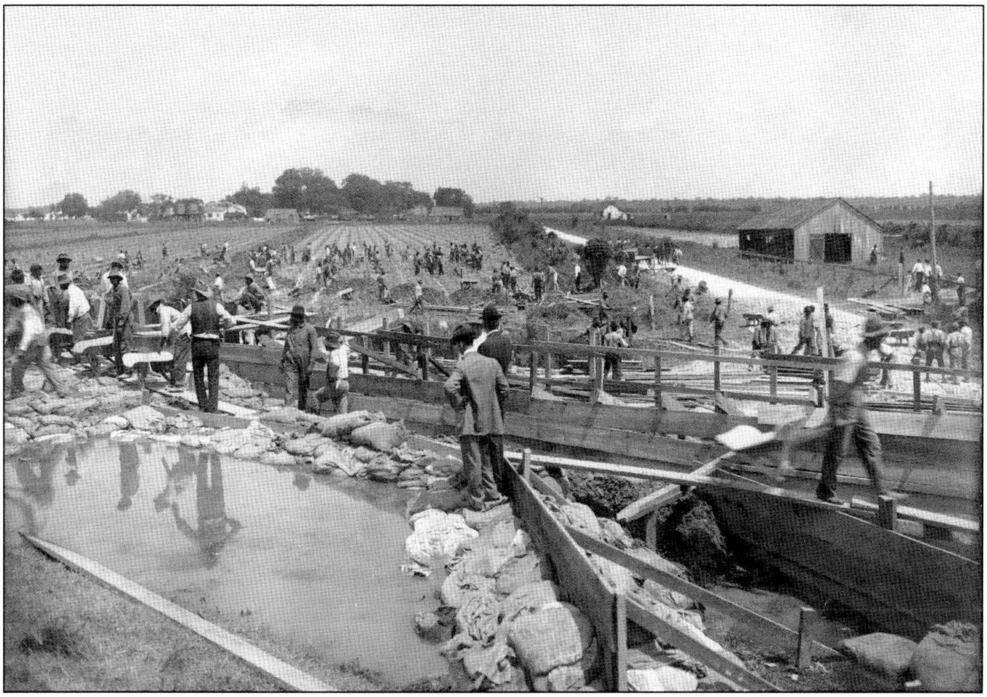

Poydras Plantation. Unidentified laborers work the Poydras plantation, located just outside of New Orleans. This image depicts the vain attempts to control the breach of the crevasses located adjacent to the plantation. In 1882, there were 284 crevasses in Louisiana; by 1922, there were only three, with one of the three at Poydras. The innovation of levees caused the demise of the use of crevasses as an effective means of flood control. The first levee in New Orleans was 3 feet high and 5,400 feet long when it was built in 1727. Two hundred years later, during the flood of 1927, the citizens of New Orleans cried out, "Cut the levee at Poydras." The men laboring in this image are representative of the task of filling over 640,000 sacks of sand to shore up the levees. (Courtesy of the Louisiana State Museum.)

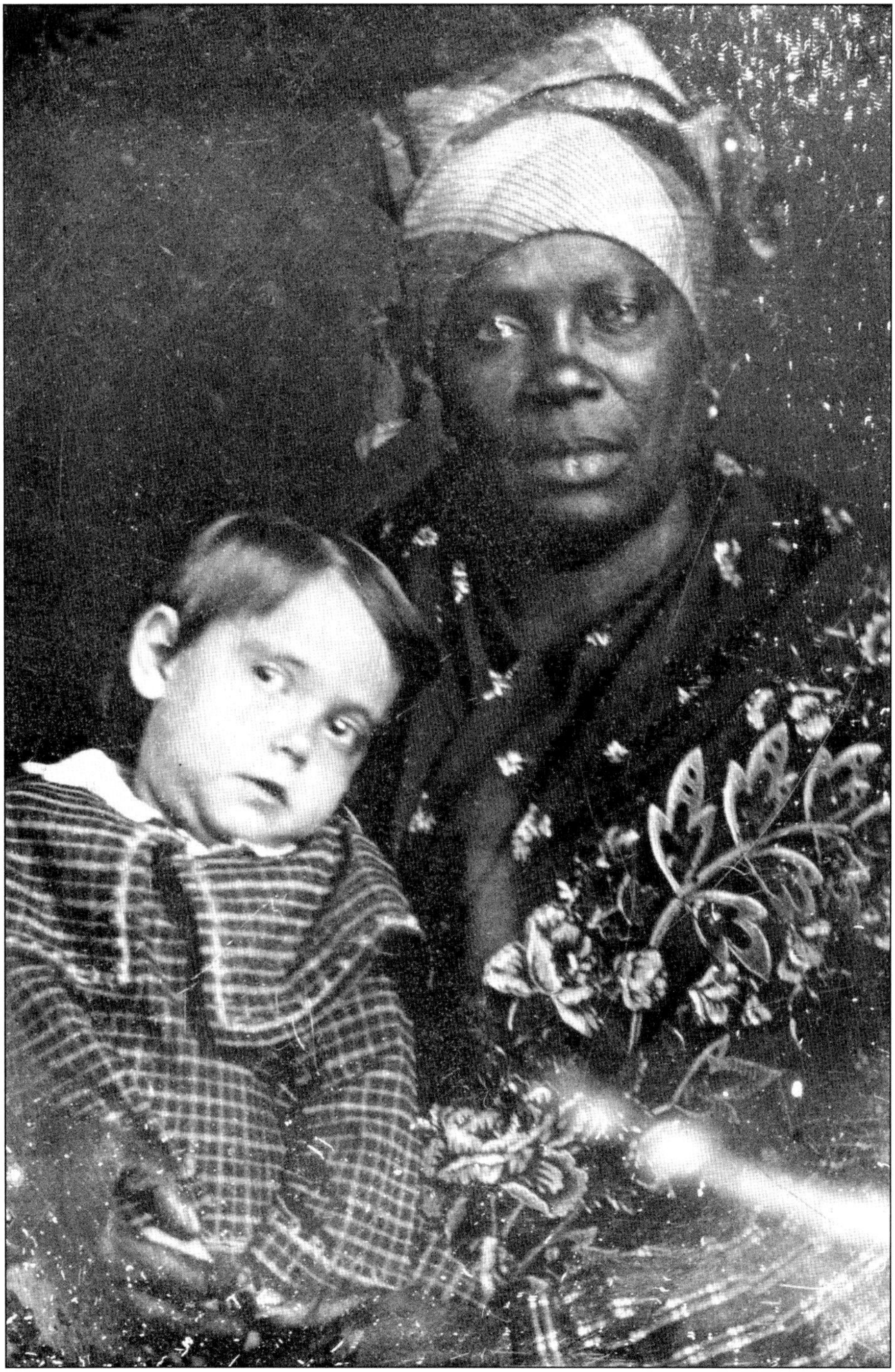

Caregiver for All. This *c.* 1850 Daguerreotype image depicts a common scene of 19th-century New Orleans. An African American woman is posed with her beloved charge, typically a young white child. Such images were generally not the idea of the domestic herself, but were intended to memorialize the affection between the servant and those she served. (Courtesy of the Louisiana State Museum.)

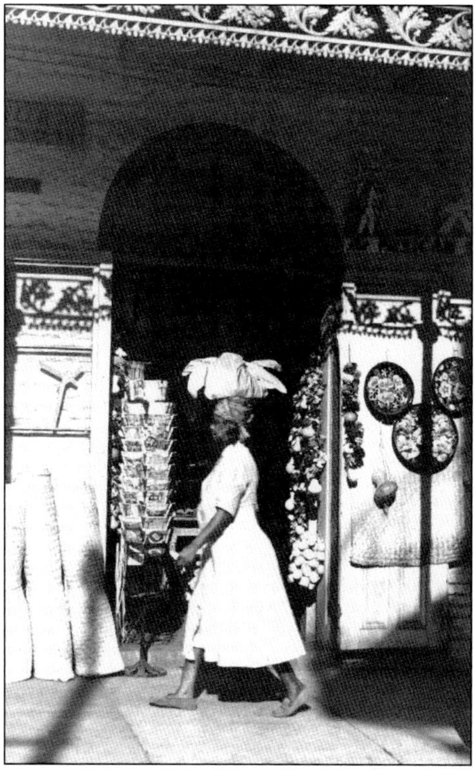

Strolling with Laundry. In this image, an unidentified woman balances a bundle of laundry on her head as she strolls past a shop in the French Quarter that sells goods from Mexico. "Taking in" other people's laundry was a specialty among domestic employments. (Courtesy of the Louisiana State Museum.)

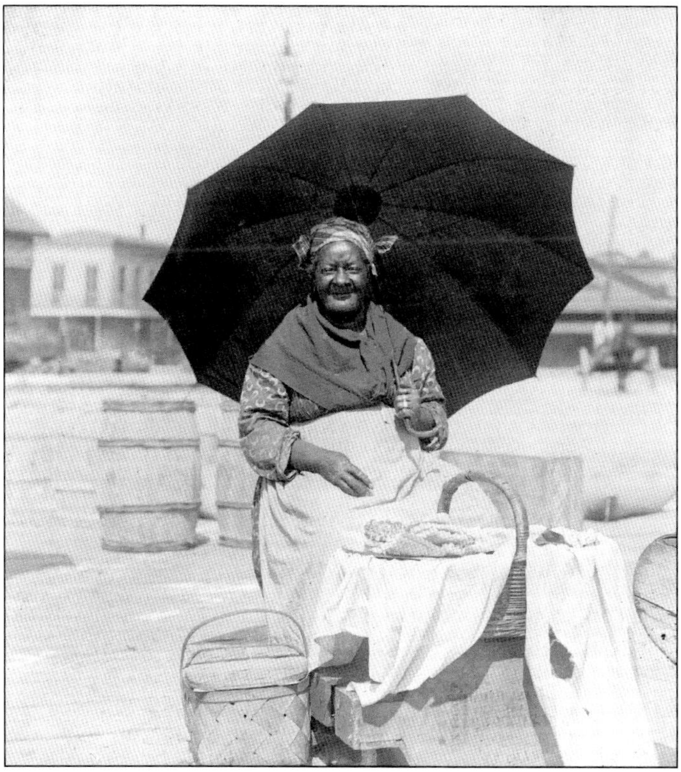

Praline Seller. During the late 19th to early 20th centuries, street vendors hawked their wares to pedestrian passersby. This image depicts a common scene in New Orleans: off Decatur Street near the French Market, a praline seller with a parasol offers homemade pralines from her wicker baskets. Traditionally pralines were made of brown sugar, granulated sugar, cream, butter, and pecans, but no matter how basic the recipe, no two praline sellers' delicacies were alike. (Courtesy of the Louisiana State Museum.)

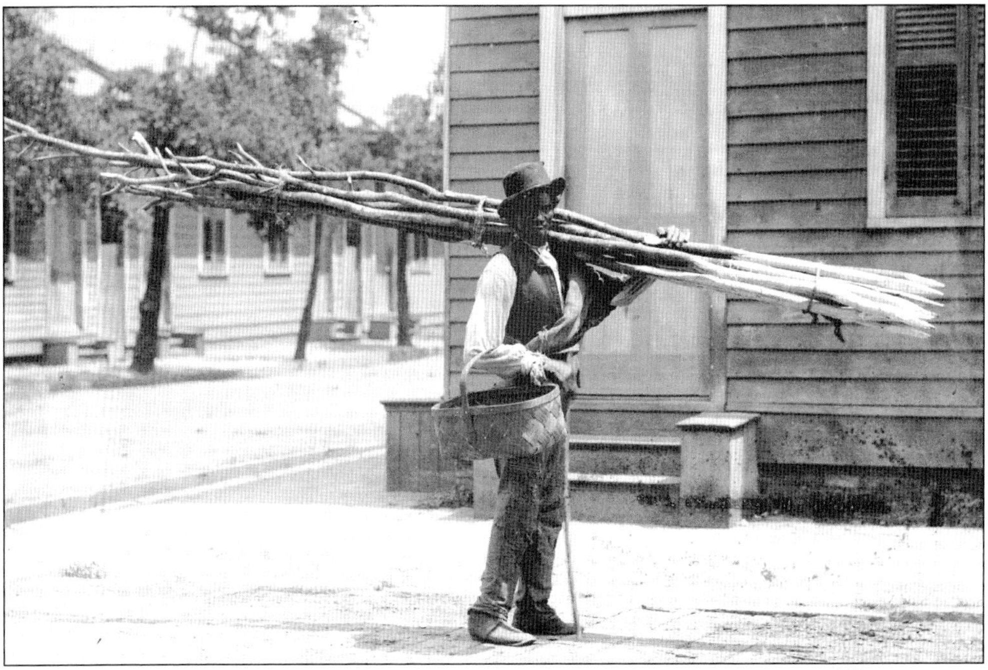

Peddler. Urban New Orleans supported cottage industries as well as common peddlers. Here an unidentified man with a wicker basket on his arm and a bundle of poles hoisted upon his shoulder walks the streets of New Orleans selling his wares. (Courtesy of the Louisiana State Museum.)

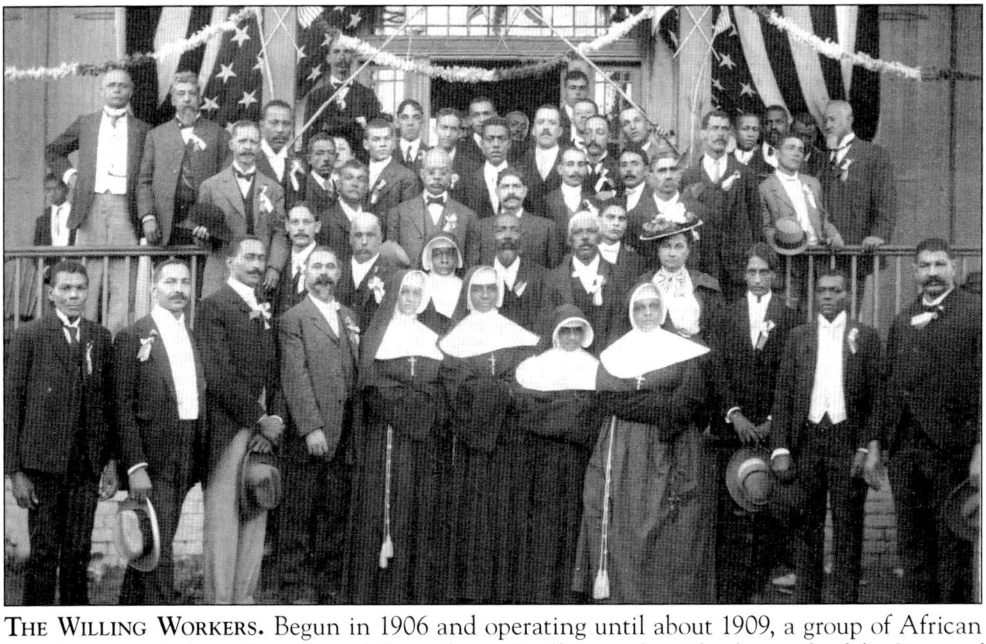

The Willing Workers. Begun in 1906 and operating until about 1909, a group of African American men informally organized themselves as "willing workers" for the needs of the Sisters of the Holy Family. It is very likely that these men had children who attended the schools operated by the sisters. It is also very likely that the men pictured here were some of the skilled craftsmen who constructed and performed many of the artistic works seen within the Catholic churches of New Orleans' African American communities. (Courtesy of the Sisters of the Holy Family.)

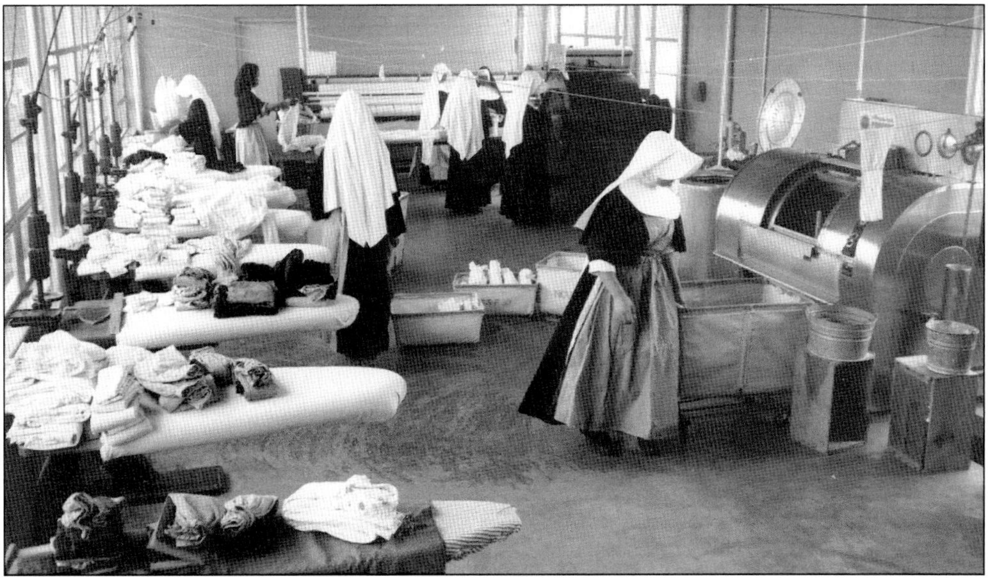

Laundry Day at the Motherhouse. This 1959 image taken by Don Rutledge depicts a typical laundry day at the Motherhouse for the Sister of the Holy Family. Note the industrial-size machinery and the organized manner in which the sisters ironed clothing. (Courtesy of the Sisters of the Holy Family.)

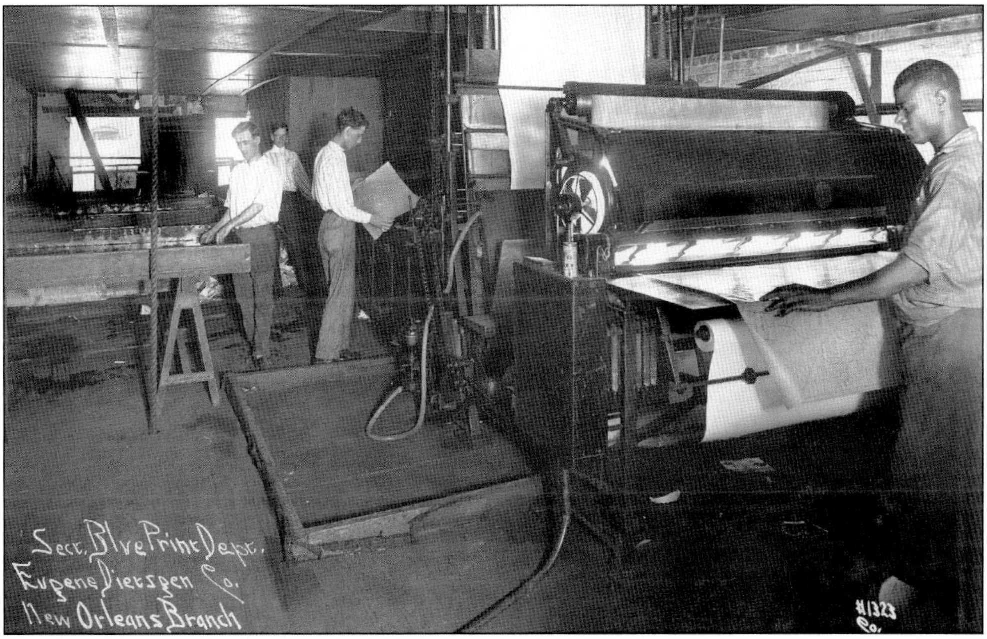

Blue Printing. Unidentified men work in the New Orleans branch of the Eugene Dietzgen Company's blueprinting department. Note that African Americans and whites are working side by side on the same tasks. Born in Germany, Eugene was the son of socialist philosopher Joseph Dietzgen. The parent Eugene Dietzgen Drafting Company, headquartered in Chicago, provided its workers with a healthy work environment that included fresh air and flowers. Judging by this 1930s image, the company's New Orleans branch offered an environment of equality. (Courtesy of the Louisiana State Museum.)

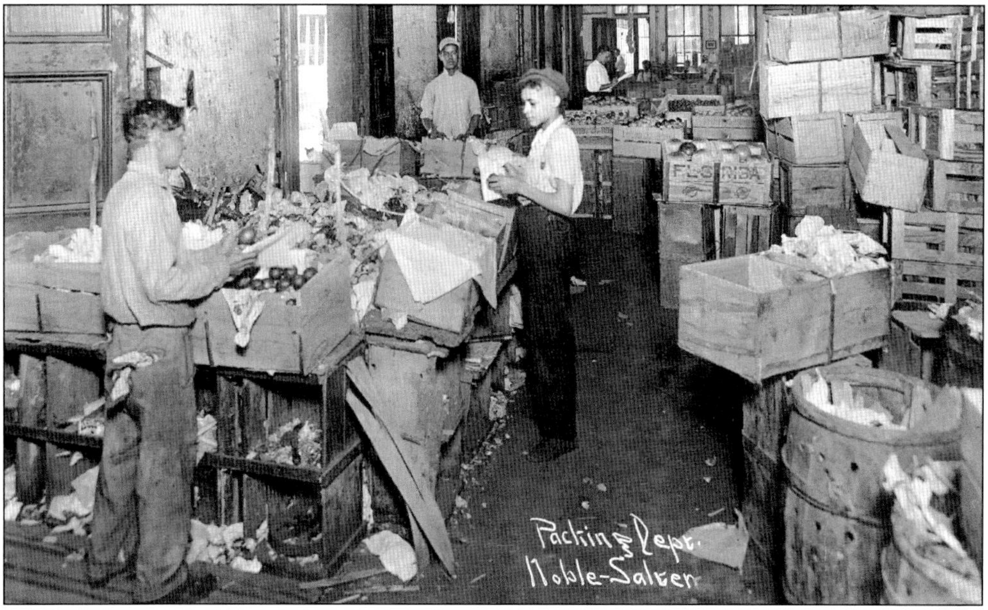

GLOBAL SUPPLIERS. The unidentified workers in this image are preparing fruits and vegetables for market inside the packing department of the Noble-Salter Commercial Merchant Company. The produce company originally had an address in the 100 block of Gravier Street on the uptown side of Canal Street in New Orleans. After 1893, however, many of the street addresses of New Orleans underwent dramatic changes. Though the business stayed in the same location, its street number changed to 300 Gravier Street. The company appears on the Industrial Roll of Honor as a U.S. company that provided goods or services to the building of the Panama Canal. (Courtesy of the Louisiana State Museum.)

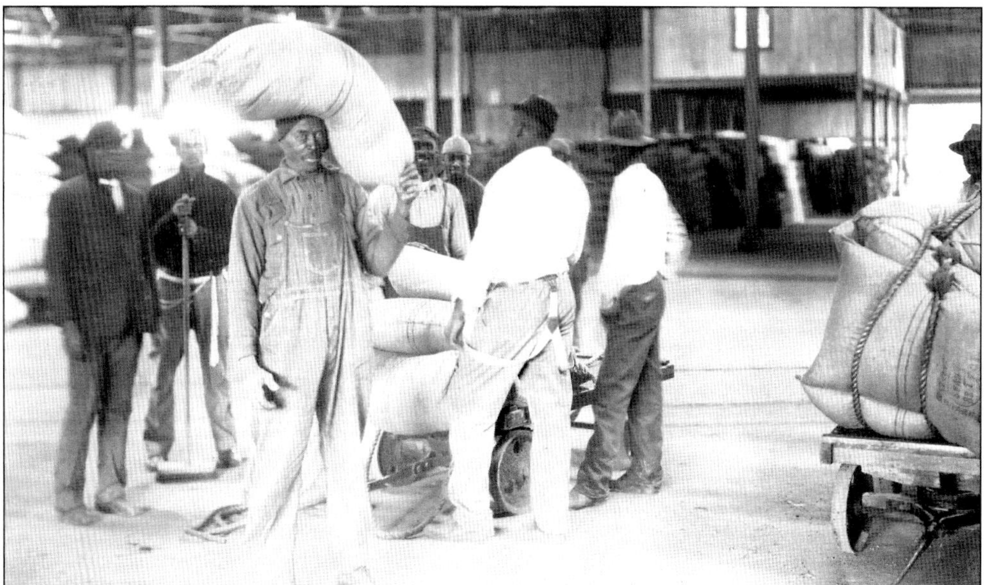

UNIDENTIFIED WORKERS. These workers at the New Orleans port, around 1900, have hoisted sacks of what could be rice—one of Louisiana's prime exports. Note the steel wheels of the flatbed pull carts. (Courtesy of the Louisiana State Museum.)

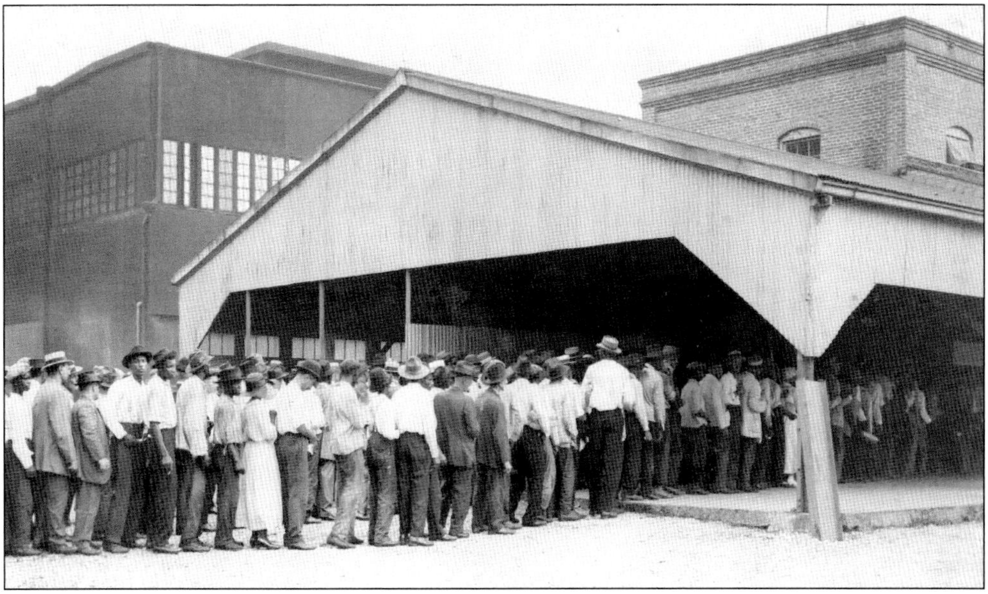

The Long Line. Depression-era men, women, and young boys wait in line for a chance to work a day labor job. (Courtesy of the Louisiana State Museum.)

Extraordinary Plasterer. Leroy Vignaud learned the art of plasterwork from his father. Vignaud is responsible for most of the plasterwork that adorns the interior and exterior of the mansions on St. Charles Avenue. Vignaud also worked on several Catholic churches and buildings in New Orleans, including the St. Louis Cathedral in the French Quarter, the Notre Dame Seminary on Carrolton Avenue, and the Castle on the Irish Bayou. Vignaud passed on the tradition of artisanship to his sons, and the family collectively created the intricate cornice work, plaster medallions, and crowns at the Seanger Theatre in New Orleans. Vignaud's sons are dedicated to continuing the family business: creating awe-inspiring art that continues to fascinate visitors to New Orleans. (Courtesy of Leroy and Christopher Vignaud.)

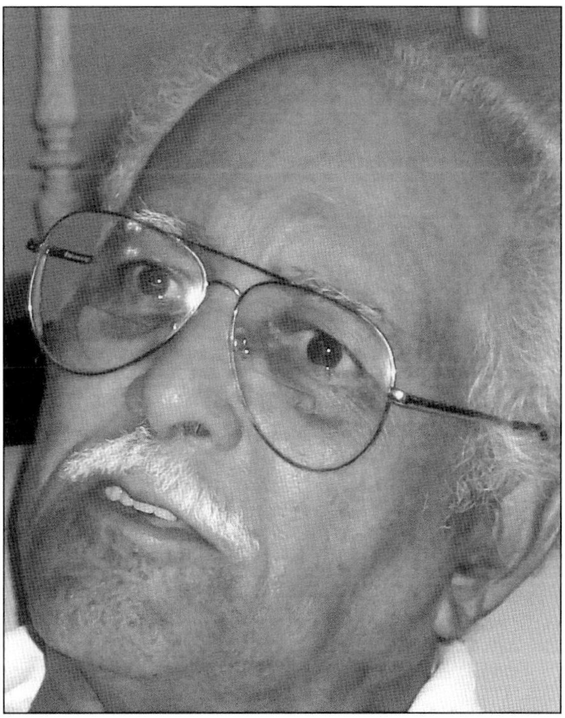

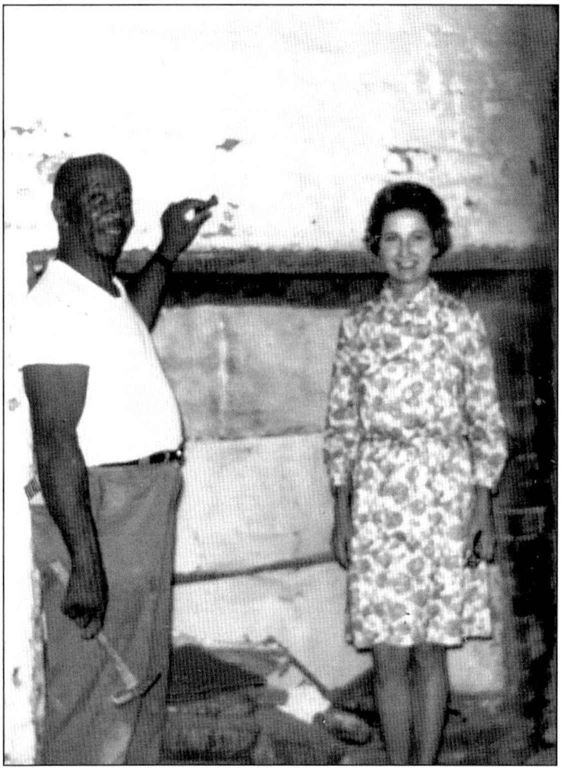

COOKING IN THE KITCHEN. The first organization chartered in New Orleans by and for women, the Christian Women's Exchange was established in 1881 and is still in operation. Originally founded to assist indigent white women, the mission of the Women's Exchange shifted to historic preservation and today owns the Hermann-Grima and Gallier Historic Houses located in the French Quarter. The hearth kitchen is pictured here with brick mason Pete Tucker, who performed much of the brickwork at the historic home, and Ethel Dameron Manard, board manager emeritis of the Women's Exchange. The hearth was restored in the early 1960s and remains the only operating 1830s hearth kitchen in New Orleans. (Courtesy of the Women's Exchange Archives and the Hermann-Grima/Gallier Historic Houses.)

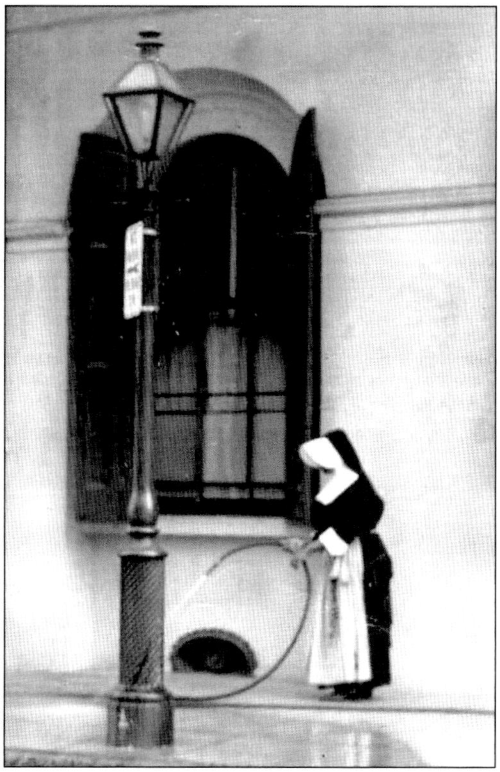

MORNING DUTY. Sr. M. Immaculate Conception, Provost of the Sisters of the Holy Family, washes the sidewalk in front of the 717 Orleans Street Motherhouse. No one was immune to the task, not even the nun seen here in this 1940s image. The early morning washing of sidewalks is still a daily occurrence in present-day New Orleans. (Courtesy of the Sisters of the Holy Family.)

Two

Hallelujah!

I believe in God. I hope in God. I love and I want to live and die for God.

—Mother Henrietta Delille (1813–1862)

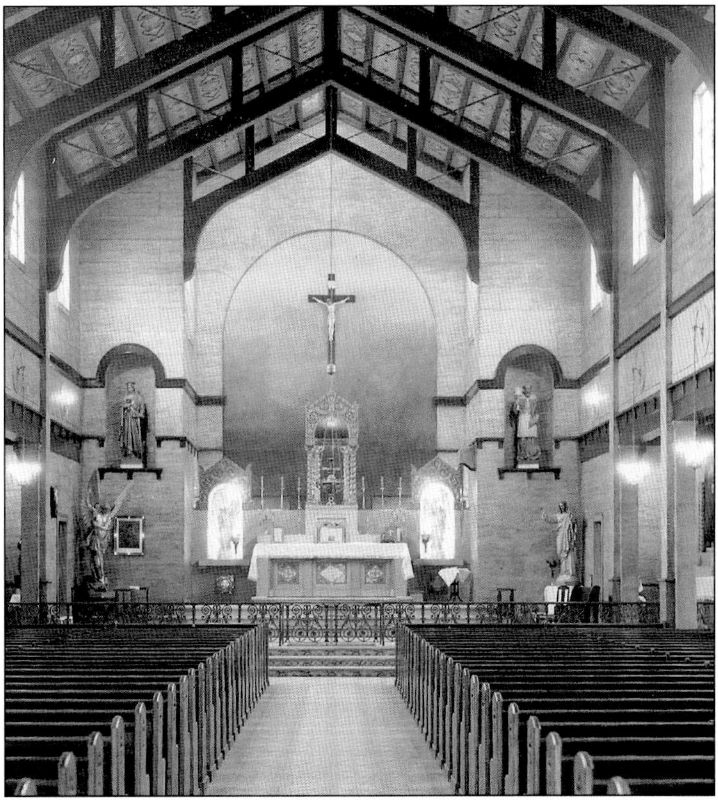

Corpus Christi. This photograph shows the interior of Corpus Christi Catholic Church located in the historical Creole of Color Seventh Ward. The detailed archways and wrought iron altar railings are examples of the highly praised artisanship found throughout historic structures in New Orleans. (Courtesy of the Society of St. Joseph of the Sacred Heart, Baltmore, Maryland.)

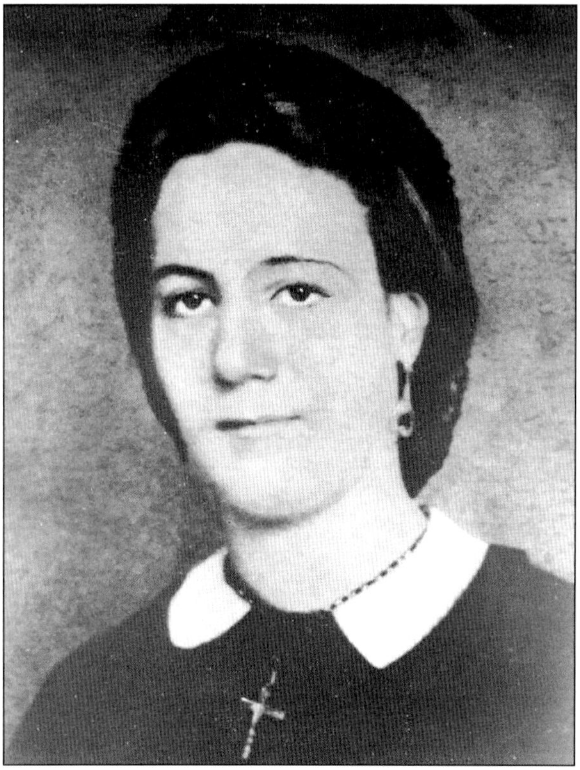

Mother Henriette Delille. A free woman of color born in New Orleans in 1812, Mother Delille cofounded and then served as the mother superior of the Sisters of the Holy Family from 1842 until her death in 1862. The Sisters of the Holy Family is America's second-oldest Catholic order for women of color and focused on the care of the elderly and religious instruction to the then-enslaved. Mother Delille is in line for canonization as a Roman Catholic saint. If she is canonized, she will be the first woman of African descent to be canonized by the church. (Courtesy of the Sisters of the Holy Family.)

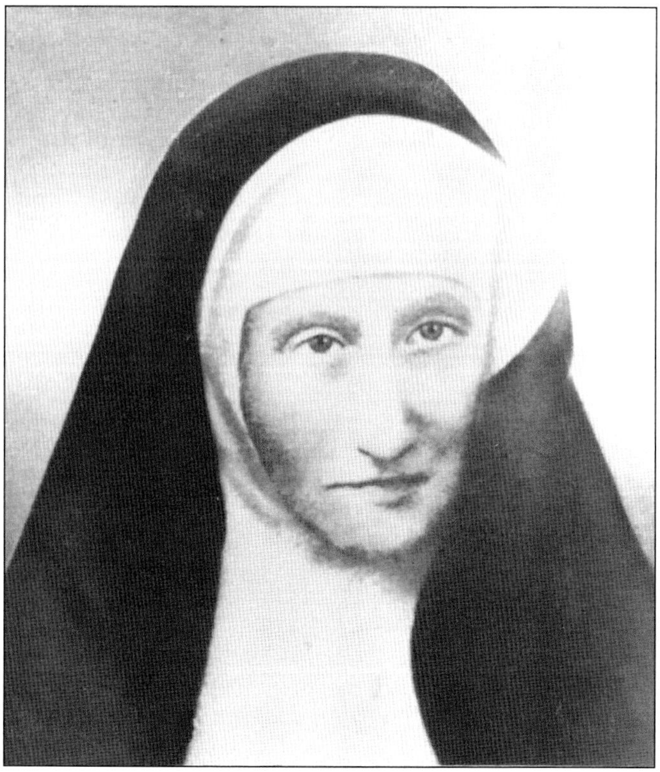

Mother Juliette Gaudin. Gaudin was cofounder of the order of the Sisters of the Holy family. Born in Cuba, Mother Gaudin became superior general of the order upon the death of Henriette Delille and served in this capacity from 1862 to 1867. (Courtesy of the Sisters of the Holy Family.)

Mother Mary Josephine Charles. The third cofounder of the Sisters of the Holy Family, Charles assumed the position of superior general upon the death of Juliette Gaudin, serving from 1867 to 1882. Sister Josephine designed the habit worn by the order in 1867; however, the order was not permitted to wear the habit until 1872, and it was not presented to the public until 1877, at St. Mary's Chapel on Chartres Street. (Courtesy of the Sisters of the Holy Family.)

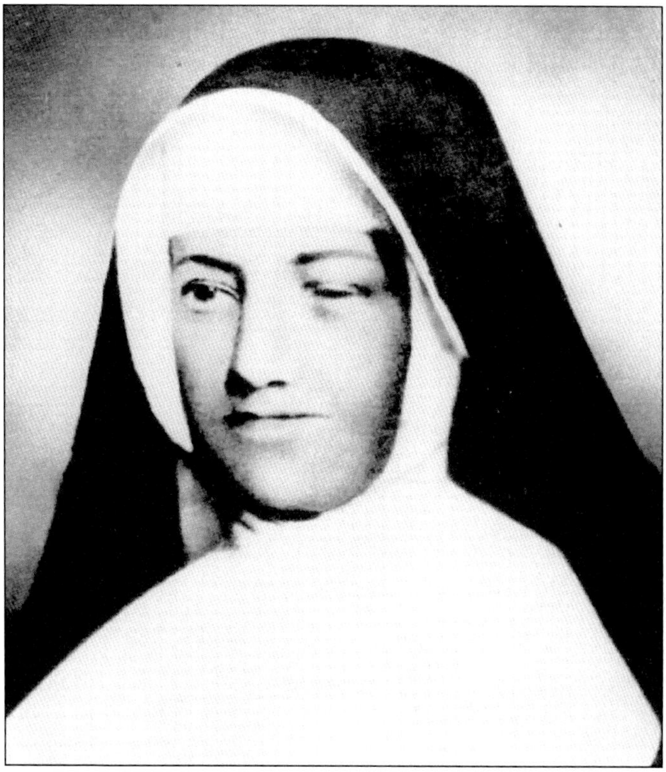

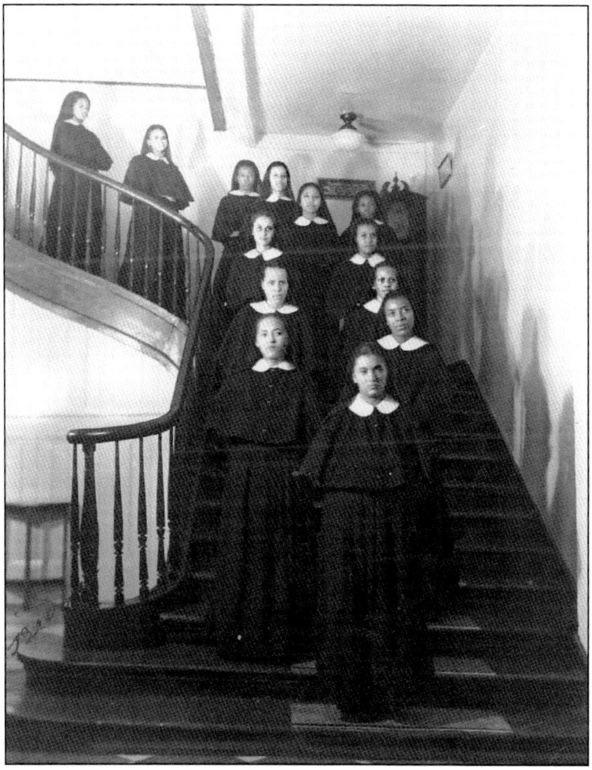

Postulants. A. P. Bedou photographed these postulates of the Sisters of the Holy Family around 1945. The sisters took occupation of 717 Orleans Street in October 1881. The property served as the Motherhouse (a training facility for novices), as well as a boarding school and day school. Before the sisters moved in, 717 Orleans Street had served as the Orleans Ballroom. (Courtesy of the Sisters of the Holy Family.)

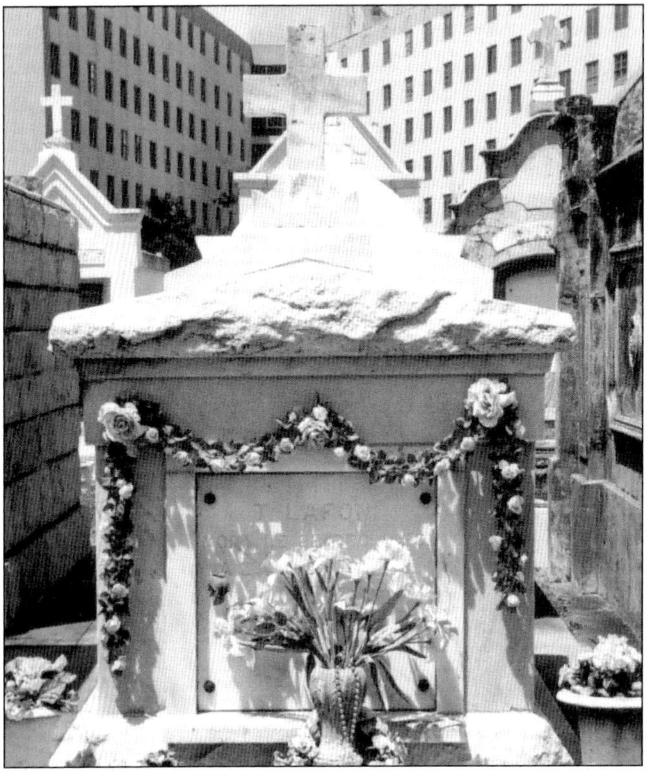

Thomy Lafon. Lafon was born in New Orleans in 1810 and became one of the city's greatest philanthropists. He was able to amass a sizable fortune as a merchant and real estate broker. During Lafon's lifetime, he established the Lafon Orphan Boys' Asylum and the Home for Aged Colored Men and Women. Upon his death in 1893, Lafon left $592,000 to numerous educational and charitable organizations, among them the Sisters of the Holy Family. Shown here is the tomb of Thomy Lafon in St. Louis Cemetery No. 3. Barbara Trevigne and Karen Livers are known as the "grave keepers." They are responsible for decorating Lafon's tomb for holidays and special occasions. (Courtesy of Phoenix Savage.)

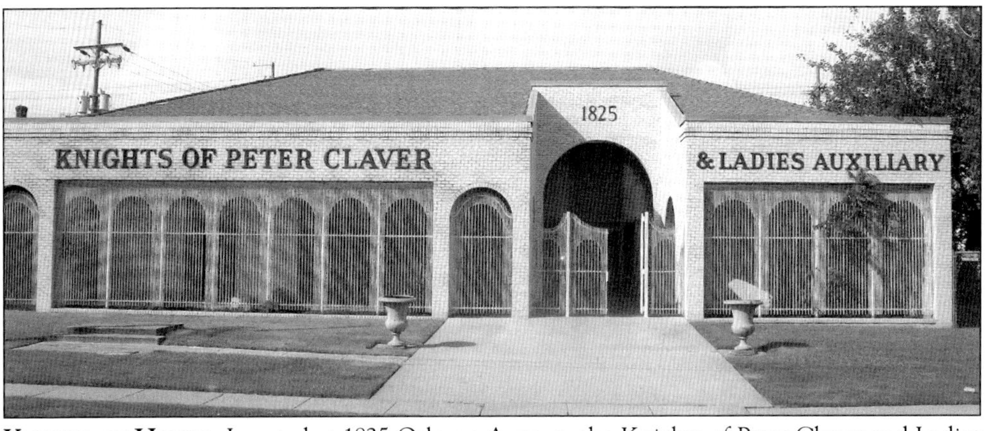

Knights of Honor. Located at 1825 Orleans Avenue, the Knights of Peter Claver and Ladies Auxiliary are the largest African American Lay Catholic organizations in the United States. The knights were established in Mobile, Alabama, in 1909, when seven priests of the St. Joseph's Society of the Sacred Heart (one of them an African American) and "forty colored men" formed the nucleus of the fraternal society, which they would call the Knights of Peter Claver. (Courtesy of Phoenix Savage.)

ANDRÉ AND NOEL TREVIGNE. This *c.* 1963 image shows the Trevigne children, André (left) and Noel, commemorating their First Holy Communion, received at Corpus Christi Church on St. Bernard Avenue. (Courtesy of Barbara Trevigne.)

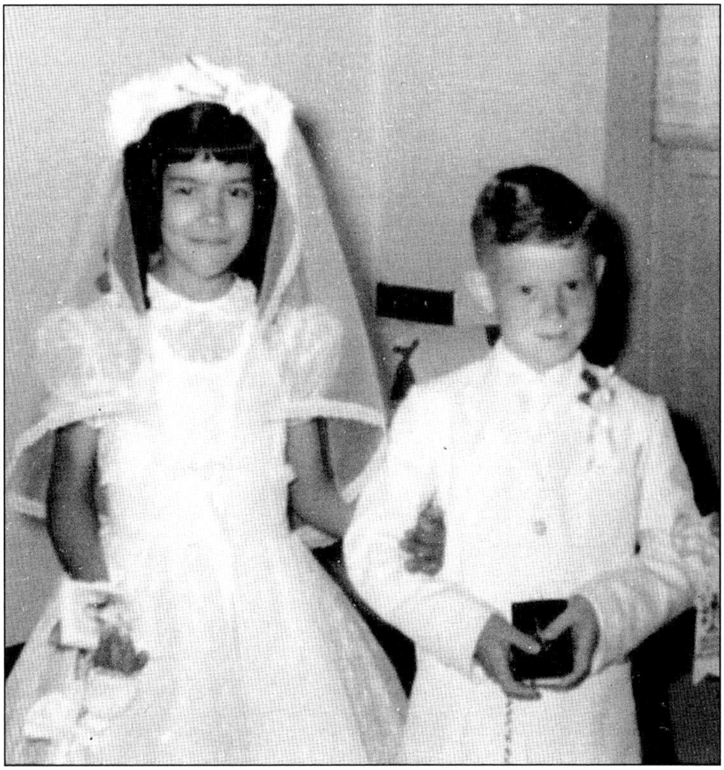

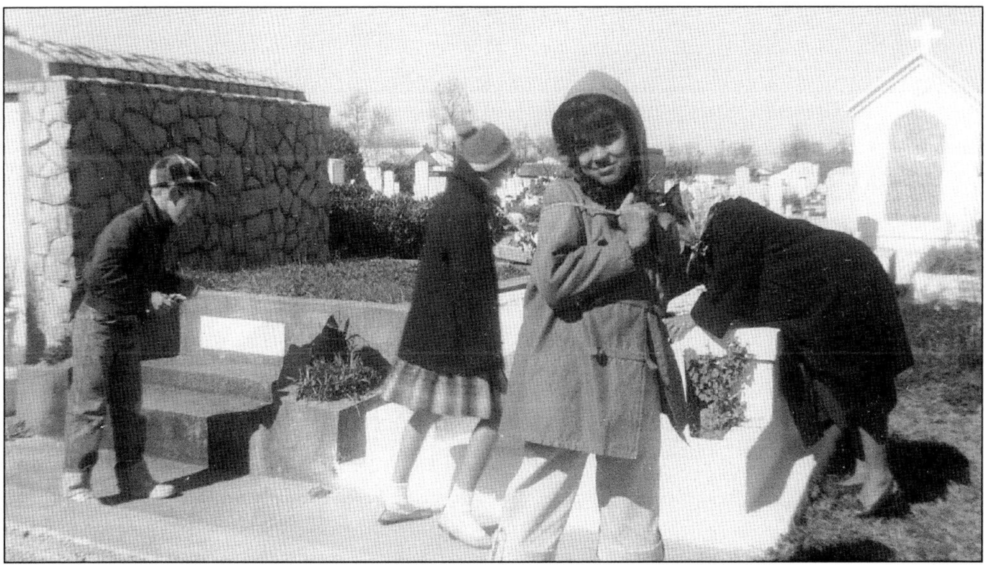

ALL SAINTS DAY. Sometimes called "The City of the Dead," New Orleans keeps its graves above ground due to flooding, creating beautiful cemeteries that dot the landscape with whitewashed tombs. Flowers are brought to the tombs of loved ones on All Saints Day. In this photograph, Barbara, André, and Emily Trevigne (along with their paternal grandmother) visit Mount Olivet Cemetery to clean the Trevigne tomb. (Courtesy of Barbara Trevigne.)

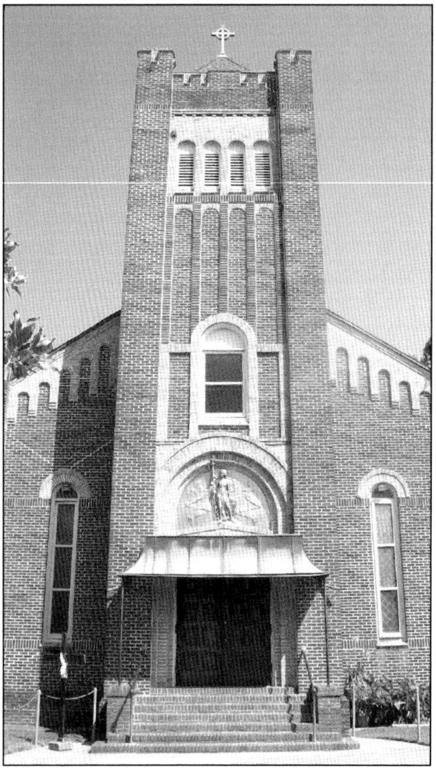

JOAN OF ARCH CATHOLIC CHURCH. Located at 8321 Burthe Street, this parish's current brick structure was built in 1923 when, after surviving a German torpedo attack while sailing to England, Father Wareing vowed that he would rebuild what the 1915 hurricane had destroyed. The German congregation of the Mater Dela Rosa Parish was originally on this site. In 1909, once Mater Dela Rosa relocated, Father Le Beau established the first Josephite parish in New Orleans. Under Le Beau, the Sisters of the Holy Family established the St. Louis School for African American children. The parish name was changed to St. Joan of Arc under Father Wareing, who succeeded Father Le Beau after Le Beau's death just prior to the 1915 storm. In that storm, while the entire church structure was destroyed, the school suffered only minor roof damage. The Sisters of the Holy Family continue to operate the St. Louis School today. (Courtesy of Phoenix Savage.)

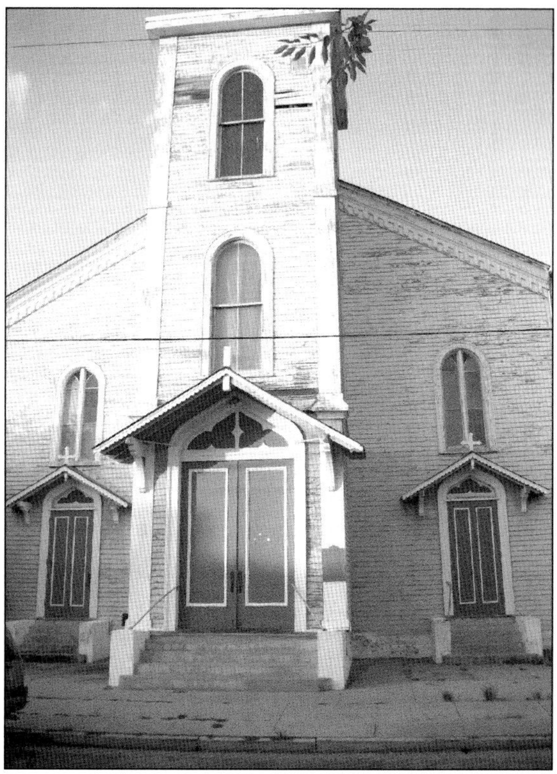

ST. FRANCIS DE SALES CHURCH. This Catholic church was founded on the principles of incorporating black culture into the traditional Catholic worship. The church stands today on the same site where it was established in 1870 under the leadership of Fr. Nicholas Simon, who served there for 40 years until his death in 1909. St. Francis De Sales Church, located uptown, continues to hold Mass regularly. (Courtesy of Phoenix Savage.)

ALTAR BOYS. These altar boys of Corpus Christi Church carry the crucifix and candles at the concluding procession of Sunday Mass. (Courtesy of the State Library of Louisiana.)

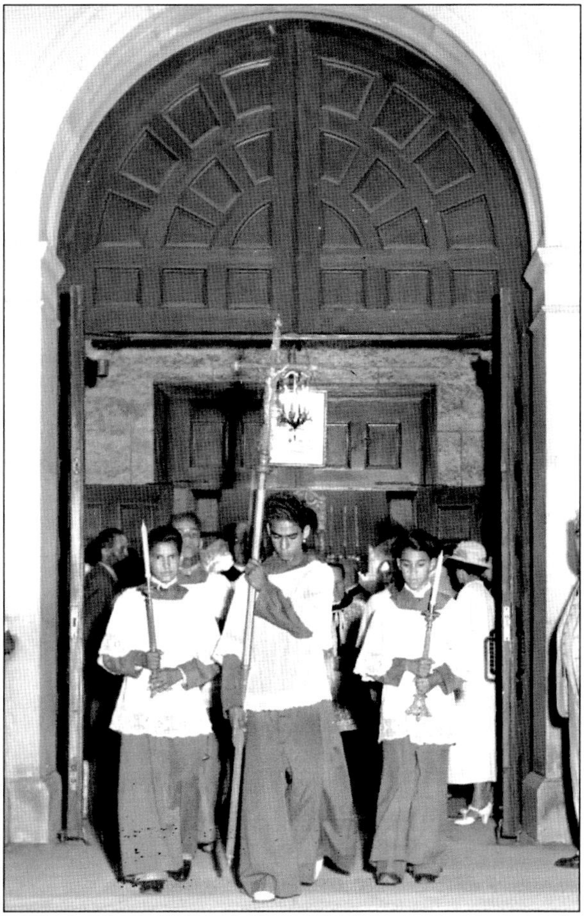

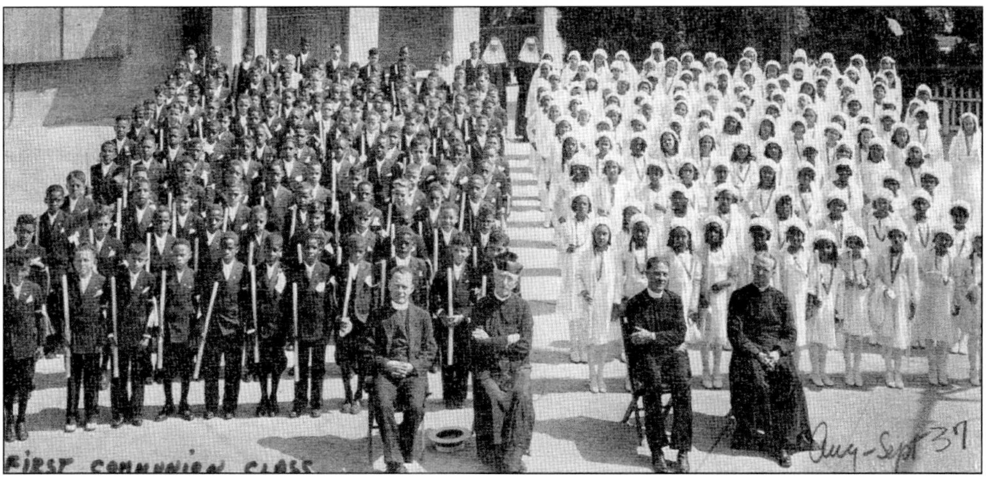

FIRST COMMUNION CLASS. Depicted in this c. 1937 image are the boys and girls of the First Communion class of Corpus Christi Church. The sacrament of the Eucharist is the central focus of every Roman Catholic Mass. This image is typical of the professional photographs taken to commemorate First Communions. (Courtesy of the Society of St. Joseph of the Sacred Heart, Baltimore, Maryland.)

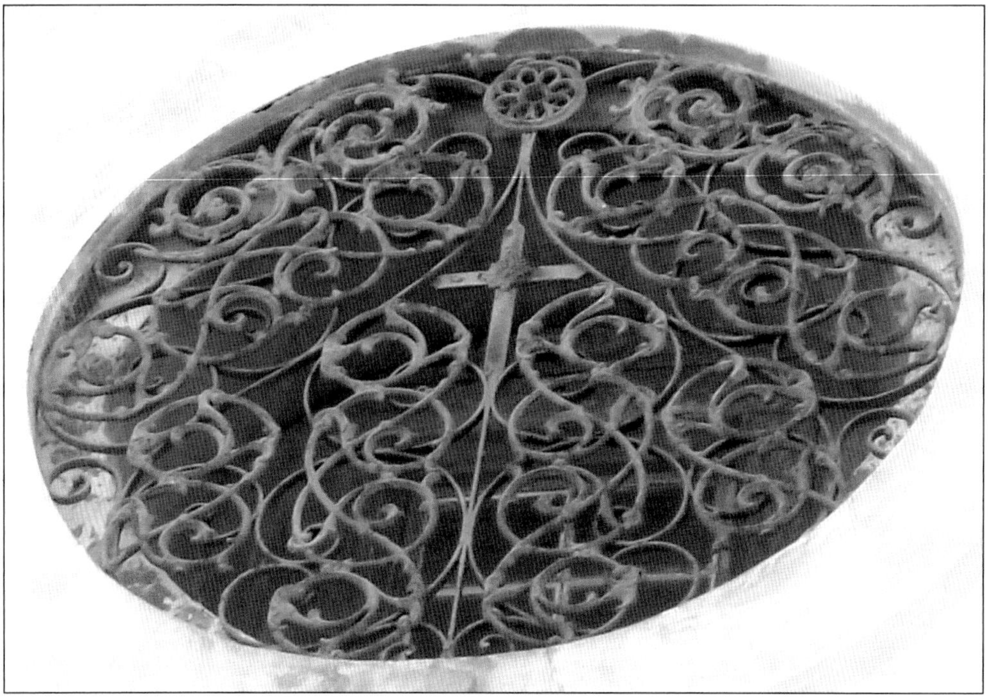

IRON CIRCLE OF ST. AUGUSTINE CHURCH. St. Augustine Church is located in the heart of Treme and was once the site of a brickyard operated under John Law's Company of the Indies. The ironwork depicted here is handcrafted by blacksmiths and is located in an upper circular cutout on the corner steeple of the church. The circular ironwork serves to represent the strength of Treme residents past and present, the history of the laborers, and the longevity of the community's faith in a higher power. (Courtesy of Phoenix Savage.)

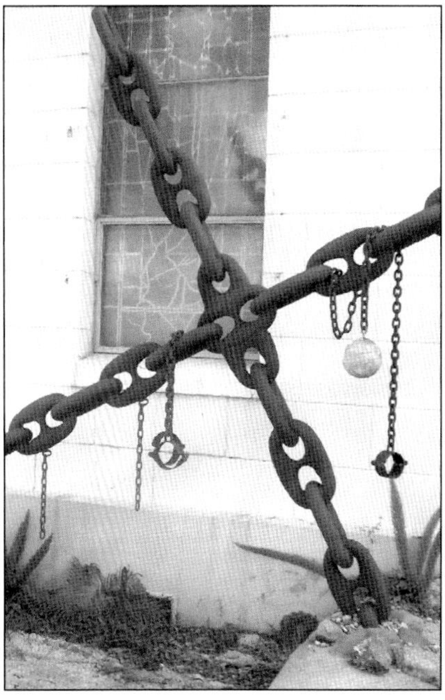

THE TOMB OF THE UNKNOWN SLAVE. The Faith Community of St. Augustine Catholic Church in historic Faubourg Treme erected this 1,500-pound memorial sculpture on October 30, 2004. The bronze dedication plaque reminds readers that St. Augustine is built on former plantation land, where enslaved Africans toiled and met their premature deaths. St. Augustine is the only Catholic church in the United States where free people of color purchased pews for the church's enslaved congregants just in time for the October 9, 1842, dedication ceremony. The concept for a memorial tomb came in a letter in 1992 from William Savoy of St. Luke Episcopal Church of New York to the senior priest of St. Augustine, Fr. Jerome Le Doux, SVD. By 2004, Anna Ross Twitchell, John Peter "Jay" Matranga, and Ophey Joseph Thibodeaux Jr. had combined their interests in the project, and not long thereafter, welder David "Thib" Thibodaux of Sorrento, Louisiana, was hard at work fabricating the sculpture depicted here. (Courtesy of Phoenix Savage.)

Three

The Walls of Jericho

And it came to pass, when the people heard the sound of the trumpet, that the people shouted with a great shout, and the wall fell down flat.

—Joshua 6:20b (NAS)

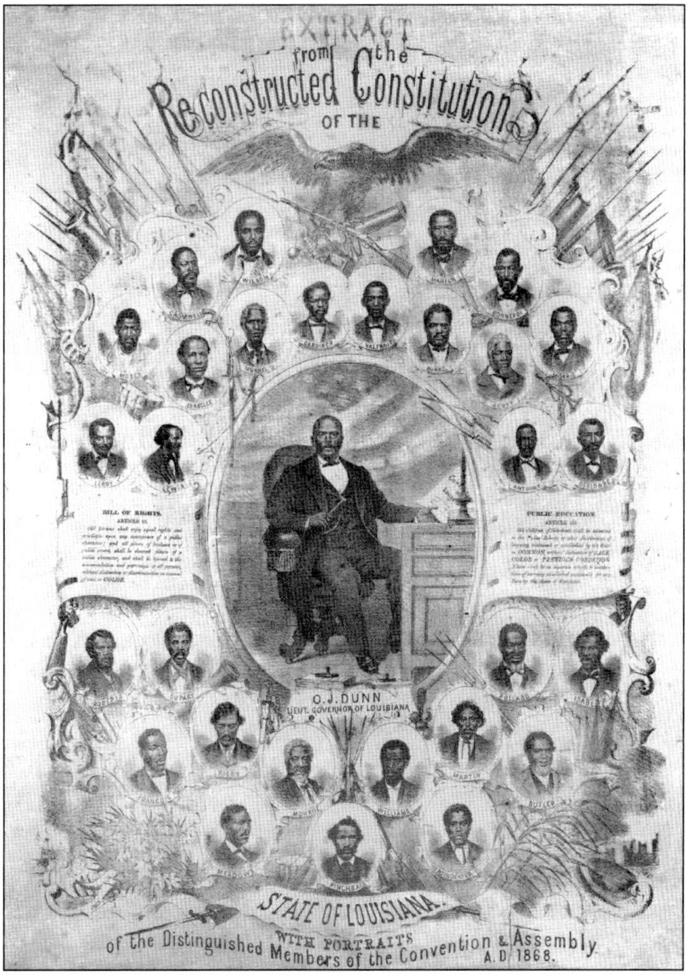

Distinguished Members. Reconstruction-era African American leaders were different from the people they represented. Most were free before the Civil War. Many were well-educated, financially secure merchants who were members of the free Negro population. Shown here is an extract from the 1868 reconstructed Constitution of the State of Louisiana, with portraits of distinguished members of the convention and assembly. (Courtesy of the Louisiana State Museum.)

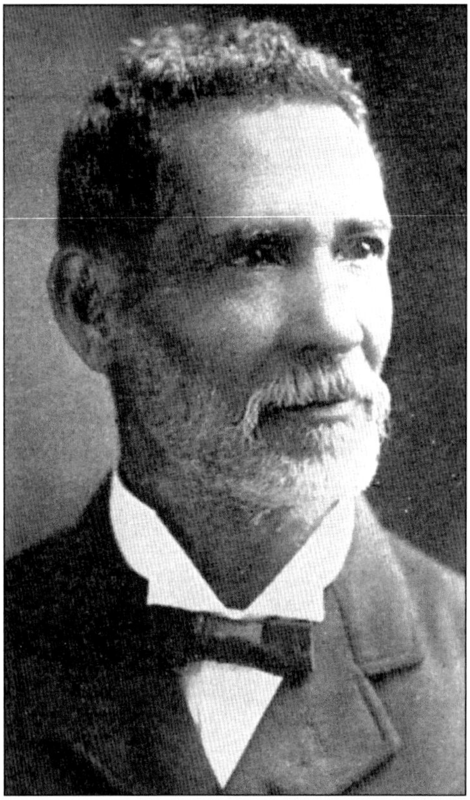

MAKER OF HISTORY. Born in New Orleans on November 15, 1849, of mixed parents who fled warring St. Domingue, Rodolphe Lucien Desdunes grew up expected to take over his family's cigar factory. Desdunes, however, aspired to be a writer. While he indeed authored the seminal treatise *Nos Homes et Notre Histore* (Our People Our History), Desdunes is more remembered for his role in the events that led to the U.S. Supreme Court decision *Plessy v. Ferguson*. Along with Dr. L. Martinet, Aristide Mary, and at least 15 others, Desdunes formed the Comité des Citoyens (Citizens Committee). These men, and possibly women, were the organizers behind the act of civil disobedience performed by Homer Plessy. Throughout Desdunes' political and creative activities, he was employed at the U.S. Customs House in New Orleans. He was at work inspecting granite that was in the process of being off-loaded from a cargo ship when a gust of wind blew dust into his eyes, leaving him blind for the remainder of his life. (Courtesy of the Louisiana Division/City Archives, New Orleans Public Library.)

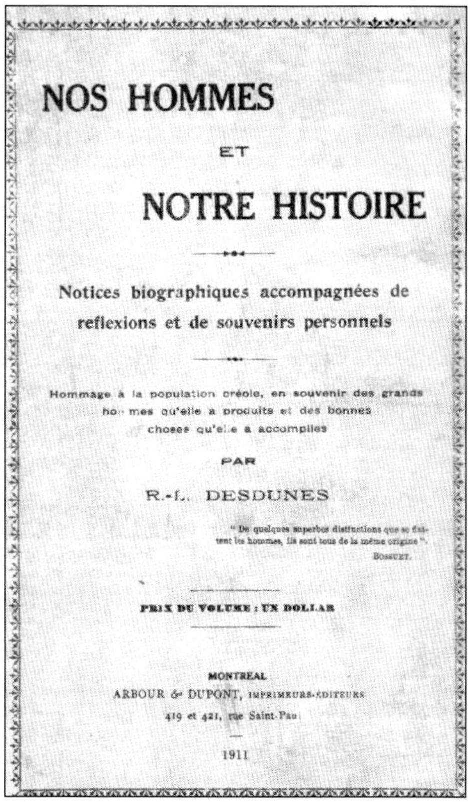

NOS HOMMES

ET

NOTRE HISTOIRE

Notices biographiques accompagnées de réflexions et de souvenirs personnels

Hommage à la population créole, en souvenir des grands hommes qu'elle a produits et des bonnes choses qu'elle a accomplies

PAR

R.-L. DESDUNES

« De quelques superbes distinctions que se flattent les hommes, ils sont tous de la même origine ».
BOSSUET.

PRIX DU VOLUME : UN DOLLAR

MONTREAL
ARBOUR & DUPONT, IMPRIMEURS-ÉDITEURS
419 et 421, rue Saint-Paul

1911

OUR PEOPLE OUR HISTORY. In 1911, Desdunes published *Nos Hommes et Notre Histoire*, a manuscript outlining the achievements and historical contributions of free people of color in Louisiana. Desdunes' literary career also included contributions to *The Crusader* (1889–1898), a journal published by Dr. L. Martinet. Desdunes died on August 14, 1928, and is interred in St. Louis Cemetery No. 2 in New Orleans. (Courtesy of the Louisiana Division/City Archives, New Orleans Public Library.)

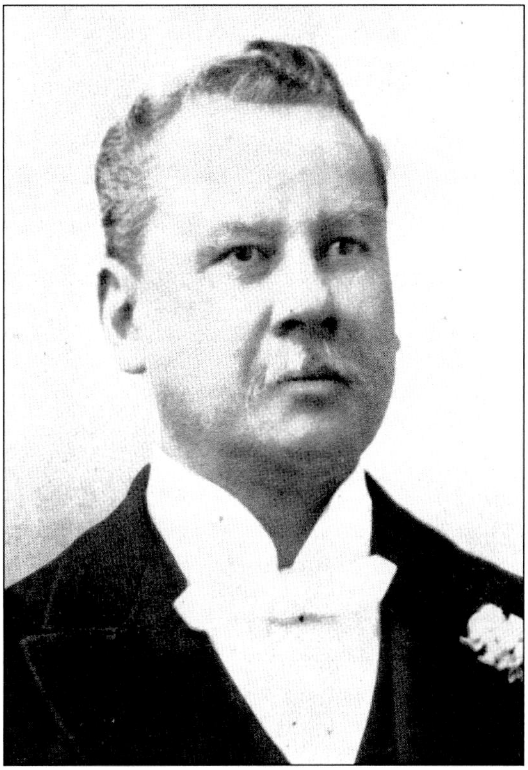

Alcee Labat. A member of the Comité des Citoyens, Labat was instrumental in crafting the legal proceedings that the committee undertook while dealing with the *Plessy v. Ferguson* case. Known for having a keen eye for detail and honesty, Labat and other members of the committee were master organizers during the time when laws worked against people of color in Louisiana. (Courtesy of the Louisiana Division/City Archives, New Orleans Public Library.)

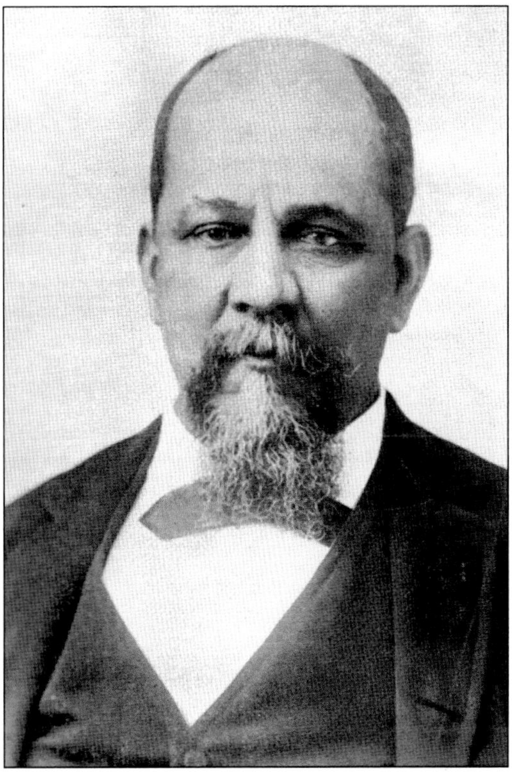

Arthur Esteves. A member of the Comité des Citoyens, whose stated mission was "to protest the adoption and enforcement of the statutes that established the unjust and humiliating discrimination against the black race in Louisiana," Esteves was focused on overturning Act 111 of the 1890 Louisiana State Legislature, which decreed that blacks and whites must travel in separate train cars. A subsequent act forbade "the mixing of races in the conveniences traveling from one place to another within the state." This act's power was eventually extended to railroad accommodations between states. (Courtesy of the Louisiana Division/City Archives, New Orleans Public Library.)

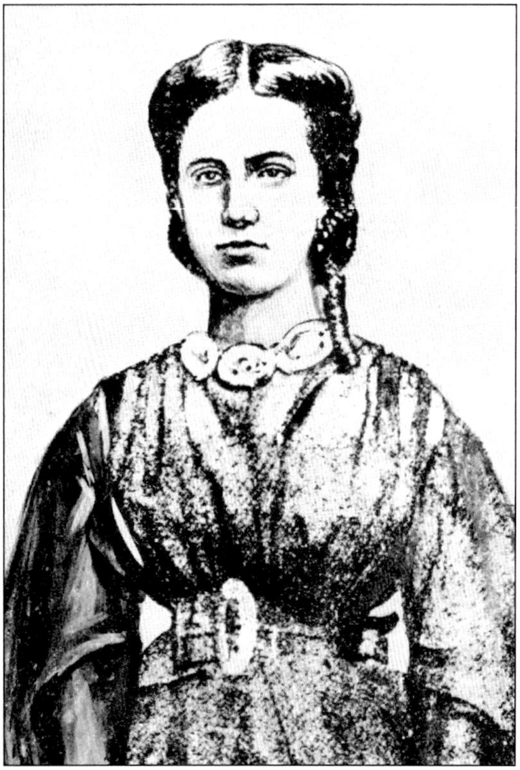

FREEWOMAN. Shown here is Victoria Lecene, believed to be the only female member of the Comité des Citoyens. Lecene was also affiliated with the Couvent School. (Courtesy of the Louisiana Division/City Archives, New Orleans Public Library.)

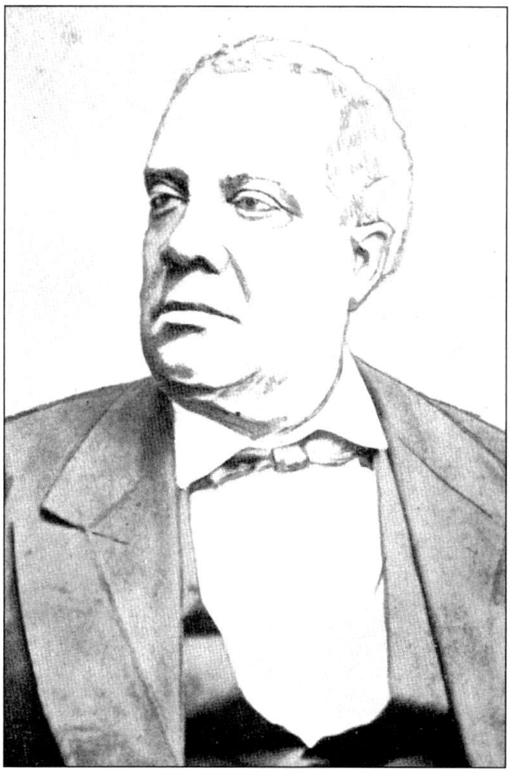

A SENSE OF DUTY. The Comité des Citoyens was formed in 1890 when the freedoms of people of color were becoming eclipsed by the law. This committee of citizens came forward to challenge the new laws. According to Desdunes, "Aristide Mary's idea was to give a dignified appearance to the resistance, which had to be implemented by lengthy judicial procedures." Members of the Comité des Citoyens were Arthur Esteves, president; C. Anotine, vice president; Firmin Christophe, secretary; G. G. Johnson, undersecretary; Paul Bonseigneur, treasurer; Laurent Auguste, shown here; Rodolphe Desdunes; Alcee Labat; Peiere Guirenovich; Louis Martinet; L. J. Joubert; M. J. Piron; Eugene Luscy; and E. A. Williams. The group organized in New Orleans on September 5, 1891. (Courtesy of the Louisiana Division/City Archives, New Orleans Public Library.)

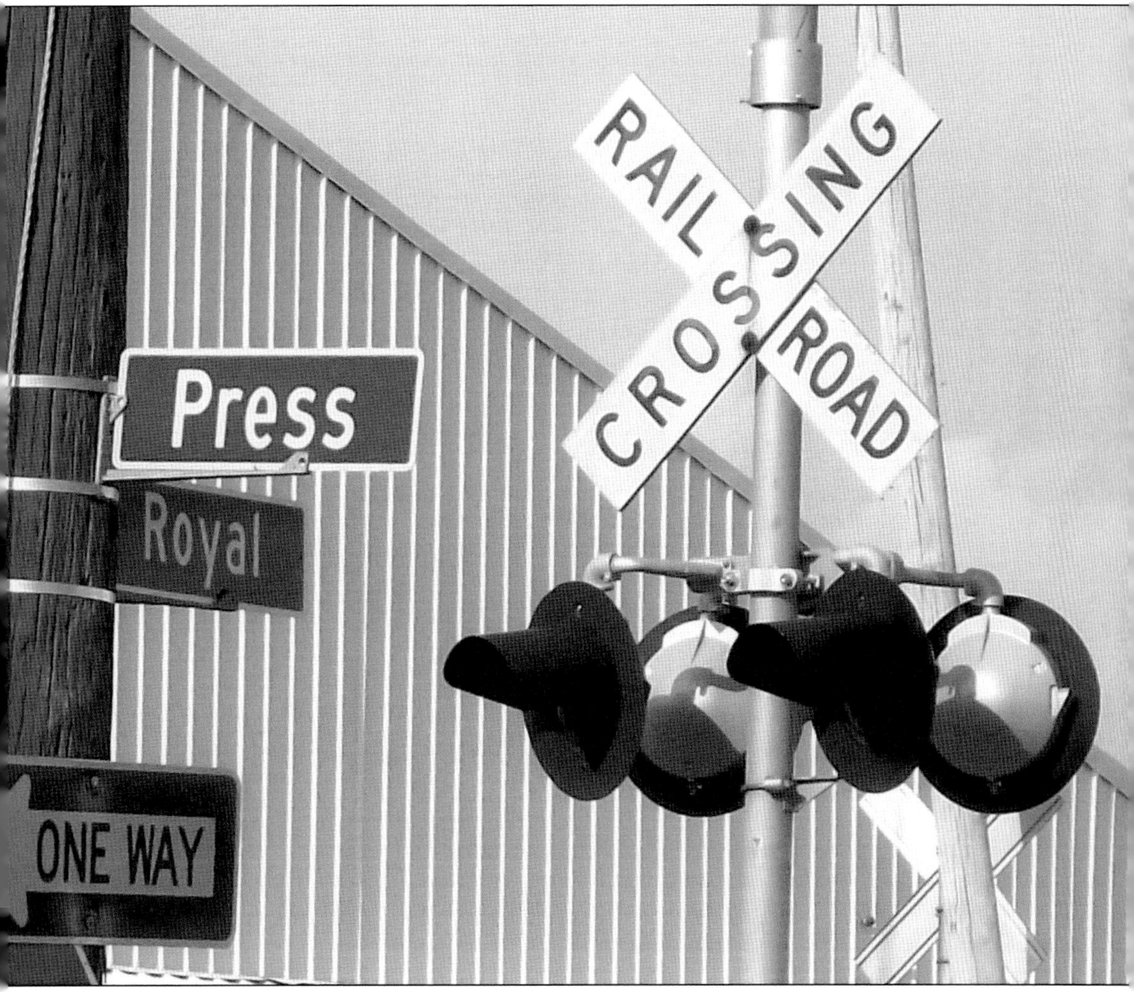

Homer Plessy at Press and Royal Streets. There are no surviving images of Plessy, born in New Orleans in 1863. As a young man, Plessy apprenticed to a shoemaker. By 1892, Plessy made a decision that placed his name in the history of American civil rights. On June 7, 1892, at the corner of Press and Royal streets in New Orleans, he boarded a train headed to Covington, Louisiana, intent on disobeying the two-year-old segregated seating law. Under the direction of the Comité des Citoyens, Plessy performed an act of civil disobedience by sitting in a car reserved for white passengers. The committee's goal was to challenge what they considered an unconstitutional law. The Plessy case went all the way to the U.S. Supreme Court. There, the court upheld the Louisiana lower court's ruling, opening the way for the spreading of the "separate but equal" concept throughout the U.S., and not only in public transportation but in all public services. Racial segregation had previously existed, but *Plessy v. Ferguson* gave legal legitimacy to discriminatory behavior. It would be 60 years before the high court overturned its ruling with *Brown v. Board of Education* in 1954. (Courtesy of Phoenix Savage.)

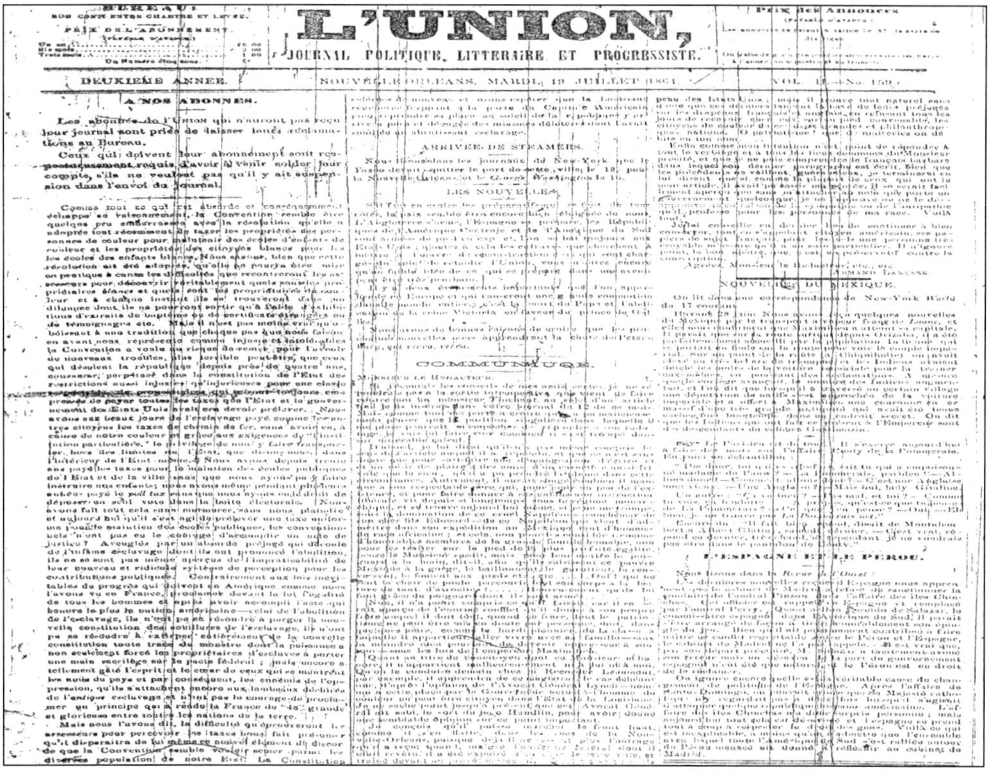

L'UNION,

JOURNAL POLITIQUE, LITTERAIRE ET PROGRESSISTE.

DEUXIEME ANNEE.

A NOS ABONNES.

Les abonnés de l'UNION qui n'auront pas reçu leur journal sont priés de laisser leurs réclamations au Bureau.

Ceux qui doivent leur abonnement sont respectueusement requis d'avoir à venir solder leur compte, s'ils ne veulent pas qu'il y ait suspension dans l'envoi du journal.

ARRIVEE DE STEAMERS.

LES NOUVELLES.

COMMUNIQUE.

NOUVELLES DU MEXIQUE.

L'ESPAGNE ET LE PEROU.

L'UNION. This newspaper was published in New Orleans in 1865 with well-known writer and linguist Paul Trevigne as the editor in chief. *L'Union* was the platform for people of color to express their thoughts about the social climate of the day. Later Trevigne was asked to serve as editor in chief of the newly formed newspaper *La Tribune de la Nouvelle Orléans*, known as *La Tribune*, founded by Dr. Louis Roudanez. (Courtesy of Dr. Laura V. Rouzan.)

LA TRIBUNE

(JULY 21, 1864)

Satisfied that we shall meet with encouragement from every friend of progress and civilization, we have purchased the interest and material of the Union paper which we acknowledge to have well filled its mission, however humble may have been this organ of the oppressed class, during the past three years of our social change and reform. We publish a new paper devoted to the principles heretofore defended by the Union.

Convinced that a newspaper under the present circumstances, representing the principles and interest that we propose to defend and advocate was much needed in New Orleans, we shall spare not means at our command to render the Tribune worthy of public confidence and respect, and these were the reasons that prompted us to its publication…

LA TRIBUNE. The mission statement at left was printed in *La Tribune* newspaper on July 21, 1864. (Courtesy of Dr. Laura V. Rouzan.)

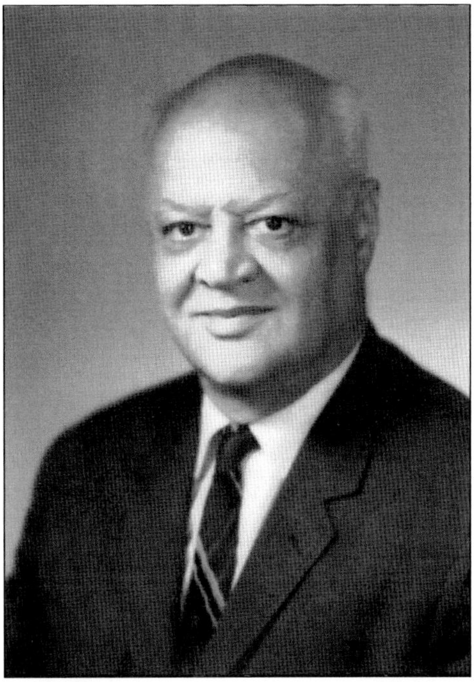

Father of the Civil Rights Movement in Louisiana. Alexander Pierre Tureaud (1899–1972) was the attorney for the New Orleans chapter of the National Association for the Advancement of Colored People (NAACP) during the civil rights movement. The NAACP chapter in New Orleans invited civil rights attorney Thurgood Marshall to represent their interests in the case of *Joseph P. McKelpin v. Orleans Parish School Board*, a case initiated by African American teachers from segregated schools, who sued the school board for salaries equal to those of their white counterparts. The case was settled out of court and the African American teachers were offered pay increases. (Courtesy of Alexander Pierre Tureaud Jr.)

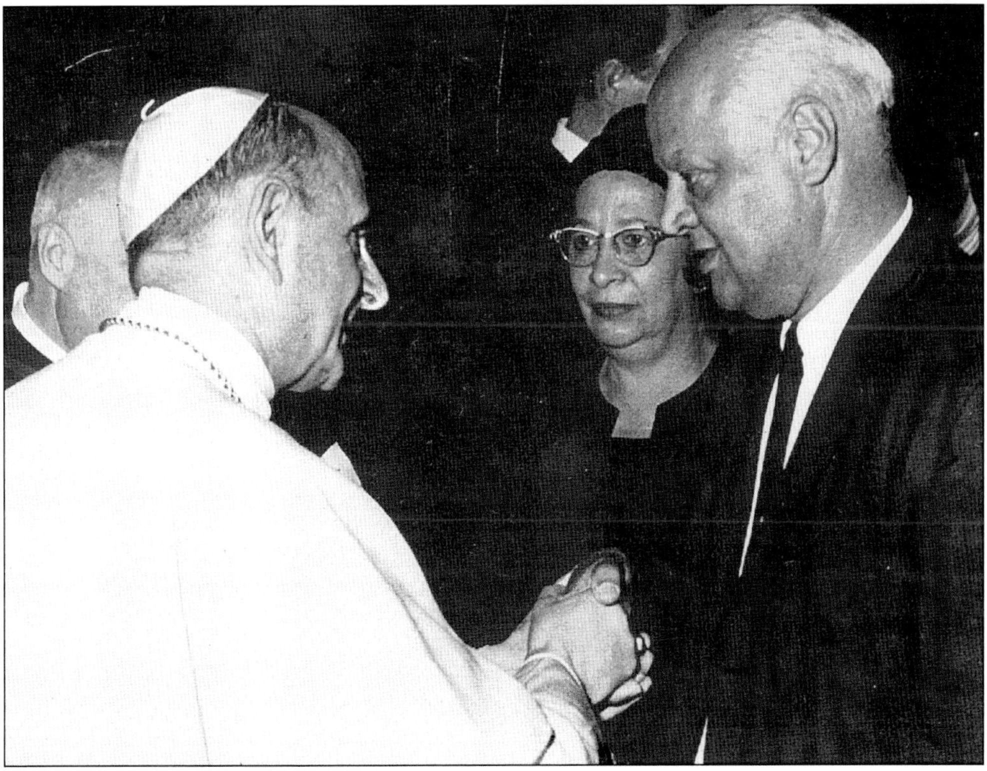

A Visit with the Pope. In 1964, the Tureaud family toured several countries in Europe. While in Italy, the Archdiocese of New Orleans arranged a visit with Pope Paul VI (1897–1978) at the Pope's summer residence in Gondolfo, Italy. (Courtesy of Alexander Pierre Tureaud Jr.)

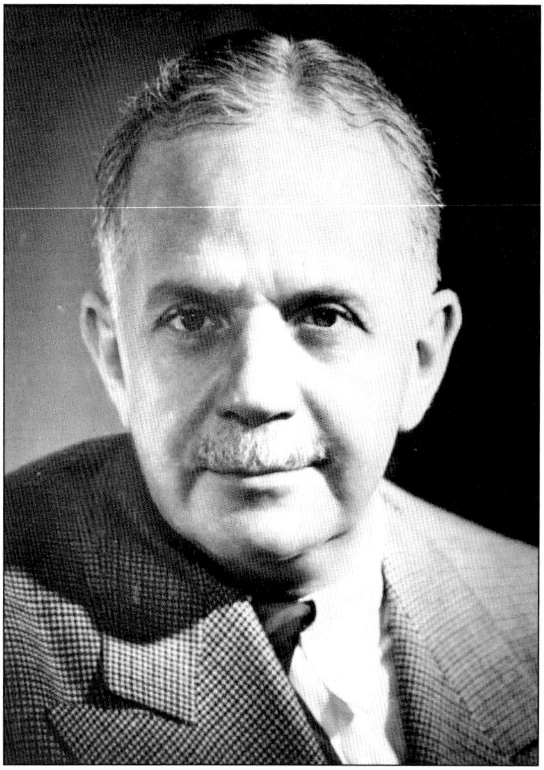

A Man Called White. Walter F. White (1893–1955) was born to George W. White and Nadiline Harrison in Atlanta, Georgia. Although phenotypically white, Walter White identified himself as African American and became a powerful spokesman for the African American community nationally. Between 1929 and 1955, White served as Executive Secretary of the NAACP. (Photograph of Walter White, undated, General Photographs-Individuals, Box 6. Courtesy of the Robert W. Woodruff Library of the Atlanta University Center.)

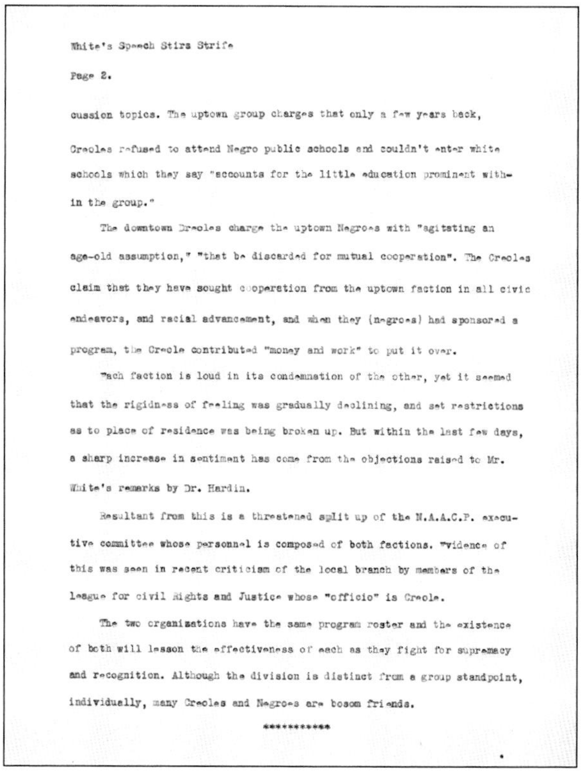

White's Speech Stirs Strife

Page 2.

cussion topics. The uptown group charges that only a few years back, Creoles refused to attend Negro public schools and couldn't enter white schools which they say "accounts for the little education prominent within the group."

The downtown Creoles charge the uptown Negroes with "agitating an age-old assumption," "that be discarded for mutual cooperation". The Creoles claim that they have sought cooperation from the uptown faction in all civic endeavors, and racial advancement, and when they (negroes) had sponsored a program, the Creole contributed "money and work" to put it over.

Each faction is loud in its condemnation of the other, yet it seemed that the rigidness of feeling was gradually declining, and set restrictions as to place of residence was being broken up. But within the last few days, a sharp increase in sentiment has come from the objections raised to Mr. White's remarks by Dr. Hardin.

Resultant from this is a threatened split up of the N.A.A.C.P. executive committee whose personnel is composed of both factions. Evidence of this was seen in recent criticism of the local branch by members of the league for civil Rights and Justice whose "officio" is Creole.

The two organizations have the same program roster and the existence of both will lesson the effectiveness of each as they fight for supremacy and recognition. Although the division is distinct from a group standpoint, individually, many Creoles and Negroes are bosom friends.

****

Walter White's Speech. This is an editorial in response to a 1938 speech given by White while he was Executive Secretary of the NAACP stating, "Negroes and Creoles maintain a division in New Orleans that is a definite hindrance to their progress." Ernest "Duth" Morial, who in 1978 became the first African American mayor of New Orleans, was adamant about not allowing this "divide and conquer" mentality to effect the work that he and many others like him wanted to accomplish. (Courtesy of State Library of Louisiana.)

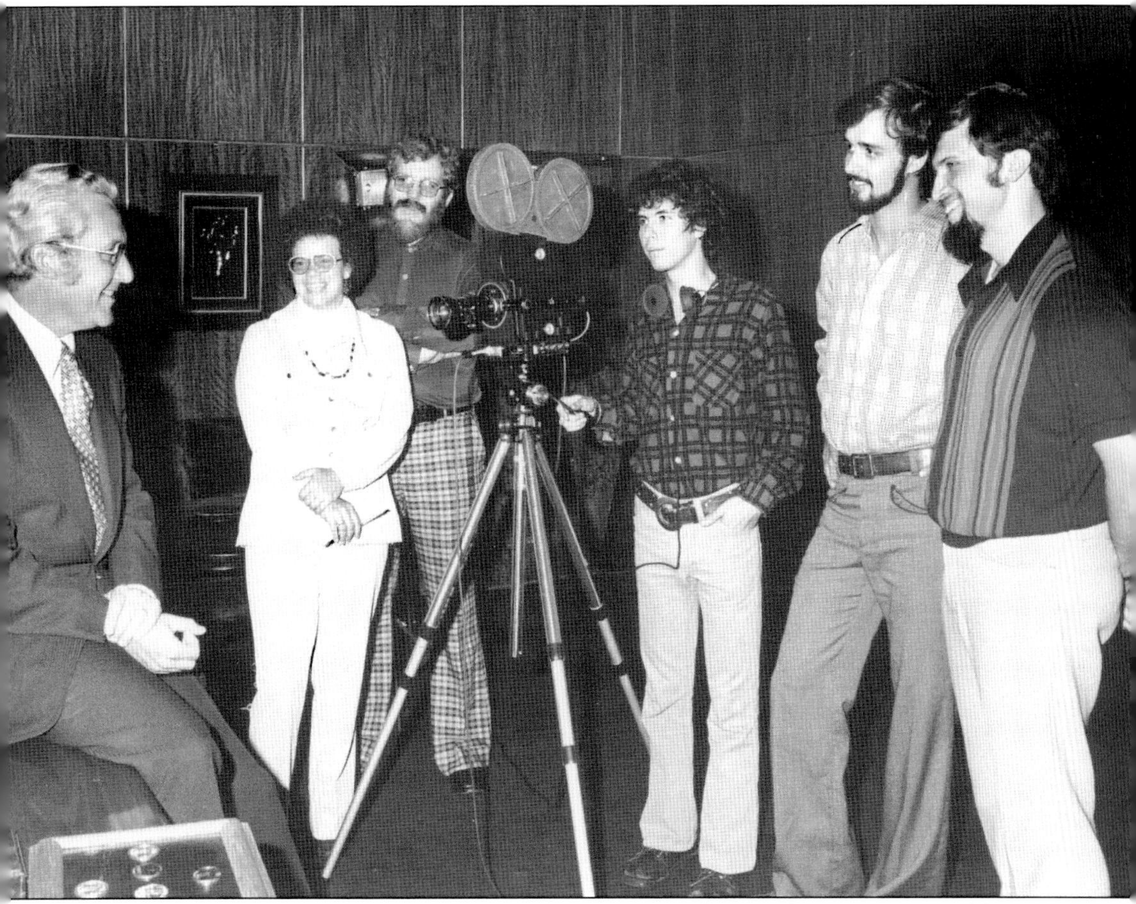

Moon. Shown here is a group shot of members of a camera crew talking with Mayor Maurice Edwin "Moon" Landrieu, who served as mayor of New Orleans from 1970 to 1978. He also represented New Orleans's 12th Ward in the Louisiana House of Representatives from 1960 to 1970. Landrieu was appointed secretary of housing and urban development under U.S. president Jimmy Carter from 1979 to 1981. During Landrieu's tenure as New Orleans' mayor, he oversaw the desegregation of the city's government and public facilities. Landrieu appointed African Americans to key positions in city government, including appointing the city's first African American chief administrative officer. Landrieu also appointed civil rights activist Rev. A. L. Davis to fill a vacancy on the city council, making Davis New Orleans's first African American city councilman. (Courtesy of the Louisiana Division/City Archives, New Orleans Public Library.)

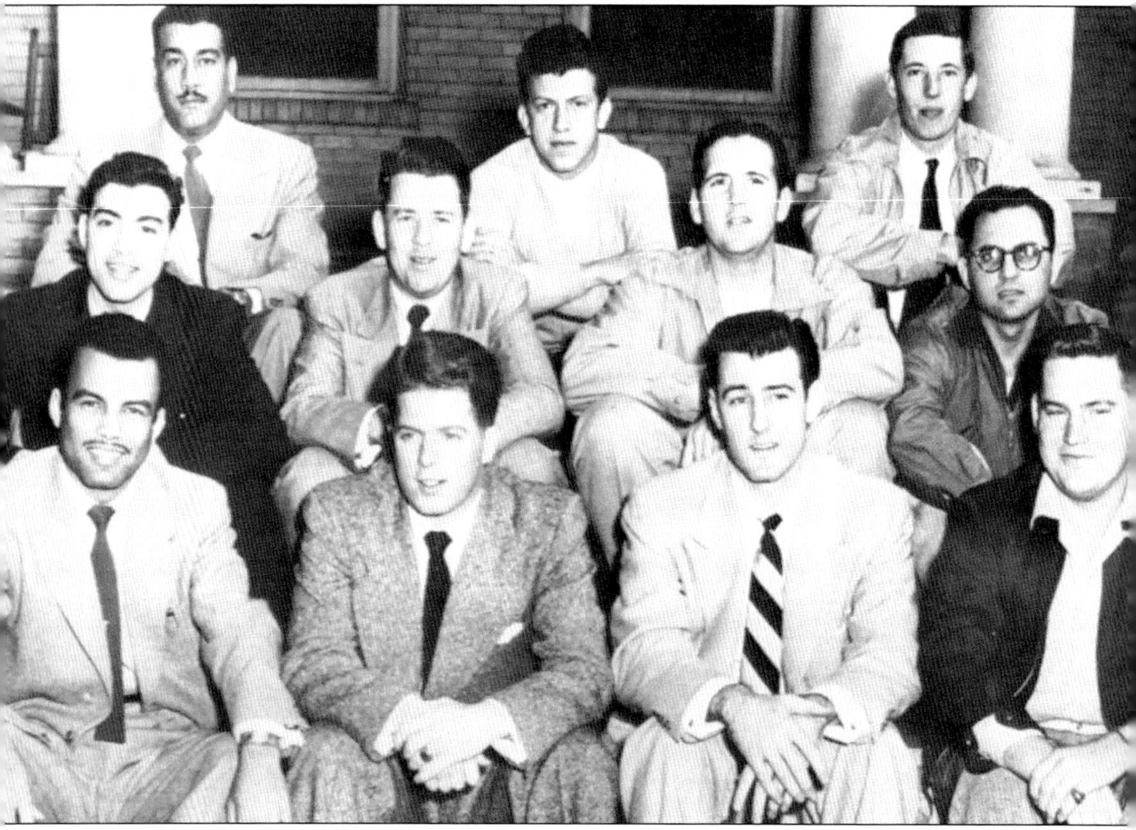

NORMAN FRANCIS AND BEN JOHNSON. This photograph of Norman Francis (first row, far left) and Ben Johnson (third row, far left) was taken with other students at the Loyola University Law School of New Orleans. Francis and Johnson were the first African Americans to attend the school. According to Dr. Norman Francis, the desegregation of Catholic schools began with strategy sessions that involved African American, white students, and Jesuit priests. These sessions generated discussions addressing the steps necessary for a successful integration of the schools. A commission was established to begin the change, and it chose Loyola University School of Law as the first target of desegregation. The plan was to take one senior from Xavier University of Louisiana and have him apply to Loyola. In 1950, Harry T. Alexander applied to Loyola Law School, but he was not accepted. Alexander went on to Georgetown Law School and became a federal judge. A second applicant from Xavier, Richard Gumble, applied in 1951. He too was not accepted, went on to Georgetown Law School, and became a judge. In 1952, Norman Francis was admitted, becoming the first African American to attend the Loyola University School of Law. His classmate and friend Ben Johnson was admitted shortly afterwards. (Courtesy of the President's Office of Xavier University of Louisiana.)

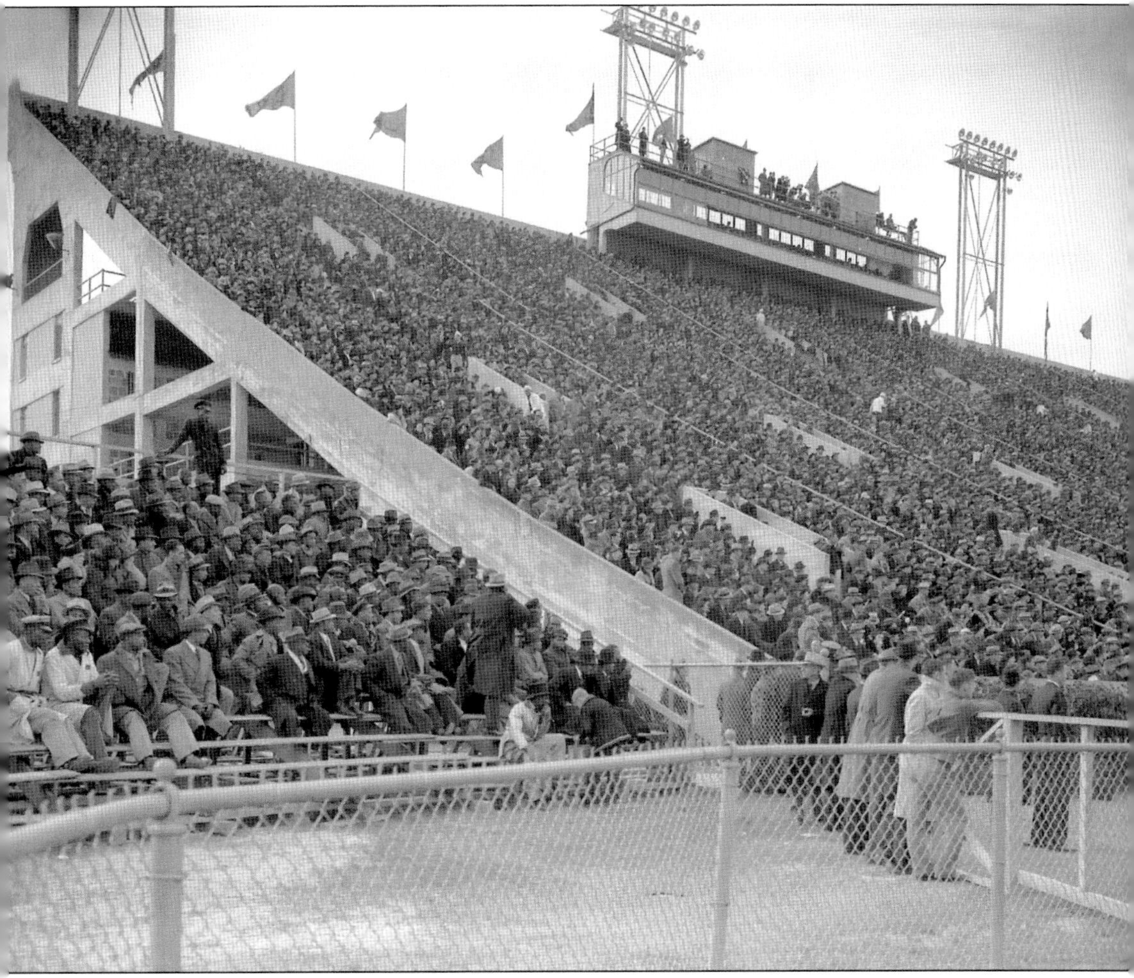

TULANE STADIUM. Built by the Works Progress Administration (WPA), this stadium on the campus of Tulane University in New Orleans was designed to accommodate the segregation of the races. Notice the bottom left-hand corner section of the stadium, designated for African Americans. (Courtesy of the State Library of Louisiana.)

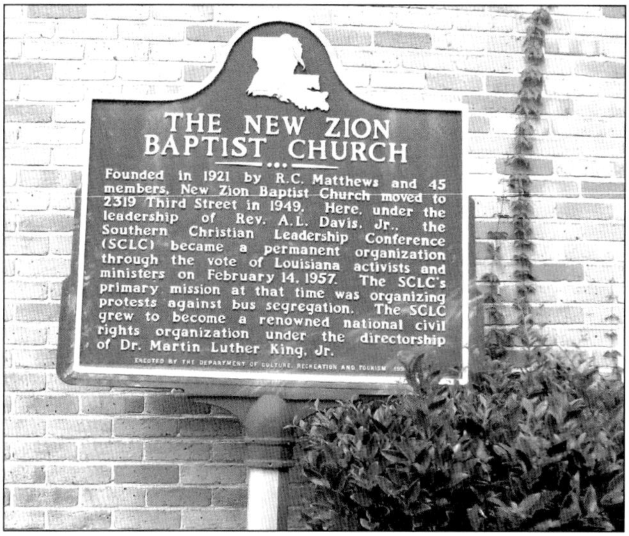

THE BEGINNING. This photograph shows a state historic marker that stands on the outside of Mount Zion Baptist Church in New Orleans. Established in 1921, Mount Zion was the site where many civil rights organizing meetings were held. Rev. A. L. Davis and other activists gathered here and established the Southern Christian Leadership Conference. Later the organization moved to Atlanta, naming the Rev. Dr. Martin Luther King Jr. as its first president. (Courtesy of Turry Flucker.)

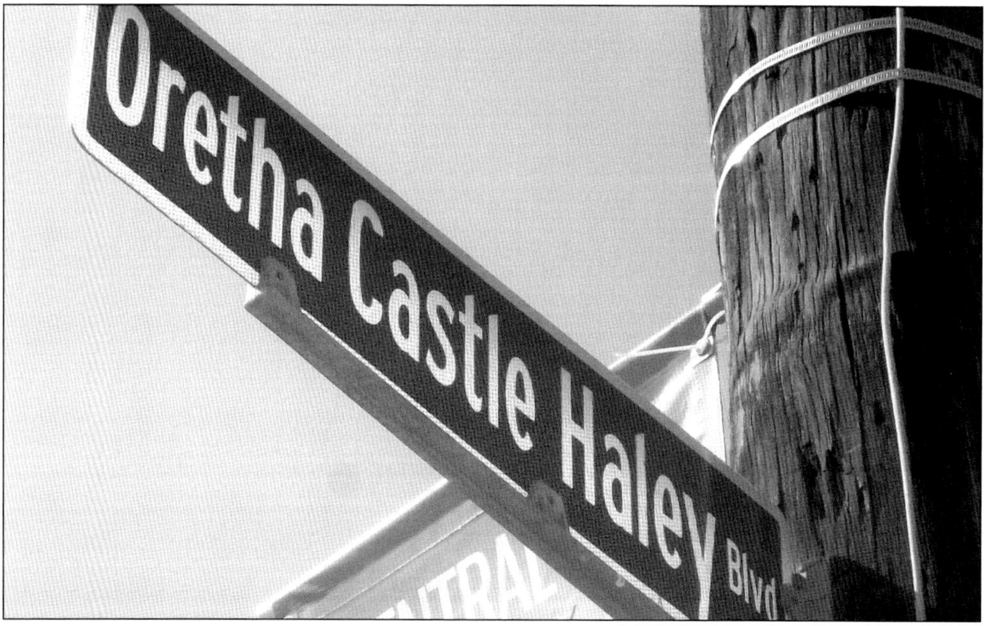

ORETHA CASTLE HALEY BOULEVARD. Located in New Orleans' Central City neighborhood, this street, originally named Draydes, was renamed for civil rights pioneer Oretha Castle Haley. Oretha Castle Haley was born in 1940 in Oakland, Tennessee. In 1947, Haley moved with parents John and Virgie Castle to New Orleans. Haley's activism began in 1959 when she was a student at Southern University at New Orleans. That spring, a boycott was staged against the merchants on Dryades Street. African Americans were concerned by the fact that stores along the street would only hire African Americans in menial jobs, even though the stores' clientele was mostly African American. The boycott successfully rendered the shopping area deserted on Good Friday, one of the busiest shopping days of the year. As a result, merchants on Dyades Street started to hire African Americans in significant positions. Haley worked mainly in Louisiana, but her sister Jean Castle and other members of the Congress of Racial Equality (CORE), took part in Freedom Rides and were jailed as a result of their non-violent protest activities. (Courtesy of Phoenix Savage.)

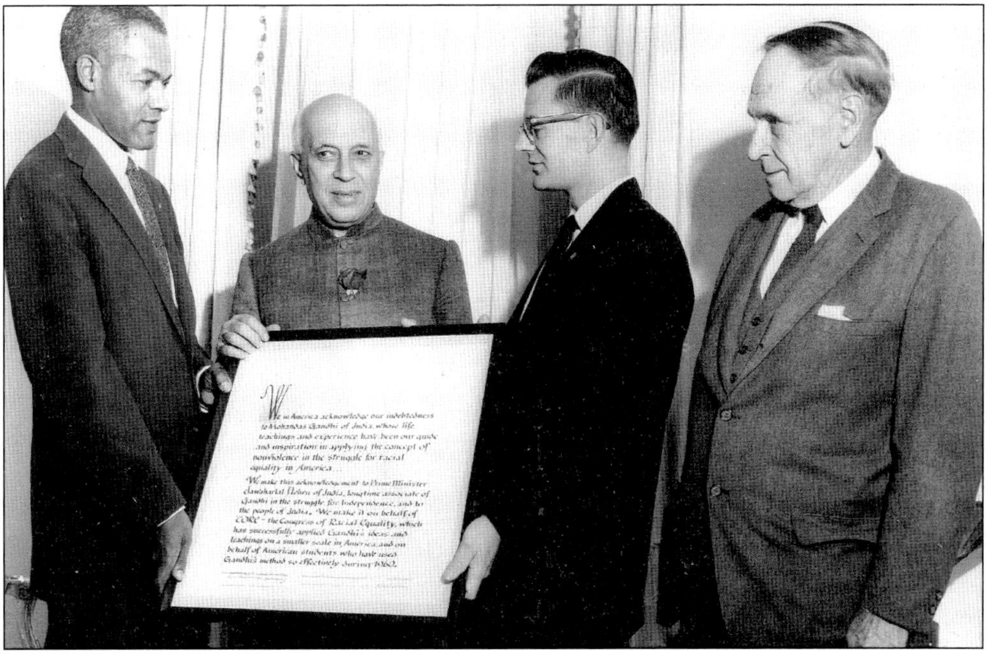

Richard Haley. Shown here on the left-hand side with a group of world peace leaders, Richard Haley was the field secretary for the Congress on Racial Equality (CORE) in the 1960s. A music teacher by profession, Haley came to Louisiana to work at the height of the civil rights movement. In 1967, Haley married Oretha Castle, a fellow activist and member of CORE. (Courtesy of Okyeame Haley, J.D.)

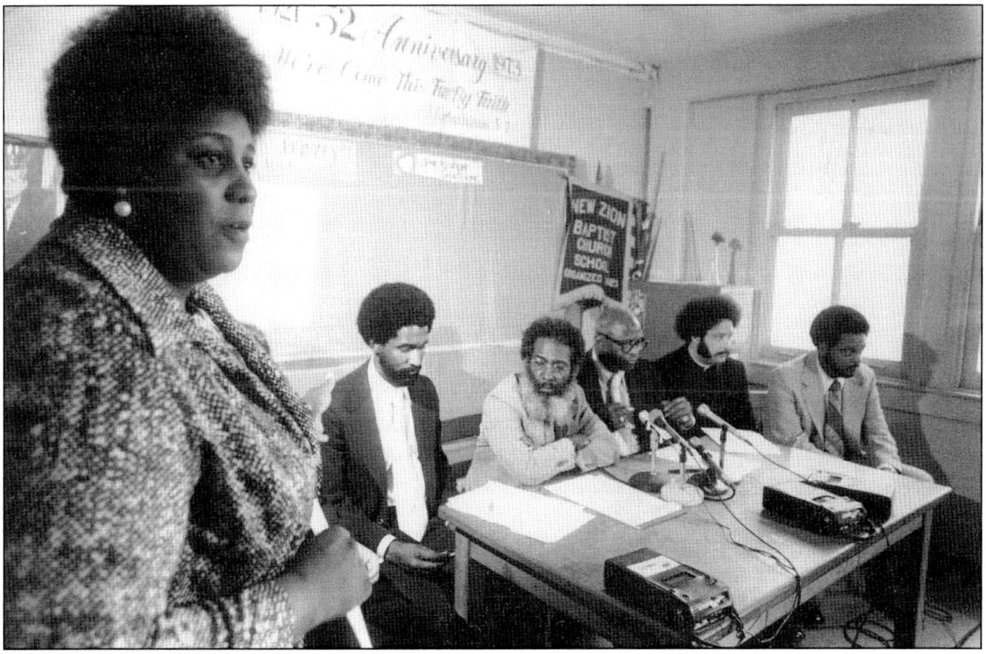

Meeting at Mount Zion Baptist Church. Shown here at Mount Zion Baptist Church are New Orleans civil rights activists including Oretha Castle Haley (standing on the left) and attorney Lolis Elie (at the table, second from left). (Courtesy of Okyeame Haley, J.D.)

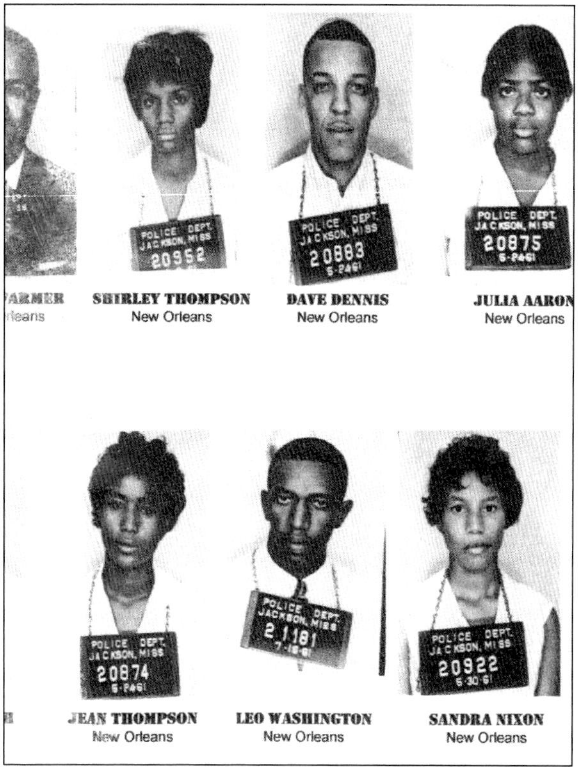

FOURTEEN FROM NEW ORLEANS. Pictured here are the mug shots of 14 Freedom Riders arrested in Jackson, Mississippi, on May 24, 1961. The Freedom Riders were inspired by the 1947 Journey of Reconciliation led by civil rights leaders and activists Bayard Rustin and George Houser. The purpose was to test an earlier Supreme Court decision banning racial discrimination related to interstate travel. The first Freedom Ride began May 4, 1961, led by CORE director James Farmer. Thirteen riders left Washington, D.C., on both Greyhound and Trailways buses. The plan was to ride through Virginia, the Carolinas, Georgia, Alabama, and Mississippi, ending with a rally in New Orleans. Pictured here are several known New Orleans activists including Jerome Smith, Doris Jean Castle, and Richard and Oretha Castle Haley. (Courtesy of Okyeame Haley, J.D.)

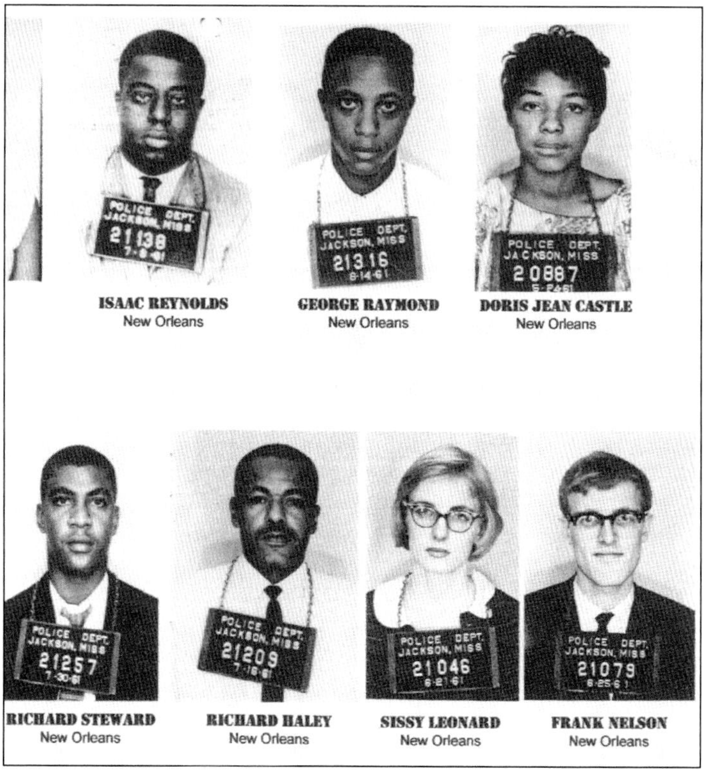

FREEDOM RIDERS. Students from New Orleans are arrested in Jackson, Mississippi, in 1961. Their crime was riding a bus. (Courtesy of Okyeame Haley, J.D.)

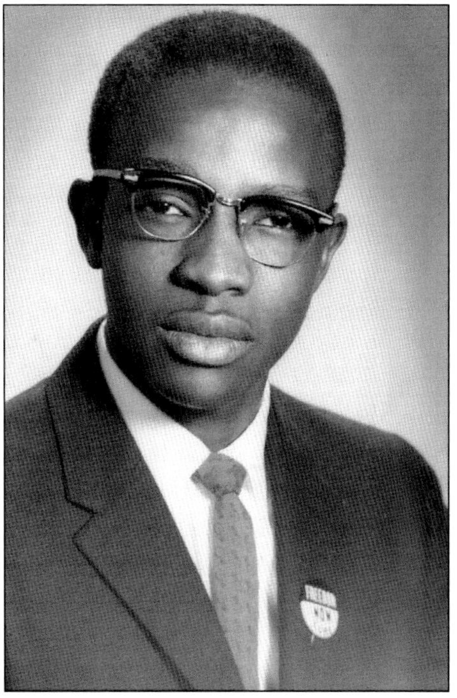

CORE. Ronnie Moore was the first CORE field secretary to support armed self-defense. Born on December 31, 1940, in Algiers, Louisiana, Moore is the youngest of seven children. Moore was 14 years old when the famous court case *Brown v. the Board of Education* was decided. He remembers riding in a car with a priest from All Saints Catholic School in Algiers when the verdict was announced on the radio. The verdict was particularly significant for him: located next to his school was a large park; the Brown ruling made Moore and his classmates wonder why they could not play in the park. In an act of defiance, Moore and several of his friends, who normally would play on the street outside the park, went into the park. All of these students, including Rudy Lombard, who would later become a major player in the civil rights movement in New Orleans, were arrested. Attorneys A. P. Tureuad and Ernest Morial worked to get the students out of jail. (Courtesy of the Amistad Research Center, Tulane University, Ronnie Moore Collection, New Orleans, Louisiana.)

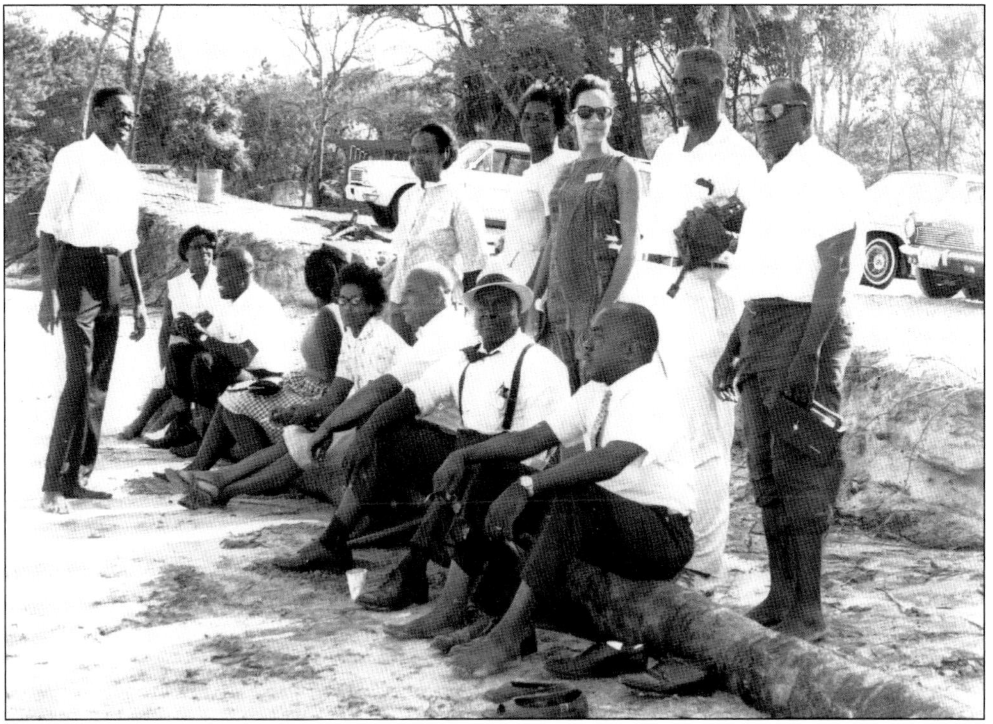

REST. This image shows Ronnie Moore (standing, far left) taking a break after being engaged in protest activities. This image was not taken in New Orleans; civil rights activists worked tirelessly to advance political and social freedoms all over the state. (Courtesy of the Amistad Research Center, Tulane University, Ronnie Moore Collection, New Orleans, Louisiana.)

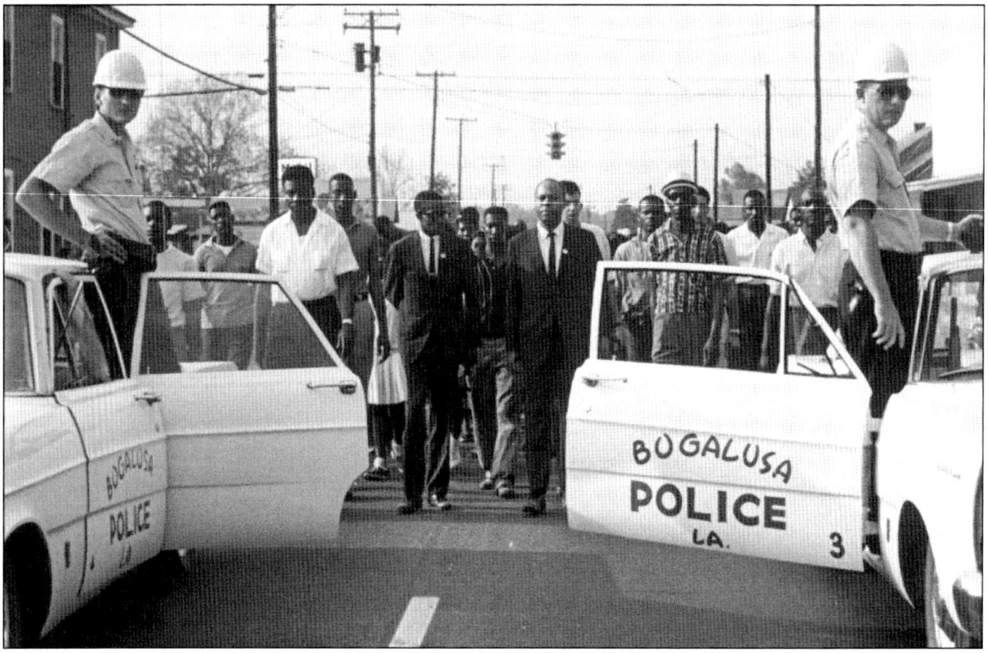

MOVING IN. This iconic shot shows a march in downtown Bogalusa, Louisiana. James Farmer, CORE's national director, is standing in front. Ronnie Moore (in a suit) is standing to the left of Farmer and A. Z. Young (in a white shirt) stands to the left of Moore. By 1965, Bogalusa was home to the largest and most powerful chapter of the Original Knights of the Ku Klux Klan in Louisiana. (Courtesy of the Amistad Research Center, Tulane University, Ronnie Moore Collection, New Orleans, Louisiana.)

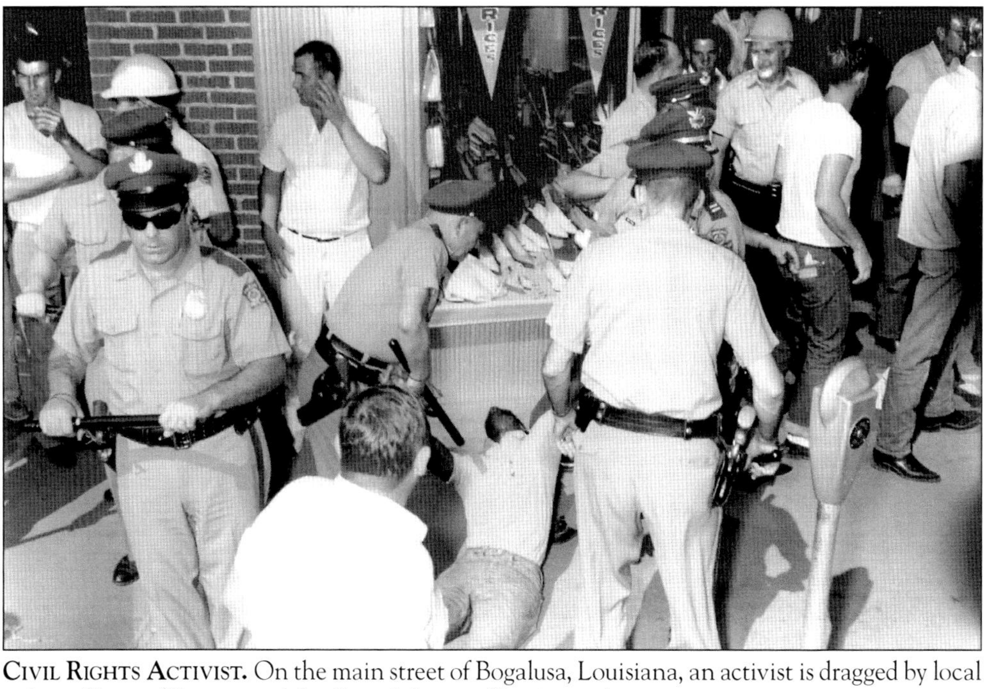

CIVIL RIGHTS ACTIVIST. On the main street of Bogalusa, Louisiana, an activist is dragged by local police officers. (Courtesy of the State Library of Louisiana.)

Jerome Smith. Shown here in overalls that were the uniform for many American civil rights activists is Jerome Smith. He was on the forefront of civil rights demonstrations in New Orleans. (Courtesy of the Amistad Research Center, Tulane University, Ronnie Moore Collection, New Orleans, Louisiana.)

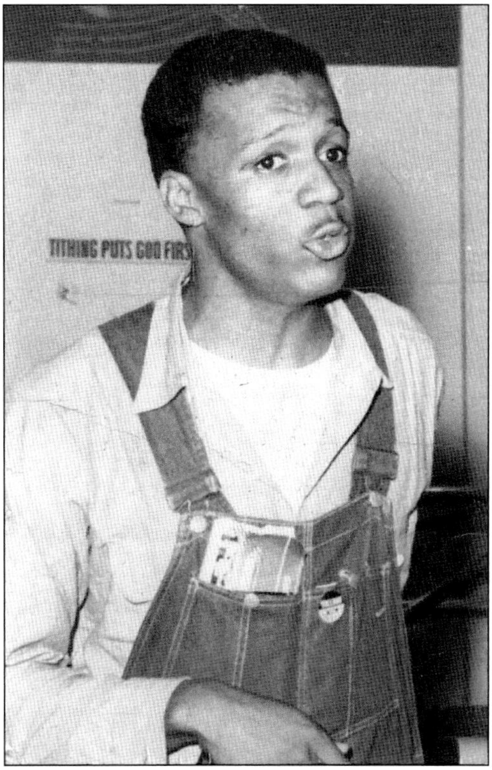

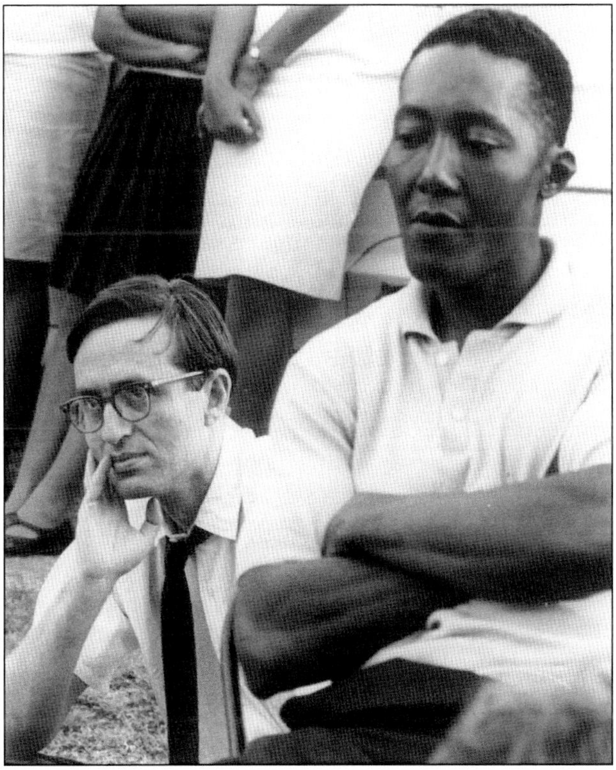

Organizer. This photograph shows Robert Hicks (right), the leader of the Bogalusa Civic and Voters League. Although never a formal member of the Deacons for Defense, Hicks organized a meeting with the group's Jonesboro, Louisiana, chapter that helped to create the Deacons for Defense chapter in Bogalusa. (Courtesy of the Amistad Research Center, Tulane University, Ronnie Moore Collection, New Orleans, Louisiana.)

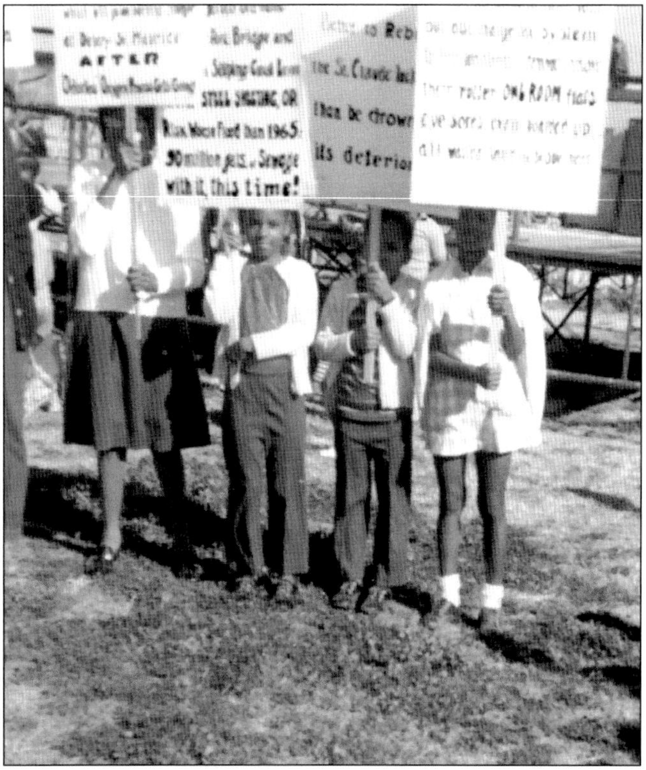

The "Ninth Ward Nine." Pictured here are lower Ninth Ward residents in New Orleans protesting the neglect of their community after Hurricane Betsy in 1965. (Courtesy of the Wisconsin Historical Society.)

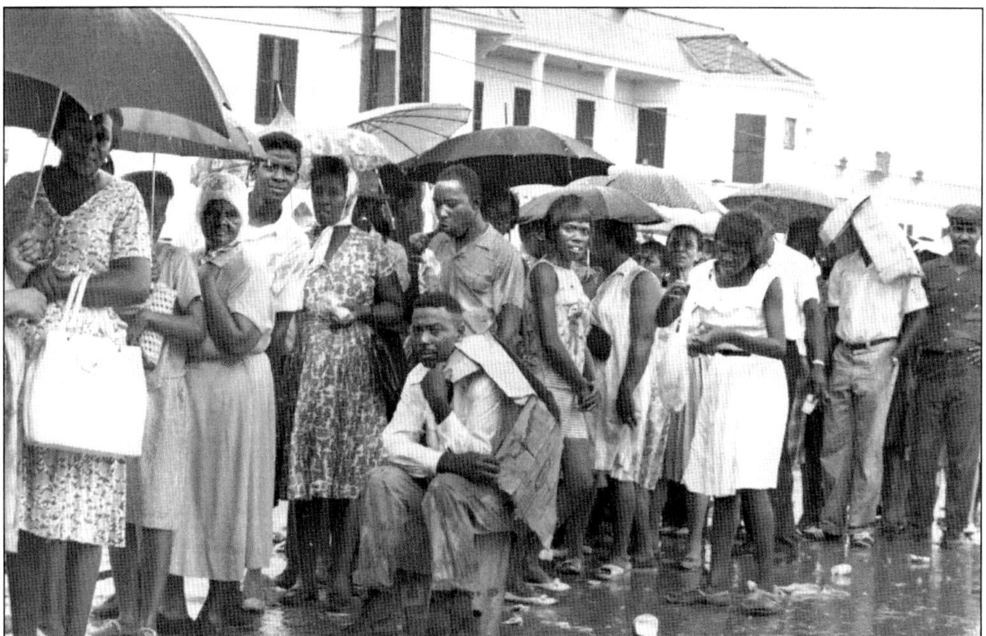

Scene at Algiers Naval Base. In 1965, thousands of New Orleanians were displaced as a result of Hurricane Betsy. Some people standing in this line would claim that employees of the Algiers Naval Base removed toilets in the first days after the storm to prevent African Americans from using them. (Courtesy of the Wisconsin Historical Society.)

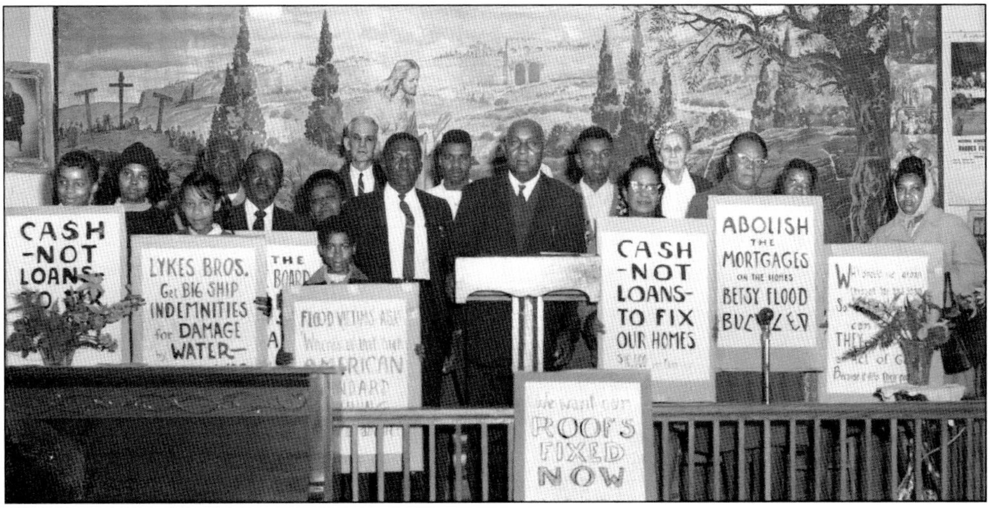

Betsy Flood Victims. A New Orleans group seeking valid compensation for lives lost and 25,000 homes ruined on September 10, 1965, met December 21, 1965, at Mercy Seat Baptist Church with Rev. Roosevelt Johnson and Rev. John Henry Craft. Included in this photograph are flood victims Walter Rogers and Elizabeth Rogers. (Courtesy of the Wisconsin Historical Society.)

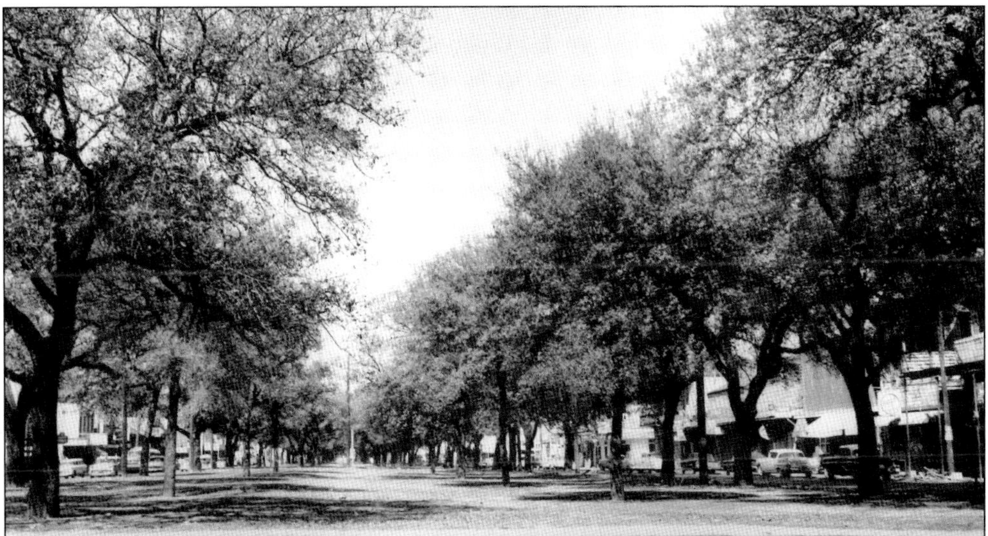

The Avenue. This photograph shows the beautiful oak trees that line the "neutral grounds" in the middle of North Claiborne Avenue in New Orleans. Many New Orleanians argue about how the broad mediums in the middle of New Orleans' streets came to be. Many believe the land that eventually became Canal Street divided the Creole section from the American section. No one can argue that the neutral grounds serve as a place where residents can gather for special events. (Courtesy of the Louisiana Division/City Archives, New Orleans Public Library.)

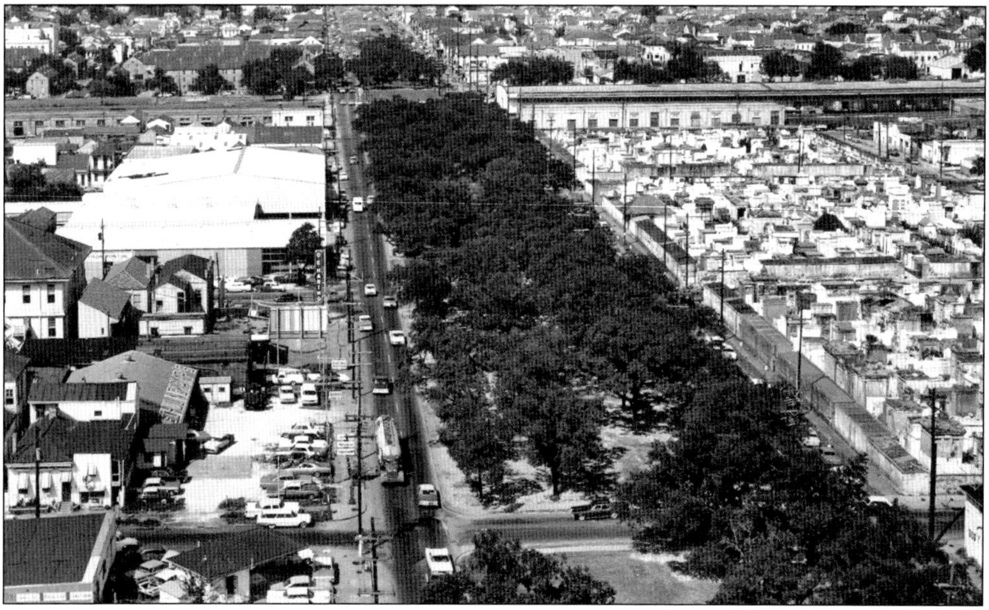

BIRD'S-EYE VIEW. This view of Claiborne Avenue from the air shows St. Louis Cemetery No. 2 on the right side and businesses on the left. Today all of the beautiful oak trees are gone, replaced with an interstate built straight through one of the oldest African American communities in New Orleans. (Courtesy of the Louisiana Division/City Archives, New Orleans Public Library.)

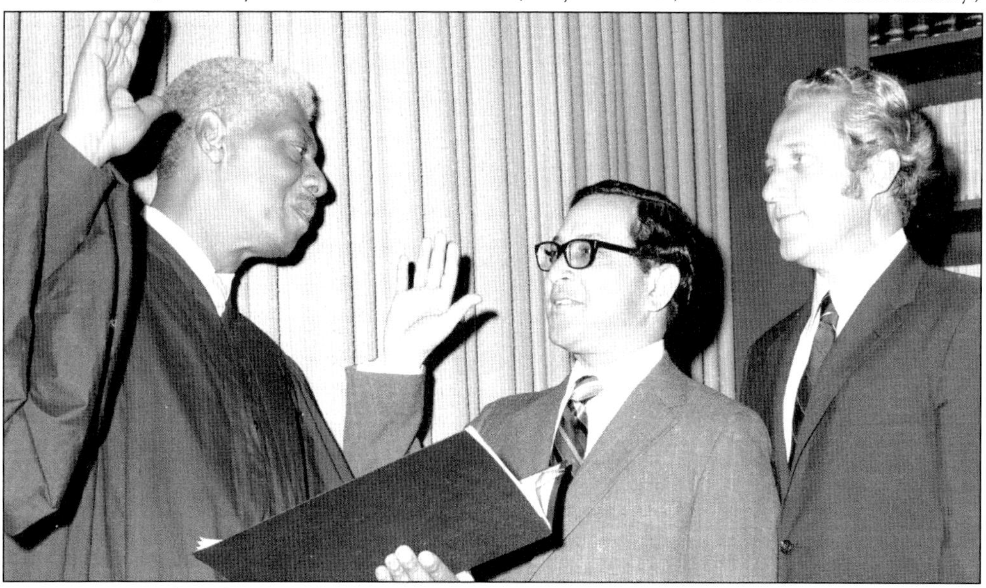

SWEARING IN. This photograph predates Ernest "Dutch" Morial's (1929–1989) election as mayor of New Orleans. It shows Morial being sworn in as judge of the Orleans Parish Juvenile Court in 1970. Judge I. M. Augustine (1924–1994) was the first African American district judge in Louisiana. Augustine was born in New Orleans and was a graduate of McDonogh 35 High School. After graduating from high school, Augustine went on to receive undergraduate and law degrees from Southern University at Baton Rouge and Lincoln University in St. Louis, Missouri, respectively. Also pictured here is Mayor Moon Landrieu. (Courtesy of the Louisiana Division/City Archives, New Orleans Public Library.)

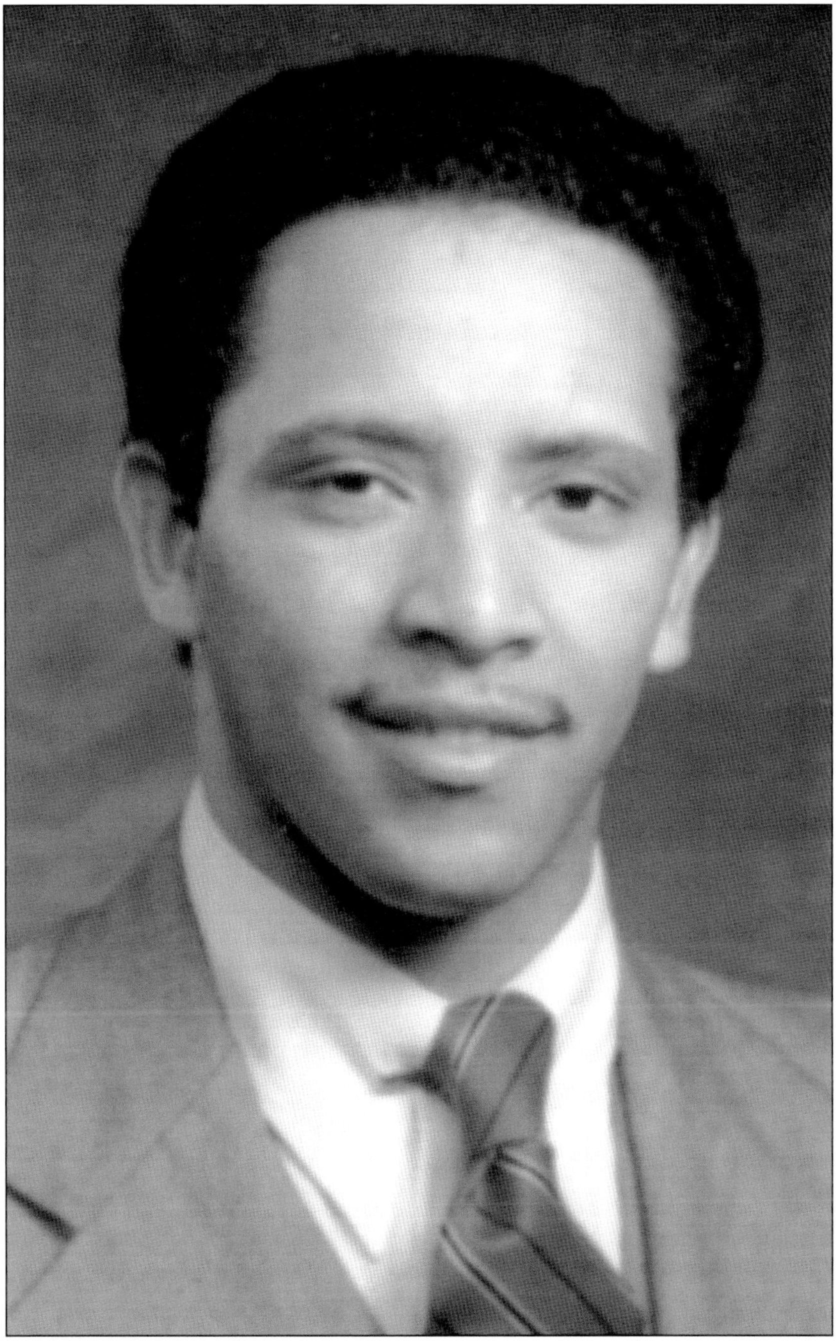

Marc H. Morial. Pictured here is Marc Morial (1958–), the son of Mayor Ernest "Dutch" Morial and Sybil Haydel Morial. Marc Morial is a graduate of the University of Pennsylvania and Georgetown Law School. According to an interview with Sybil Haydel Morial, as a youth Marc enjoyed accompanying his father to sessions of the Louisiana State Legislature sessions. Morial served as mayor of New Orleans from 1994 to 2002. Marc Morial is currently president and CEO of the National Urban League, one of the nation's oldest and largest civil rights organizations. (Courtesy of the Louisiana Division/City Archives, New Orleans Public Library.)

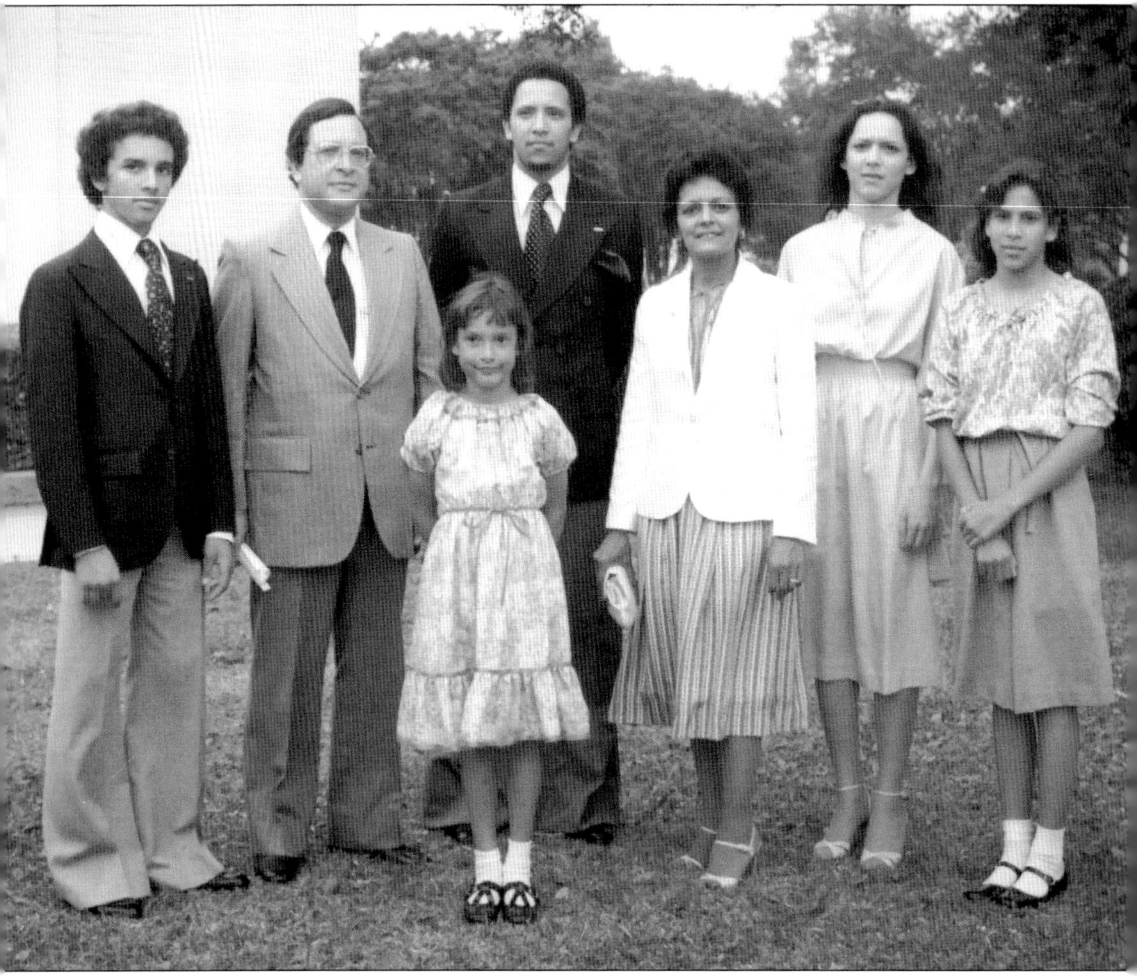

Morial Family. This photograph shows the Morial family. Pictured from left to right are Jacques Morial, Mayor Ernest N. Morial, Monique Morial, Mayor Marc Morial, Sybil H. Morial, Julie Morial, and Cherie Morial. During the 1960s, when the civil rights movement was at its peak, Sybil Morial organized the Louisiana League of Good Government. This group of young women wanted to become more informed about government. The organization invited national political figures to speak about issues of the day; it lasted for 40 years. (Courtesy of the Louisiana Division/City Archives, New Orleans Public Library.)

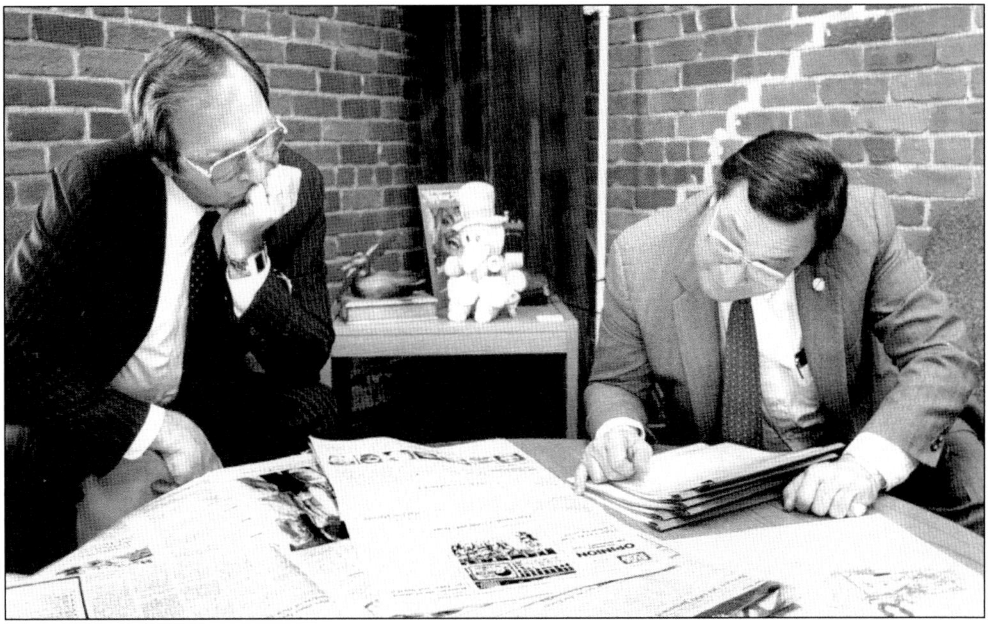

Planning a Fair to Remember. Photographed looking at plans are Peter Spurney, executive director of the Louisiana World's Exposition, with Mayor Ernest "Dutch" Morial. New Orleans played host to the 1984 Louisiana World's Exposition. (Courtesy of the Louisiana Division/City Archives, New Orleans Public Library.)

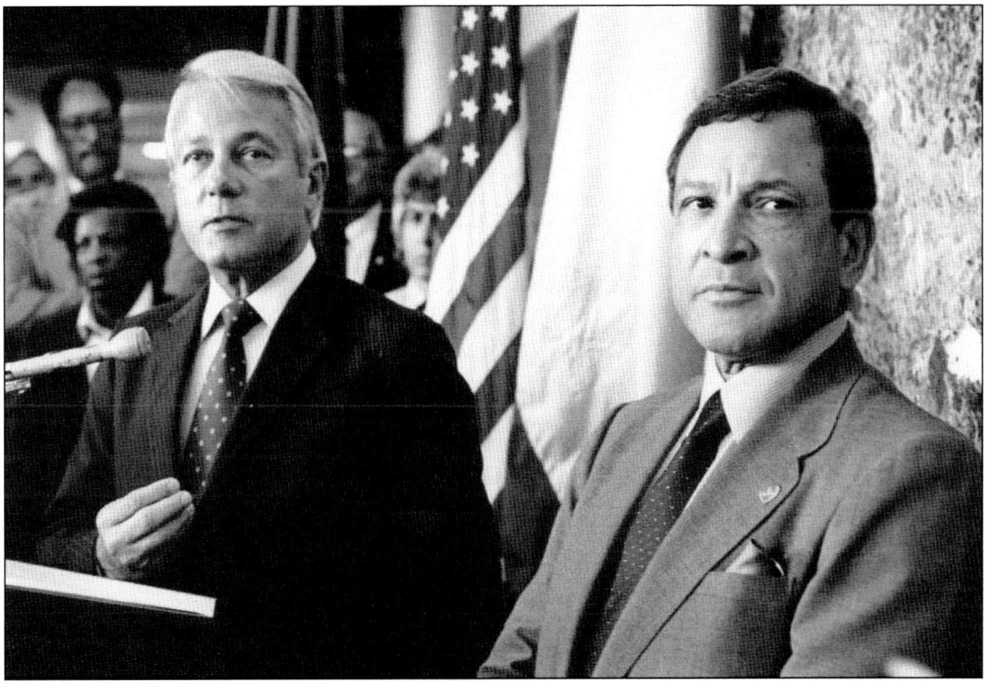

The Mayor and the Governor. Pictured here in 1978 with Louisiana governor Edwin Edwards, Ernest Morial (right) celebrates his election as mayor of New Orleans. He was reelected for a second term in 1982. (Courtesy of the Louisiana Division/City Archives, New Orleans Public Library.)

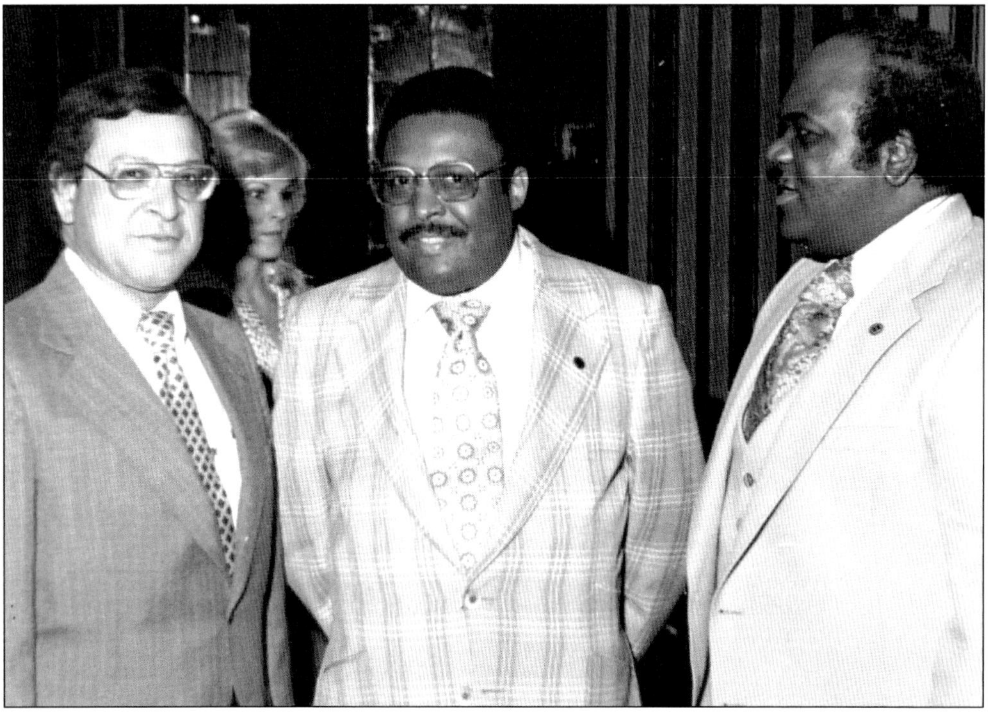

URBAN LEAGUERS. Morial poses with Howard Mills of the National Urban League and Clarence Barney of the Urban League of Greater New Orleans. (Courtesy of the Louisiana Division/City Archives, New Orleans Public Library.)

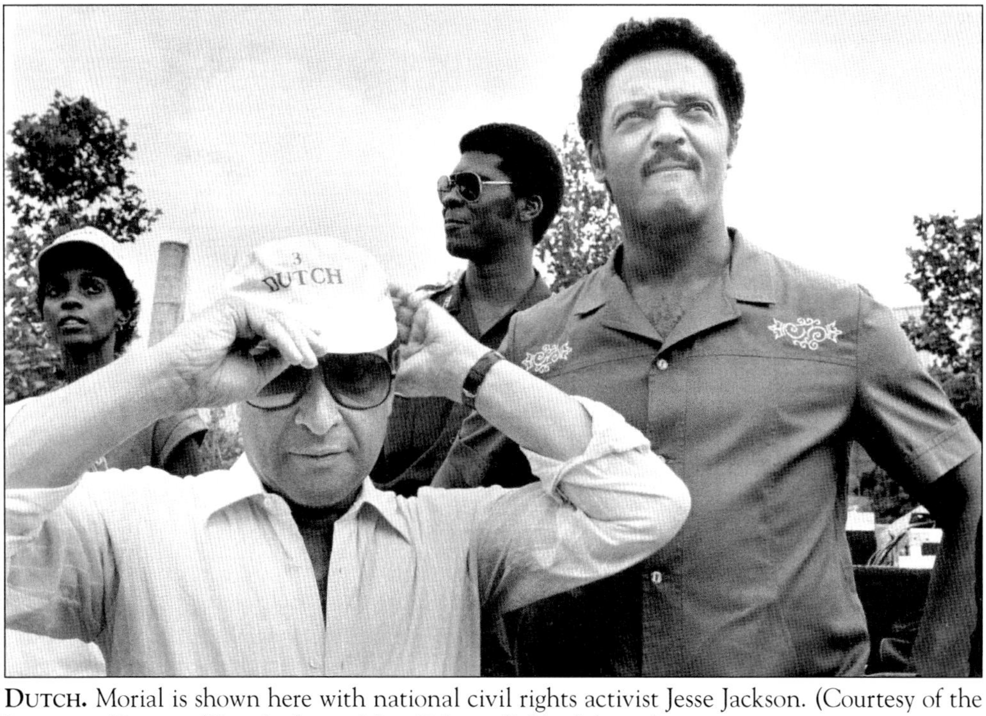

DUTCH. Morial is shown here with national civil rights activist Jesse Jackson. (Courtesy of the Louisiana Division/City Archives, New Orleans Public Library.)

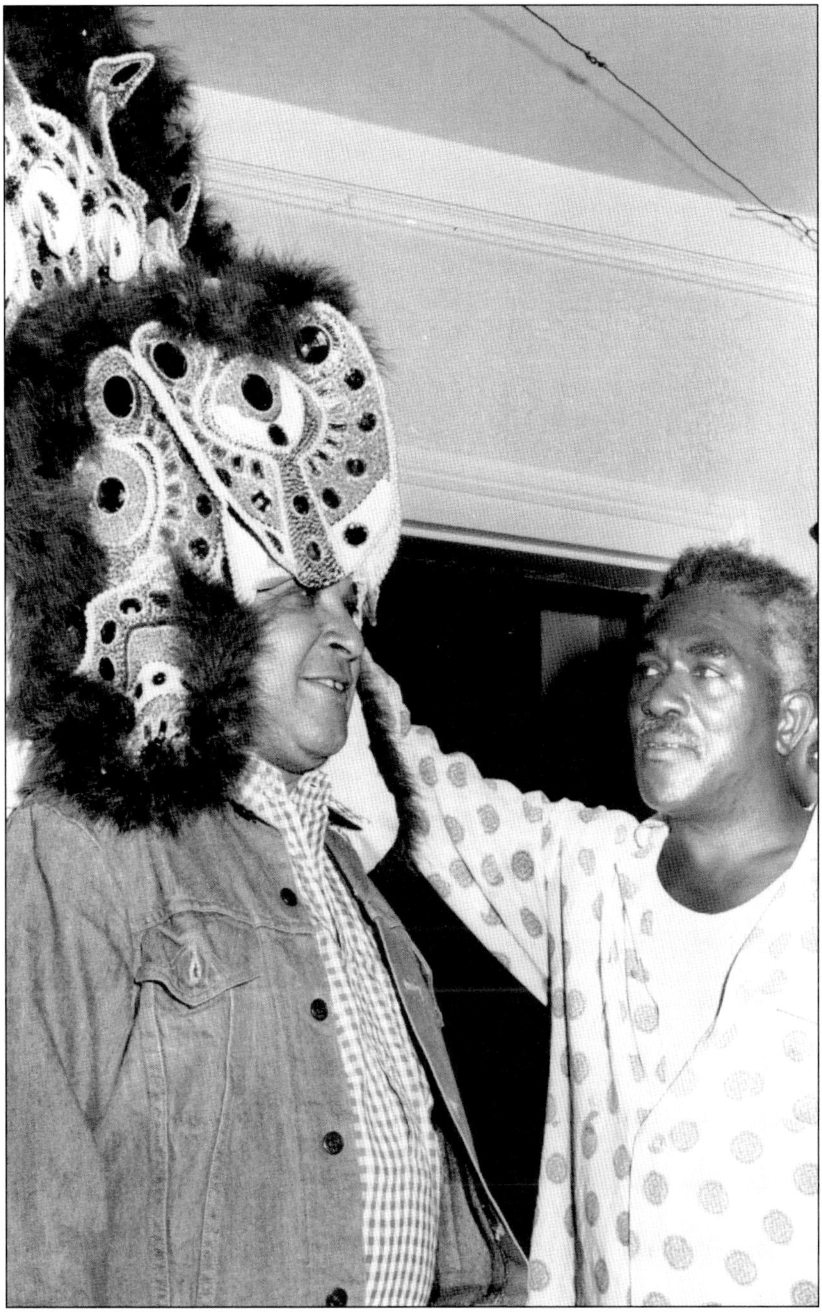

DUTCH AND BIG CHIEF TOOTIE MONTANA. This photograph shows Mayor Morial and Allison "Tootie" Montana. The century-old tradition of New Orleans' African American men dressing up in elaborate costumes for Mardi Gras is an intrinsic part of New Orleans culture. The costumes created by these men honor their Native American and African heritages. Big Chief "Tootie" Montana, pictured on the right, was a member of the Yellow Pocahontas. In 1987, he received a fellowship as a Master Traditional Artist from the Folk Art Program at the National Endowment of Arts in Washington, D.C. (Courtesy of the Louisiana Division/City Archives, New Orleans Public Library.)

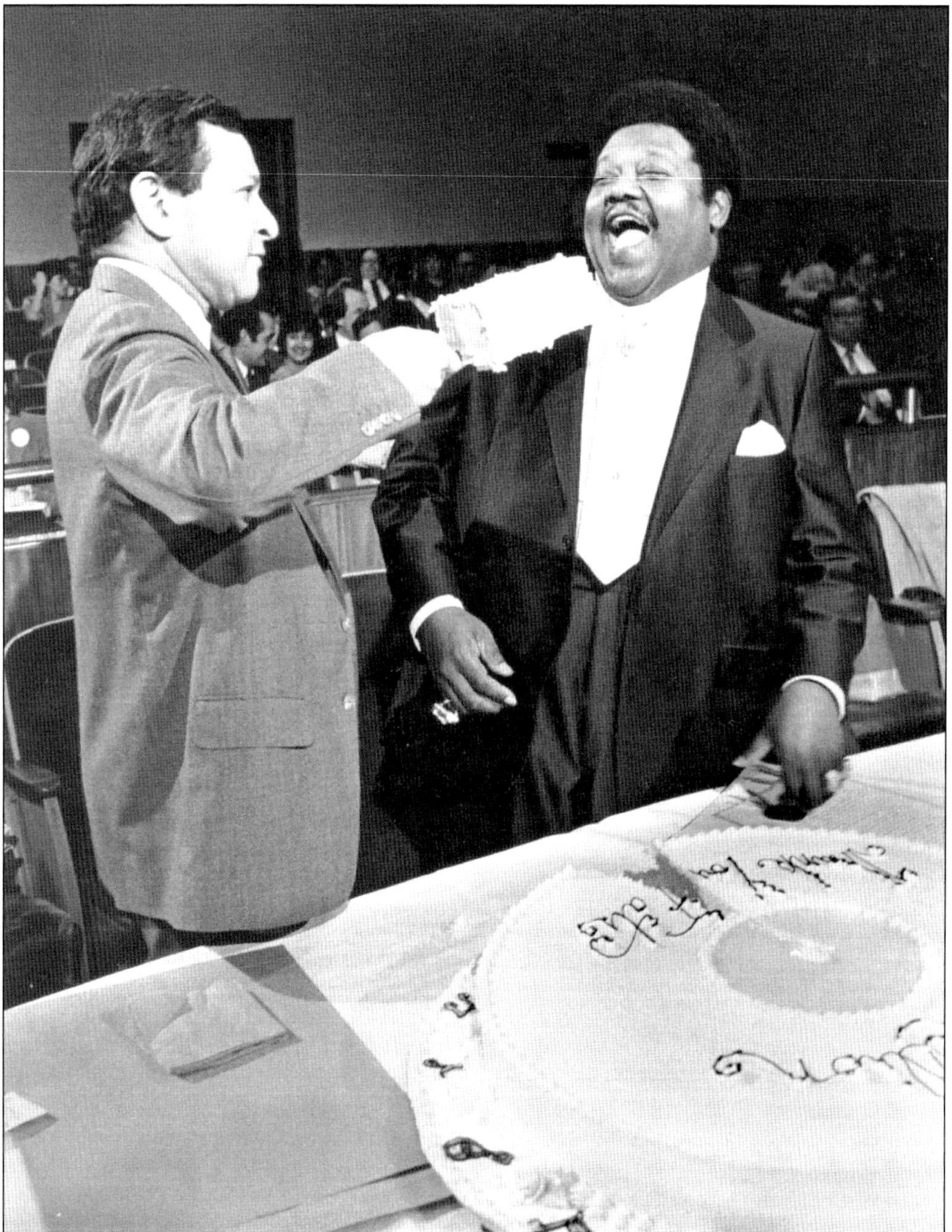

Playtime with a New Orleans Legend. Mayor Morial is shown having fun with Rhythm and Blues and Rock and Roll legend Antoine Dominique "Fats" Domino, born in New Orleans on February 26, 1928. Among his many recordings, Domino is most popular for his hits "Ain't That A Shame" and "Blueberry Hill." (Courtesy of the Louisiana Division/City Archives, New Orleans Public Library.)

Four

LEARNING

There is No Learning Without Controversy.

—Andrew Young (1932–)

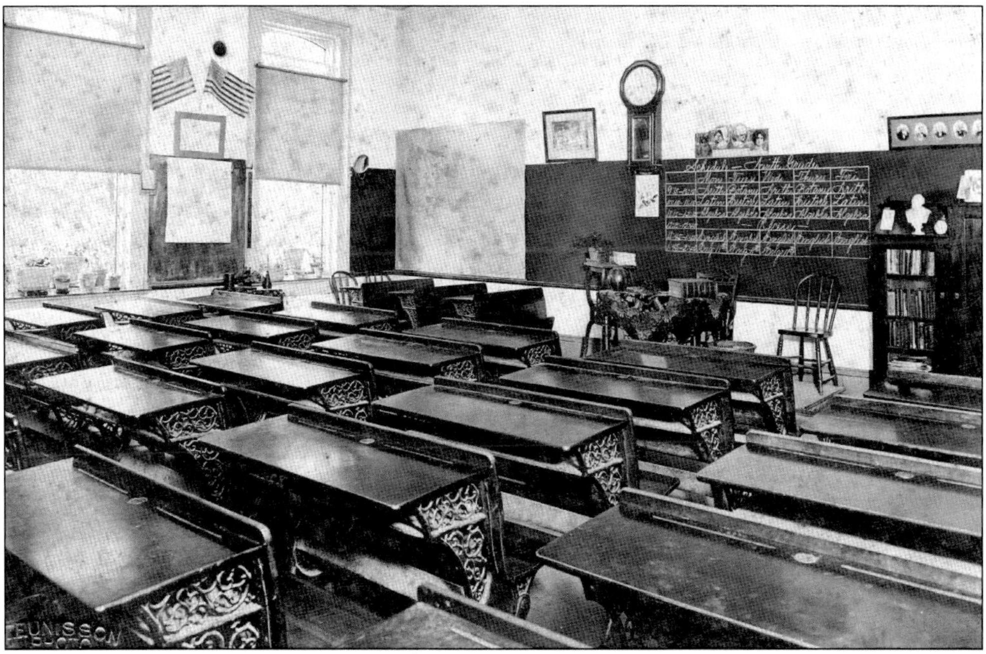

SOUTHERN UNIVERSITY. In 1880, the Louisiana General Assembly chartered Southern University in New Orleans (SUNO). With 12 students in 1881, Southern University opened its doors. The original campus in New Orleans was the former Israel Sinai Temple on Calliope Street. Due to a lack of land for expansion within New Orleans, Southern moved to Baton Rouge in 1914. (Courtesy of the Louisiana State Museum.)

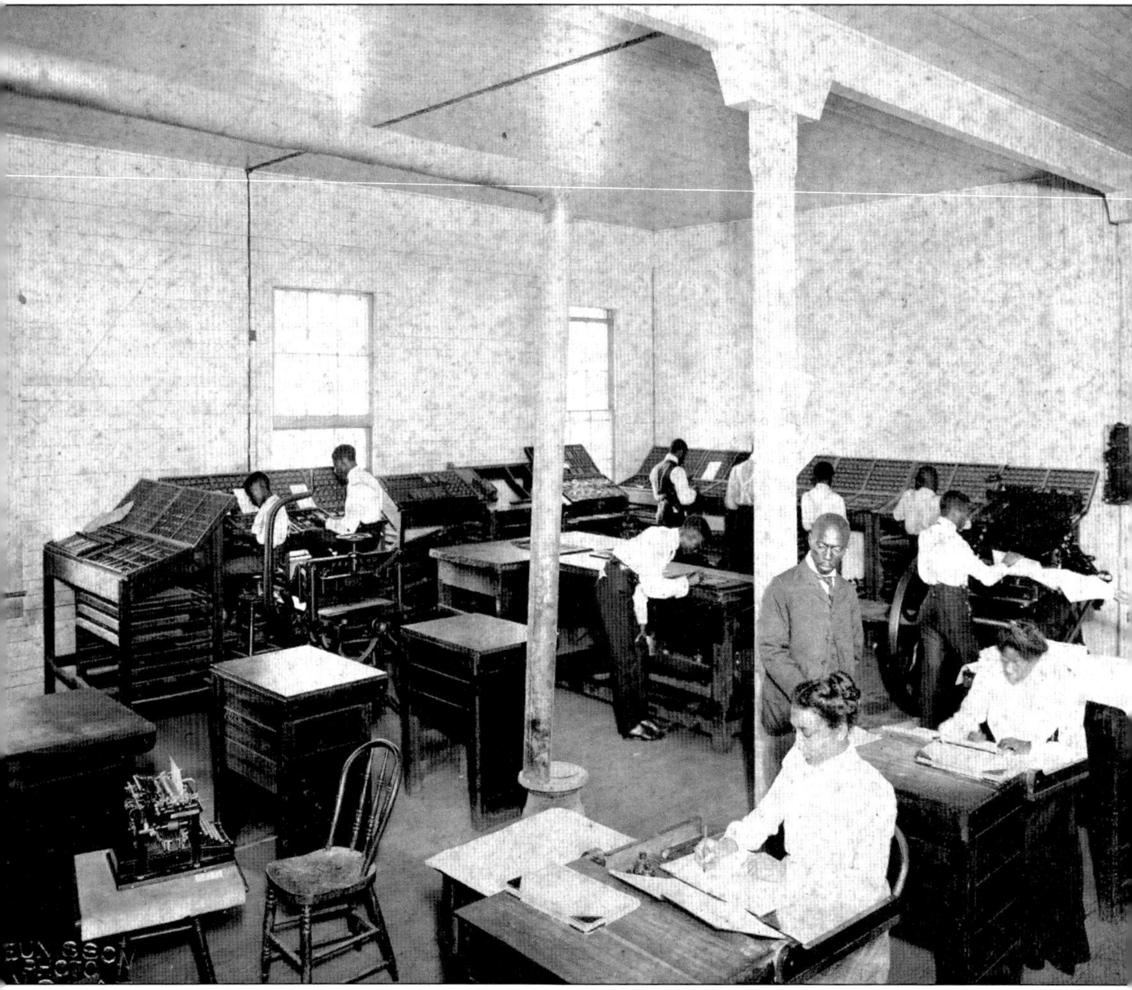

PUBLICATION LABORATORY. This early 20th-century shot captures SUNO students working on publications at the university. Among the many materials the university published, the most popular were probably the student newspaper and the annual yearbook. (Courtesy of the Louisiana State Museum.)

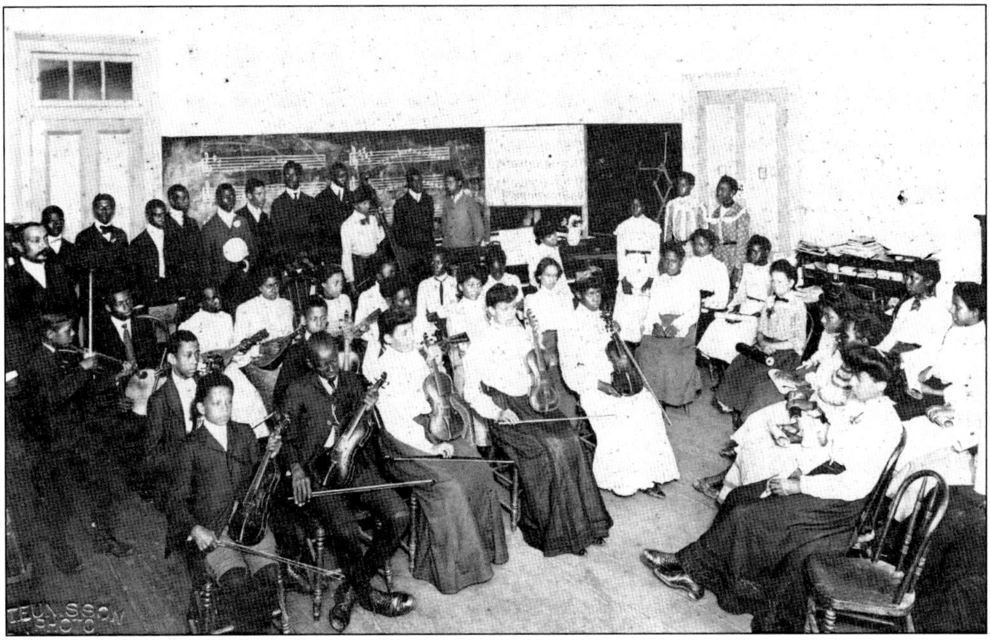

STRINGS. SUNO students with string instruments rehearse music in the practice room. (Courtesy of the Louisiana State Museum.)

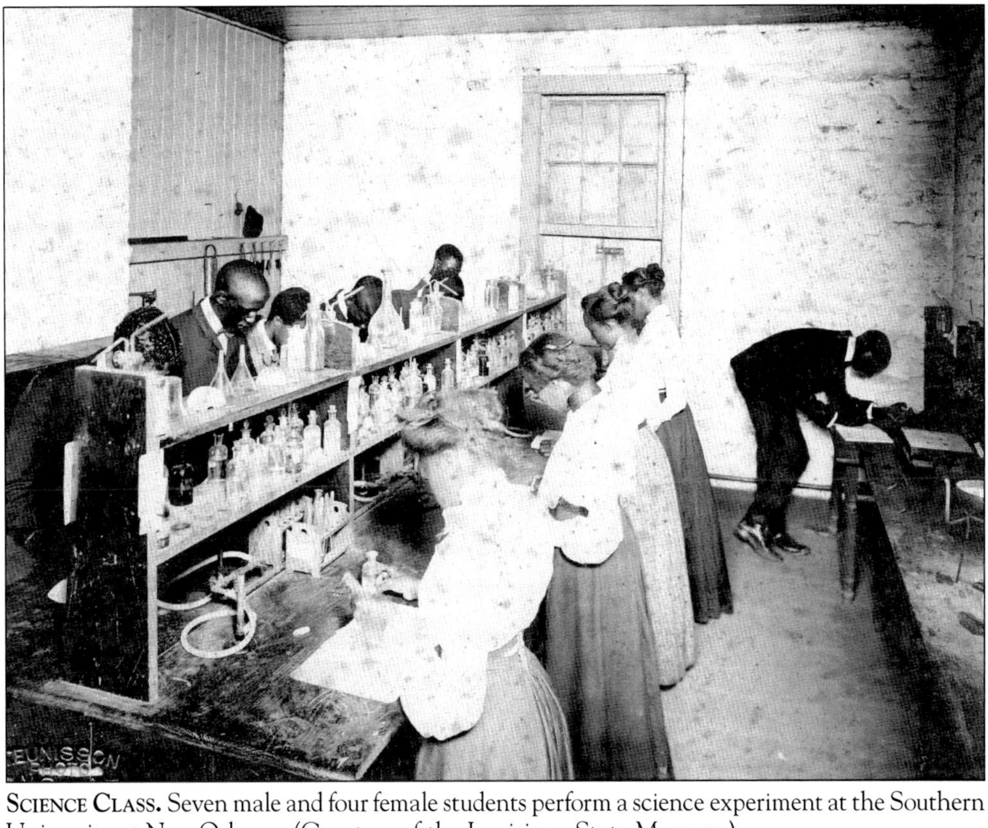

SCIENCE CLASS. Seven male and four female students perform a science experiment at the Southern University at New Orleans. (Courtesy of the Louisiana State Museum.)

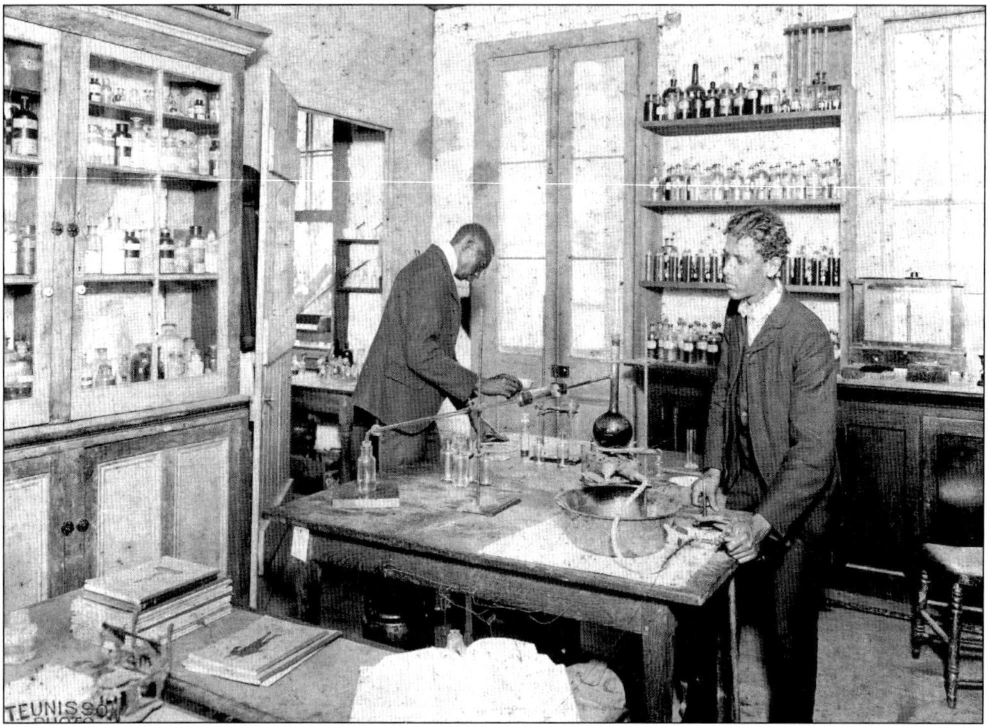

CHEMISTRY CLASS. Two SUNO students are pictured here in a chemistry class. (Courtesy of the Louisiana State Museum.)

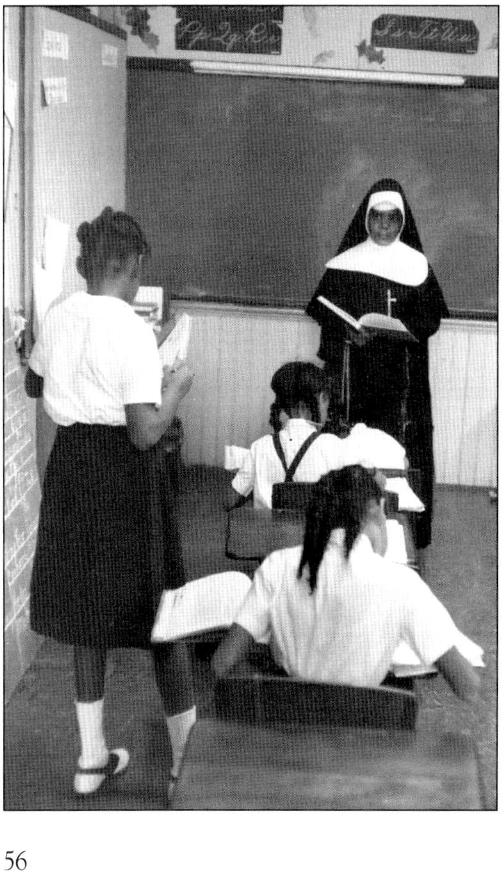

LOWER GRADES AT ST. MARY'S ACADEMY. Students read aloud as their teacher listens closely. (Courtesy of the Sisters of the Holy Family.)

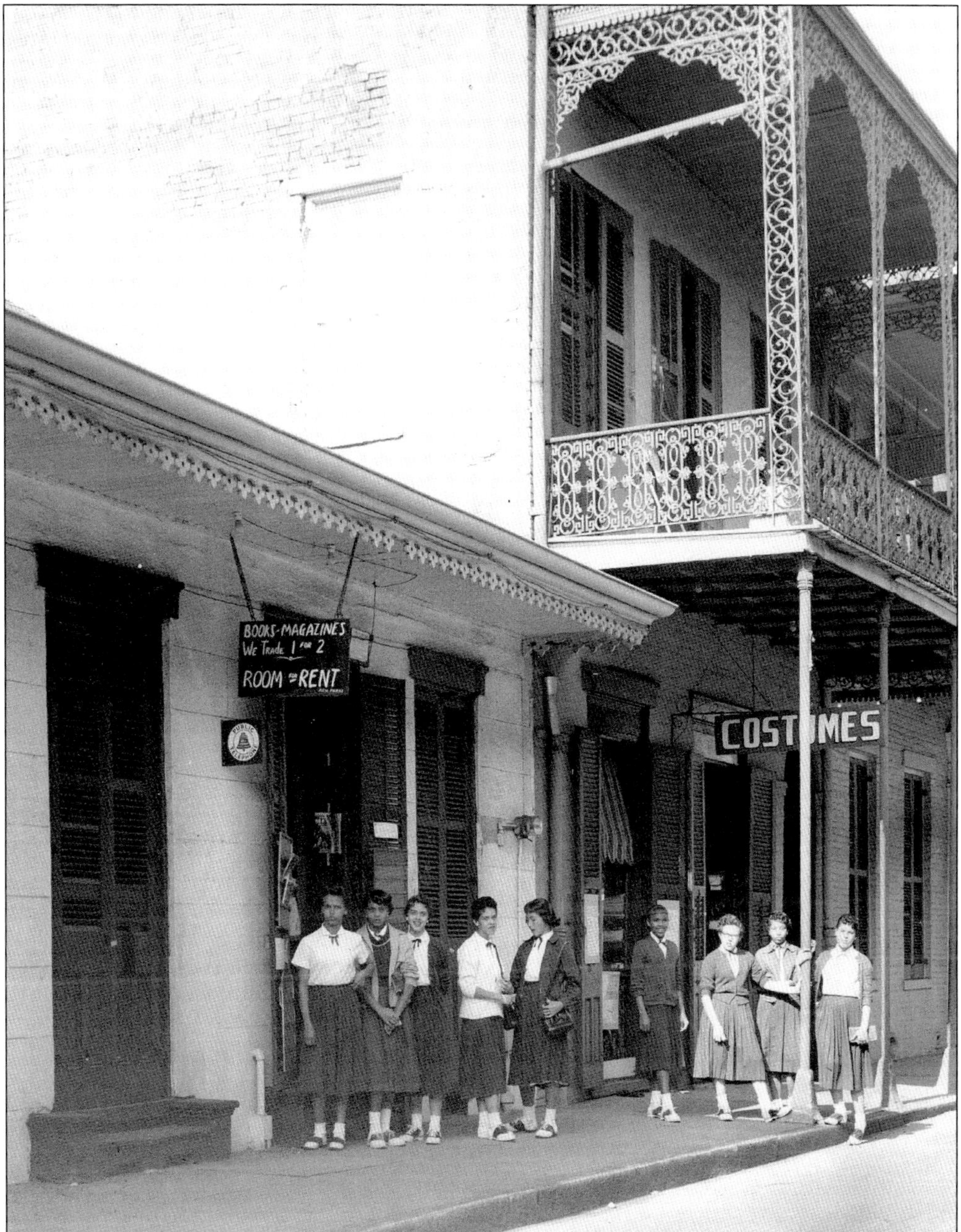

St. Mary's Academy Students in the Quarter. St. Mary's School was established in 1867 on Charters Street in New Orleans. Mother Josephine Charles was the principal. In 1878, Victoria Jordan became the school's first graduate. In 1881, St. Mary's School moved from Charters Street to 717 Orleans Street and became St. Mary's Academy, the first secondary school for girls of color in New Orleans. This photograph shows a group of St. Mary's Academy students in the French Quarter, a few blocks from St. Mary's Academy. (Courtesy of Sisters of the Holy Family.)

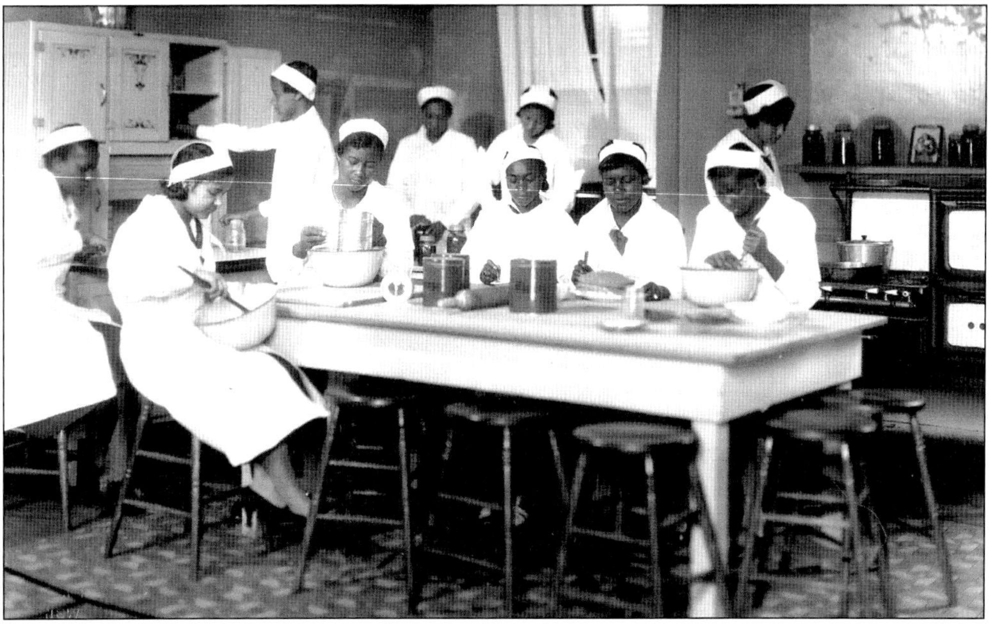

HOMEMAKING AT ST. MARY'S. In this photograph, students at St. Mary's Academy are engaged in a baking session in a Home Economics class. Home Economics teaches students about the economics and management of their homes and community. Compare this image taken in the early 1900s to the image below, taken in the 1950s. (Courtesy of the Sisters of the Holy Family.)

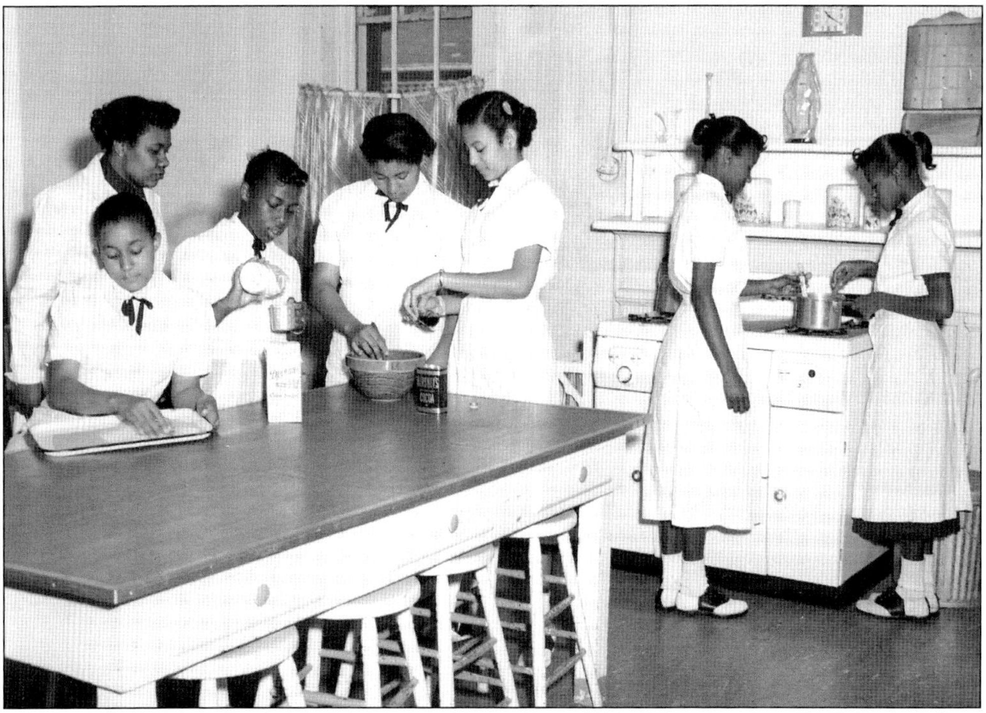

BAKING COOKIES. These St. Mary's Academy students learn measurements and mixing techniques as they prepare to bake chocolate chip cookies in their Home Economics class. (Courtesy of the Sisters of the Holy Family.)

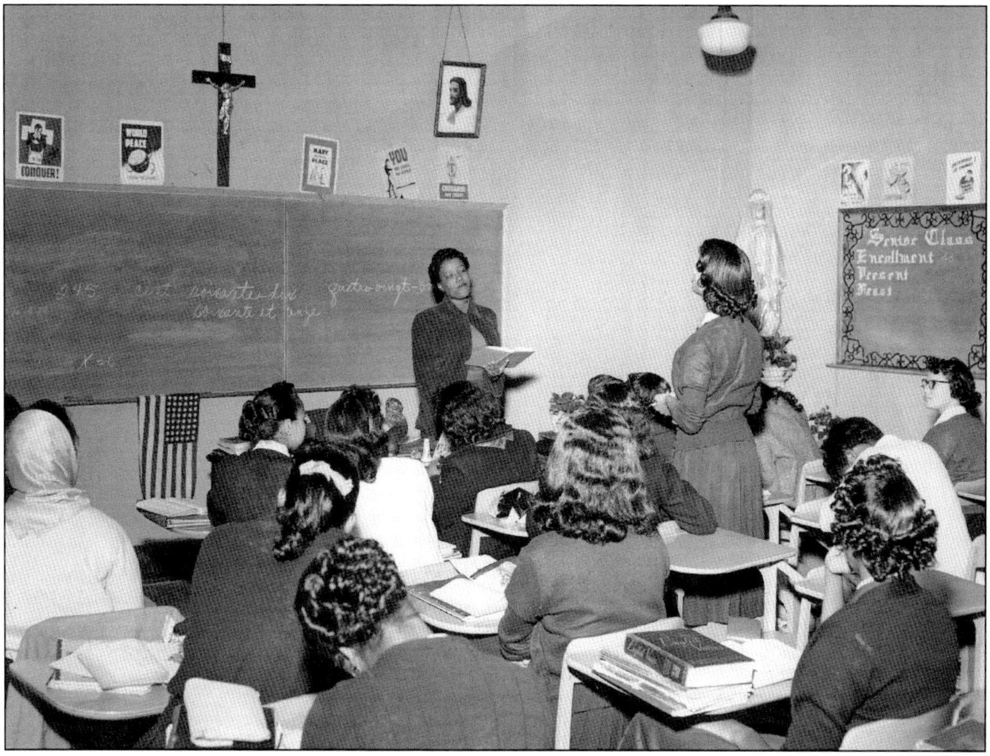

FRENCH CLASS. These students are reciting French to a lay teacher at St. Mary's Academy. (Courtesy of Sisters of the Holy Family.)

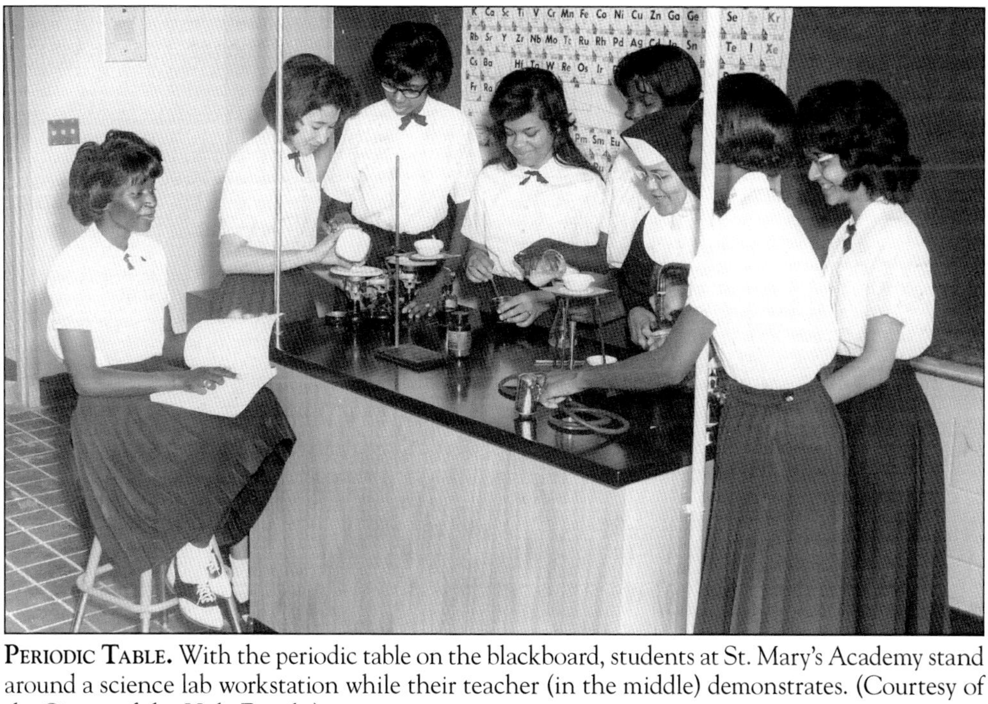

PERIODIC TABLE. With the periodic table on the blackboard, students at St. Mary's Academy stand around a science lab workstation while their teacher (in the middle) demonstrates. (Courtesy of the Sisters of the Holy Family.)

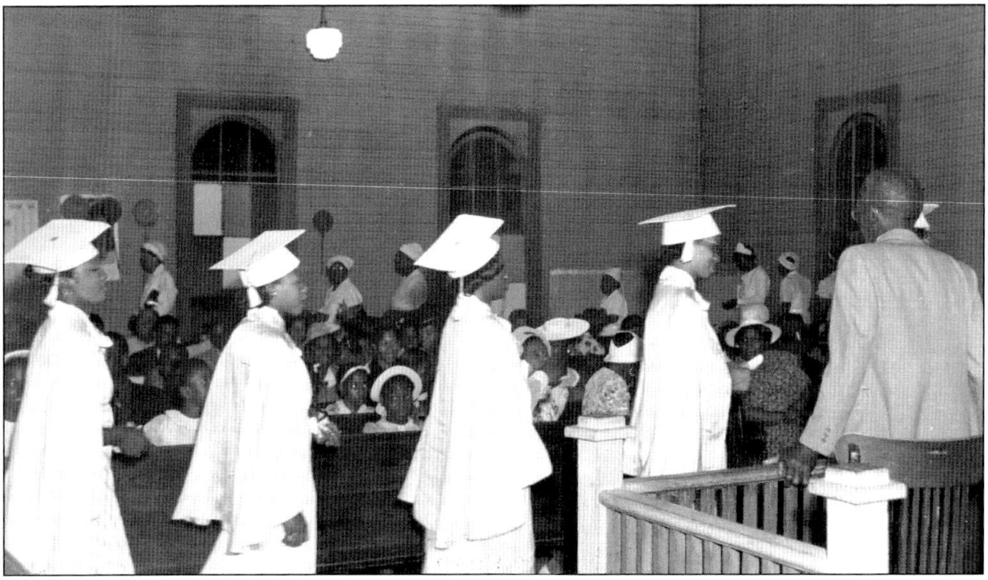

GRADUATES. This image shows graduates from St. Mary's Academy in New Orleans. Part of the mission at St. Mary's Academy is to "educate the whole person." At St. Mary's, students are taught how "to live Christian values, think critically, give service, and act responsibly in a global society." Many graduates of St. Mary's Academy have gone on to become successful entrepreneurs, educators, public administrators, physicians, and attorneys. (Courtesy of the State Library of Louisiana.)

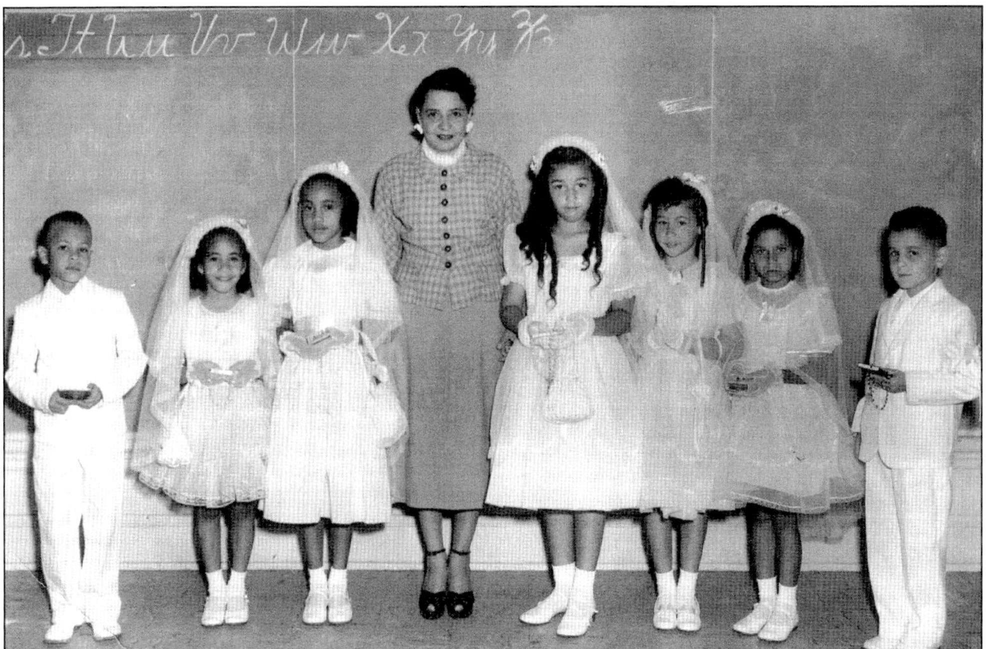

FIRST COMMUNION. "Little Communion" was held at Corpus Christi Church on St. Bernard Avenue in New Orleans, but these students loved their second-grade teacher, Carmen Rogers Robinson, so much that they went to their school to show how cute they were in their special First Communion outfits. (Courtesy of Barbara Trevigne.)

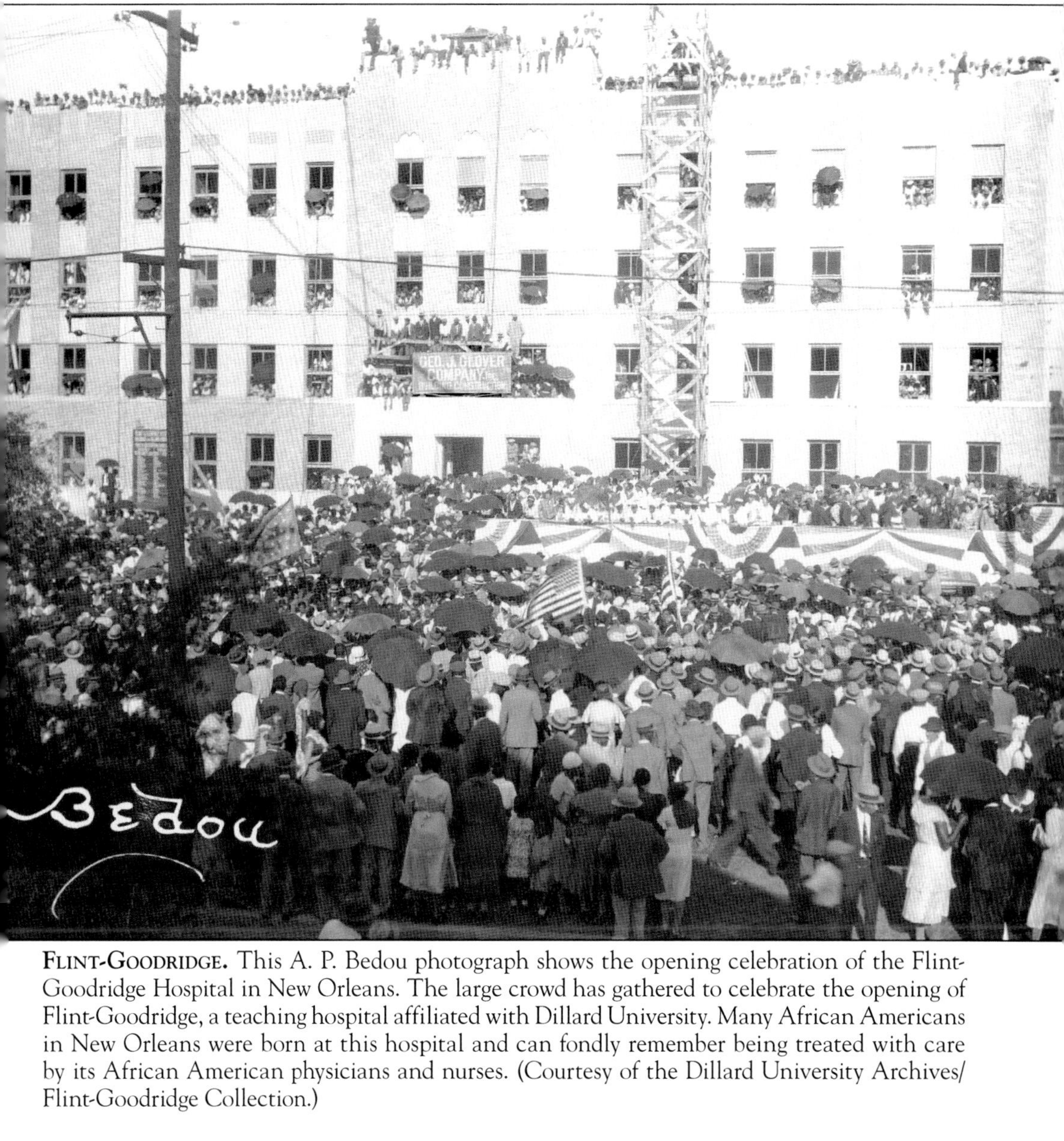

FLINT-GOODRIDGE. This A. P. Bedou photograph shows the opening celebration of the Flint-Goodridge Hospital in New Orleans. The large crowd has gathered to celebrate the opening of Flint-Goodridge, a teaching hospital affiliated with Dillard University. Many African Americans in New Orleans were born at this hospital and can fondly remember being treated with care by its African American physicians and nurses. (Courtesy of the Dillard University Archives/ Flint-Goodridge Collection.)

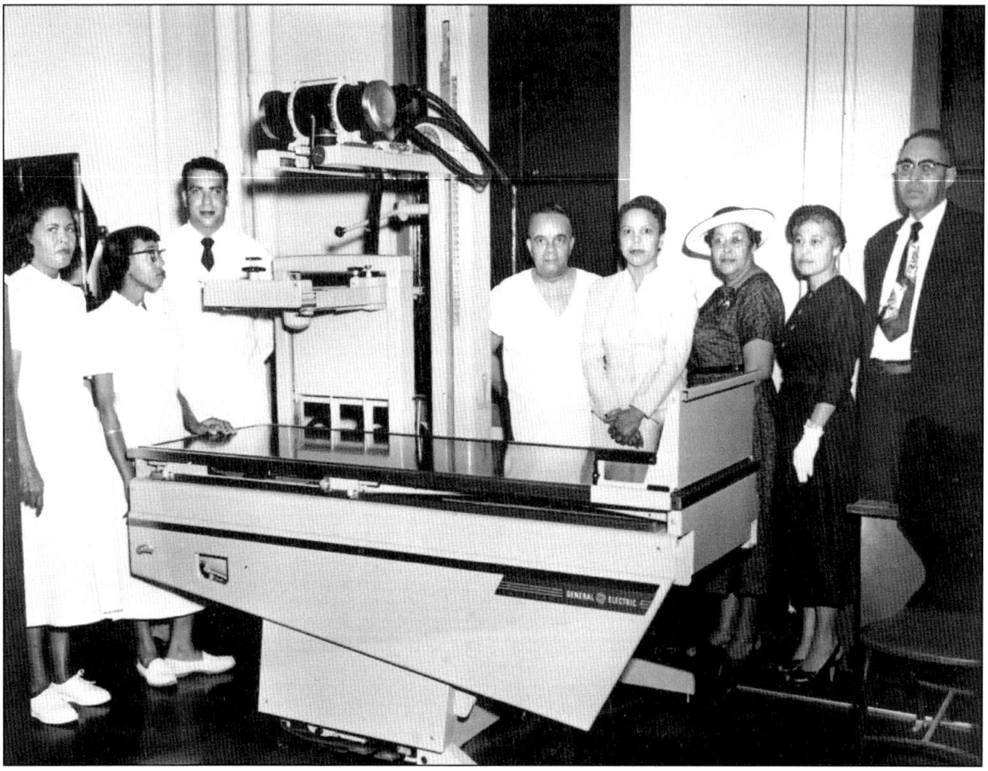

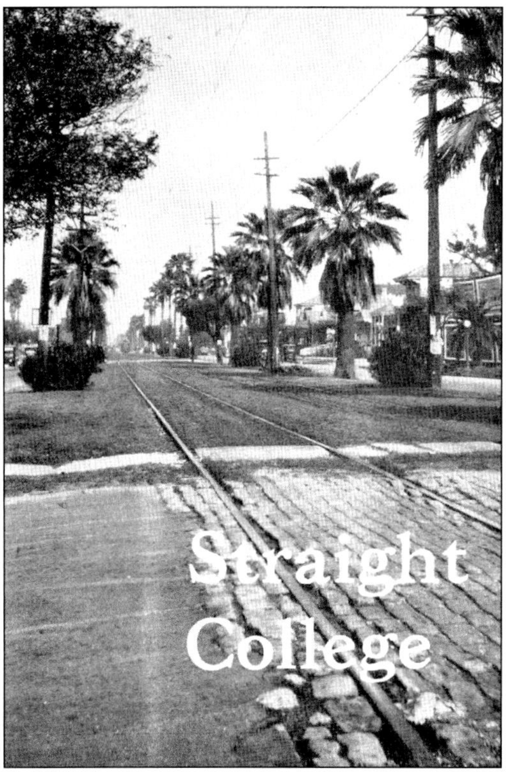

NEW MEDICAL EQUIPMENT. Doctors and nurses at Flint-Goodridge display the hospital's new medical equipment for all to see. It was common for the average African American citizen of New Orleans to donate to the hospital for the purchase of medical equipment and other needed materials. (Courtesy of the Dillard University Archives/Flint-Goodridge Collection.)

THE GREAT NEGRO UNIVERSITY IN NEW ORLEANS. Established September 24, 1935, Dillard University merged from two African American colleges founded in the mid-19th century—New Orleans University and Straight College. Dillard was named in honor of James Hardy Dillard, who was dedicated to the education of African Americans in the South. Pictured here is an advertisement symbolically representing the straight path to education. (Courtesy of the Dillard University Archives/Straight College and New Orleans University Collections.)

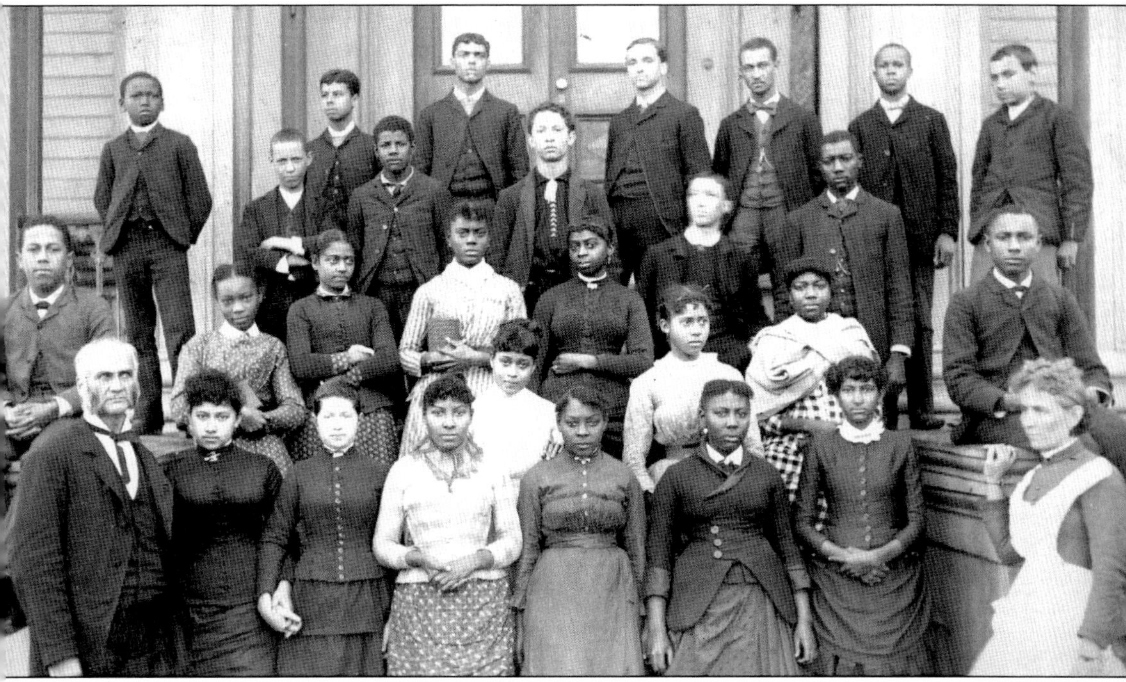

STUDENTS AT STRAIGHT. This image shows students at Straight College in the late 1800s. After the Civil War, schools were established in the American South to educate newly emancipated African Americans. Sister schools of Straight College were Tougaloo College in Mississippi, Talladega College in Alabama, and Fisk University in Tennessee. White educators and missionaries from the North usually staffed these schools. (Courtesy of Dillard University Archives/Straight College and New Orleans University Collections.)

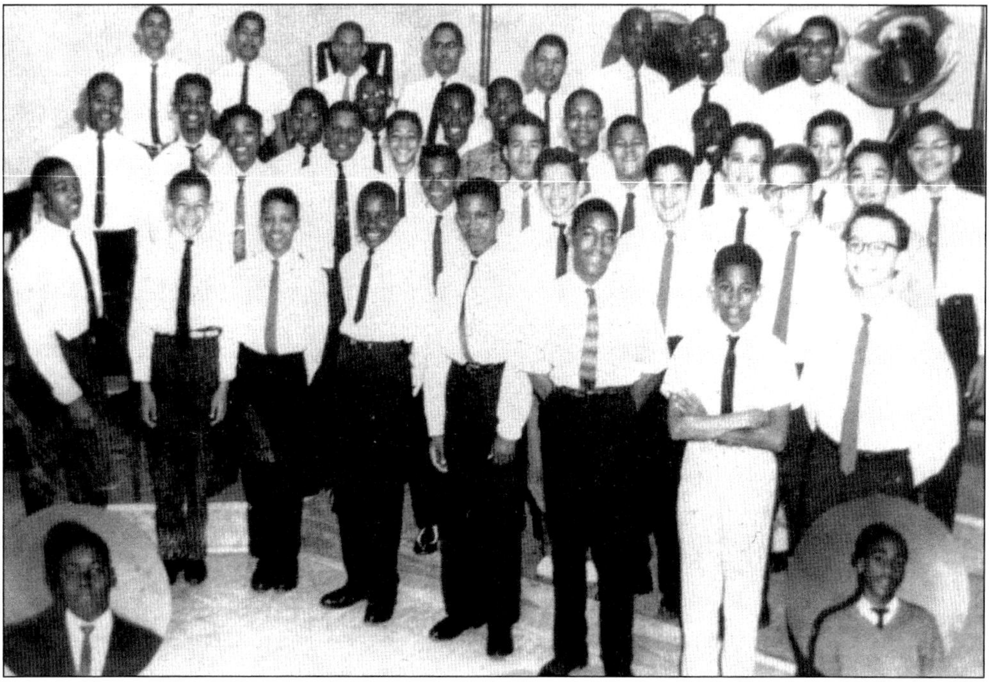

St. Augustine High School Students. This photograph shows the first eighth-grade class at St. Augustine High School in New Orleans. Established in 1951, St. Augustine is an all-boy Catholic high school. The Archdiocese of New Orleans built St. Augustine with funds provided through the Youth Progress Program. Priests and brothers of the Society of St. Joseph of the Sacred Heart operate the school. St. Augustine maintains a tradition of academic excellence and strong discipline. The famed "Marching 100" was the first African American high school band to march in the REX parade on Mardi Gras Day. (Courtesy of Keith Weldon Medley.)

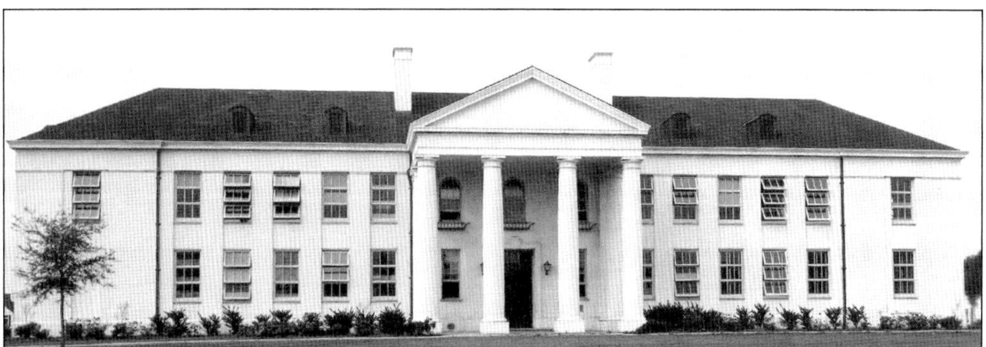

Rosenwald Hall. This was the first permanent building on the campus of Dillard University. Rosenwald Hall was originally the campus library. Built in May of 1934, the building was dedicated in 1948 to philanthropist Julius Rosenwald. (Courtesy of the State Library of Louisiana.)

DR. RAPHEAL CASSIMERE. This photograph shows Raphael Cassimere (right) receiving his degree from Louisiana State University at New Orleans (LSUNO), now called the University of New Orleans (UNO.) Cassimere was the first African American to receive a graduate degree in History from the LSUNO. Later, Cassimere became the first African American to teach at the University of New Orleans. (Courtesy of the Special Collections at the University of New Orleans.)

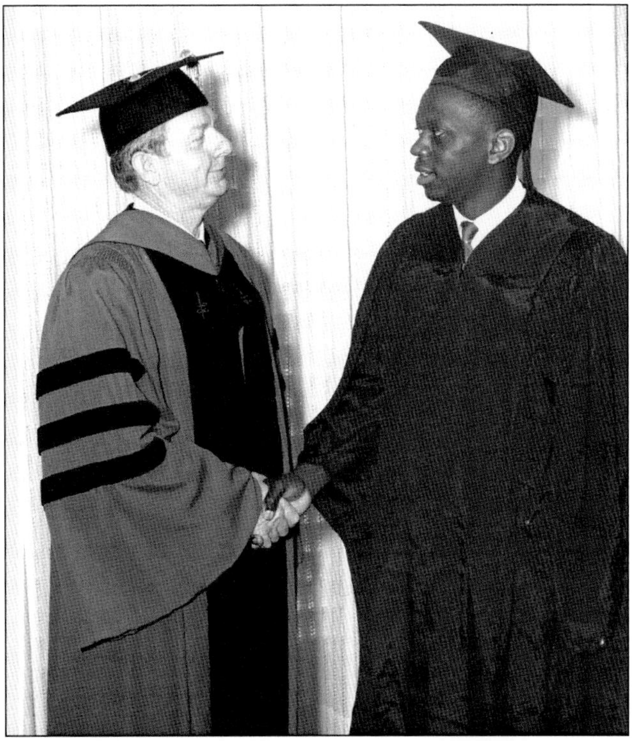

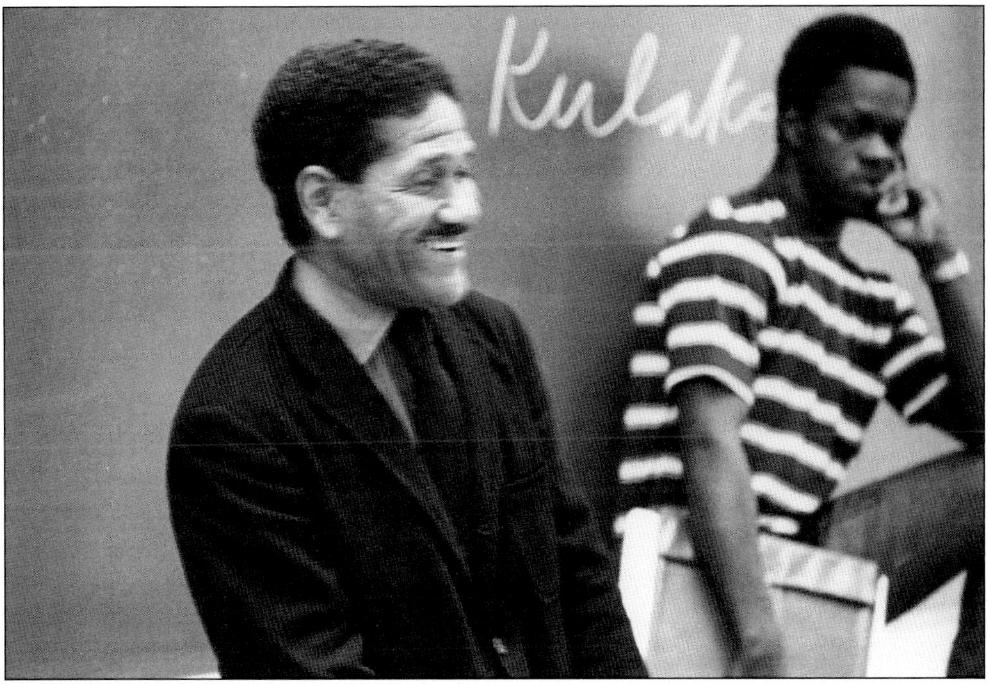

THE DEAN OF NEW ORLEANS AFRICAN AMERICAN HISTORY. Born in 1900, Marcus Bruce Christian was a poet, writer, and folklorist. The director of the Negro Writers Project at Dillard in the 1930s, Christian worked with Lyle Saxon, who was head of the Louisiana WPA Writers Project. (Courtesy of the University of New Orleans Louisiana Collection.)

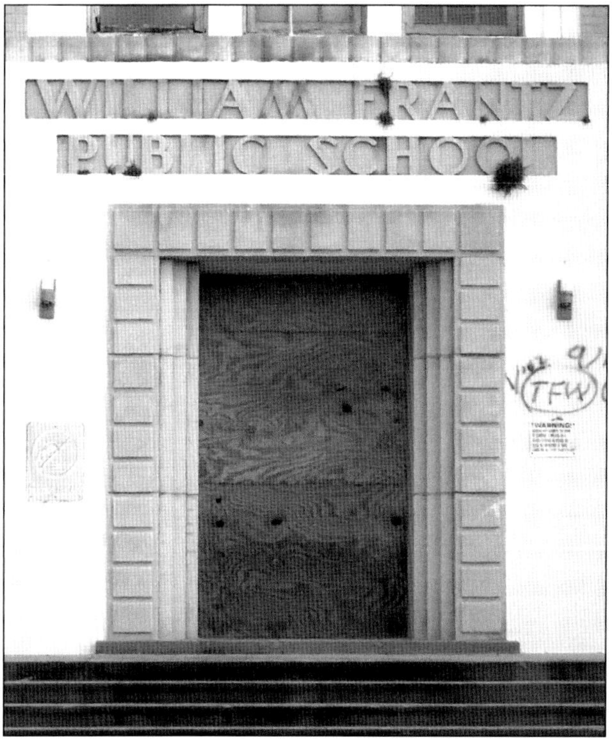

With All Deliberate Speed. Judge J. Skelly Wright said that ending segregation would "require the utmost patience, understanding, generosity, and forbearance from all of us." Wright ordered the desegregation of the public schools in New Orleans. This photograph shows the facade of William Frantz School after Hurricane Katrina. First grader Ruby Bridges desegregated Frantz School November 14, 1960. Bridges entered the school escorted by Federal Marshals walking through a crowd of angry protesters, mostly white women from the surrounding neighborhood. (Courtesy of Phoenix Savage.)

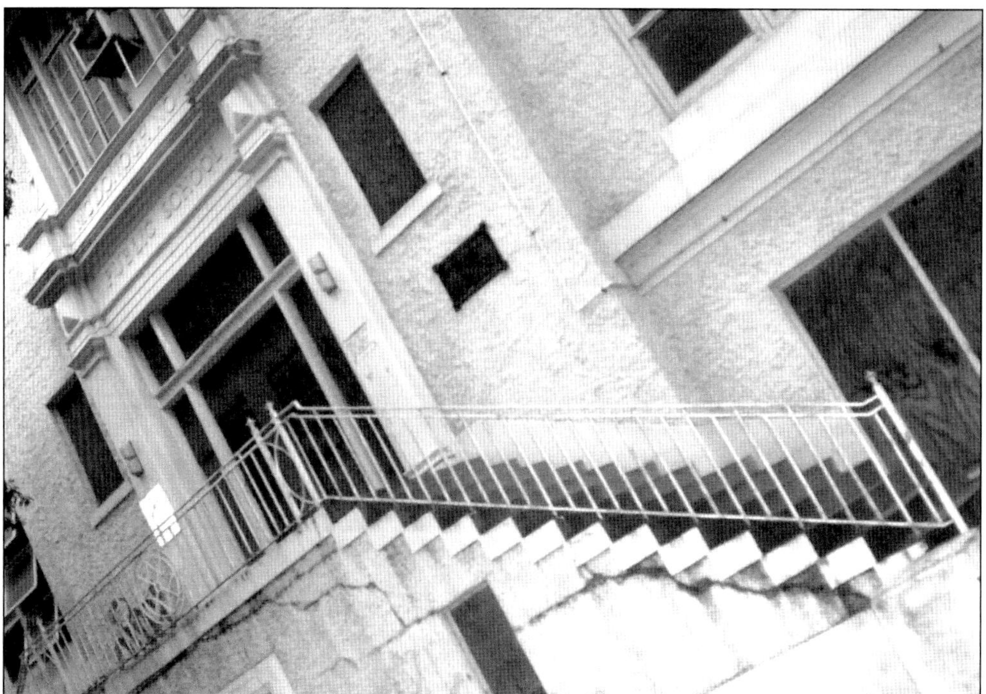

Pioneers. On November 14, 1960, three little girls desegregated McDonogh 19 Elementary School in New Orleans. Leona Tate, Tessie Prevost, and Gail Etienne walked up the stairs shown here and stepped into history. (Courtesy of Phoenix Savage.)

Five

Because I Am Here

Beauty is here because I am here.

—Anonymous African Dutch Woman, 1600s

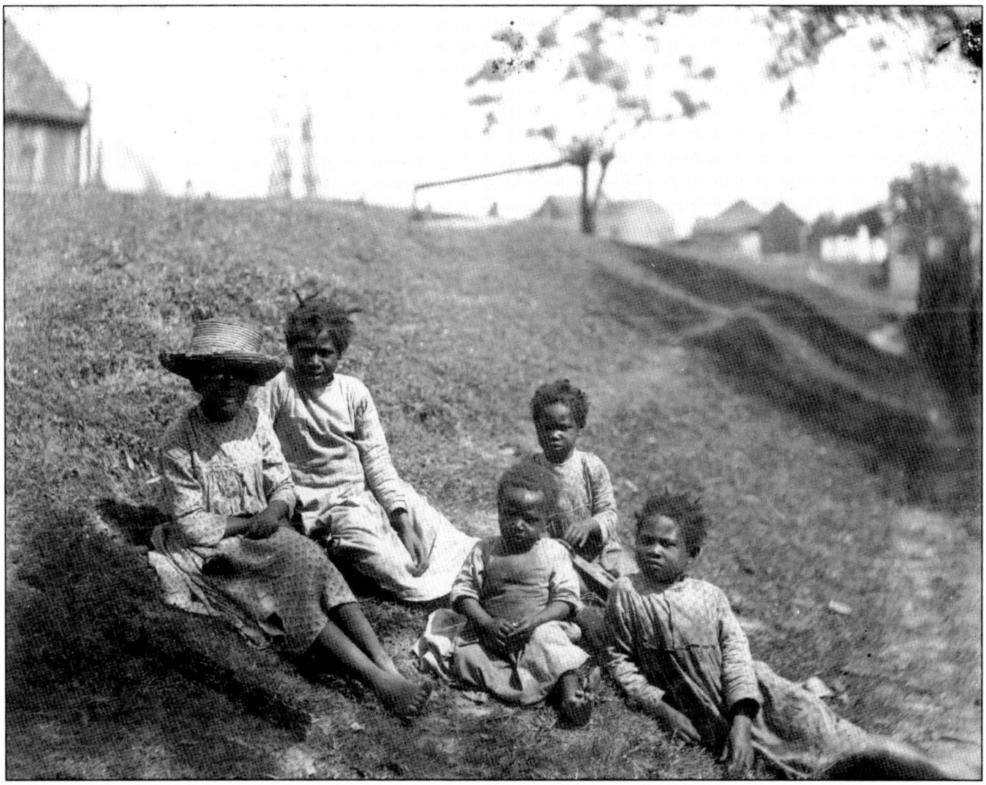

Children Sitting on the Side of a Hill. This photograph shows five children on a hillside, possibly on the outskirts of the original city of New Orleans. (Courtesy of the Louisiana State Museum.)

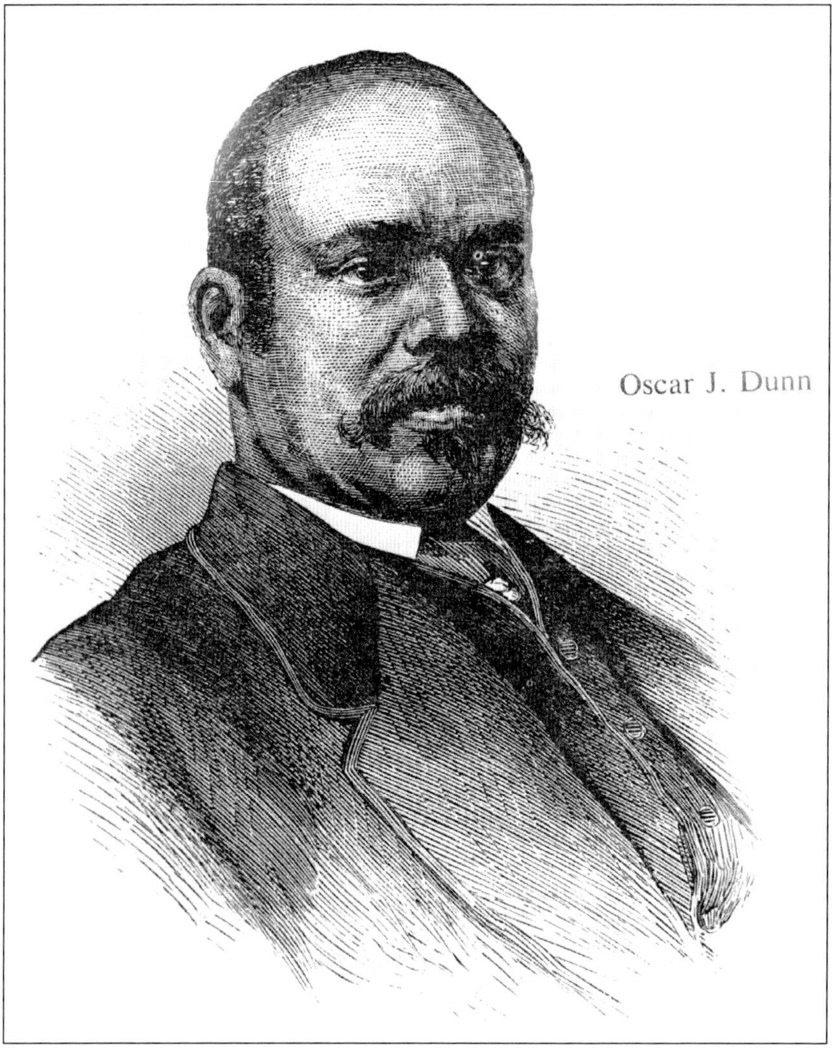

Oscar Dunn. Born enslaved in 1826, Oscar James Dunn's freedom was purchased by his father. He would grow up to become the first African American to serve as lieutenant governor of Louisiana. As a young man, Oscar Dunn apprenticed in the plastering and painting trades. He also taught violin lessons. An English-speaking African American in Reconstruction-era New Orleans, Dunn became involved with the Prince Hall Masons. He served as grand master of the Eureka Grand Lodge of Louisiana, owned and operated an employment agency for freedmen, and was a vocal supporter of the Universal Suffrage movement. Dunn also served as secretary of the Advisory Committee of the Freemen's Savings and Trust Company of New Orleans. By 1867, Dunn was elected to serve as a city alderman, where he chaired the committee that advocated free public education for all children between the ages of 6 and 18. In 1868, the Louisiana State Legislature adopted the city's resolution into state law. After Francis E. Dumas refused the nomination to lieutenant governor, Republicans nominated Dunn to run on their party's ticket with gubernatorial candidate Henry Clay Warmoth. The Warmoth/Dunn ticket won by a vote of 64,941 to 38,046. Their election to the highest seats in the state marked the beginning of Radical Republican rule in Louisiana. Dunn died unexpectedly while in office on November 22, 1871. Over 50,000 citizens crowded Canal Street as a funeral procession carried Oscar James Dunn to his final place of rest at St. Louis Cemetery No. 2. (Courtesy of State Library of Louisiana.)

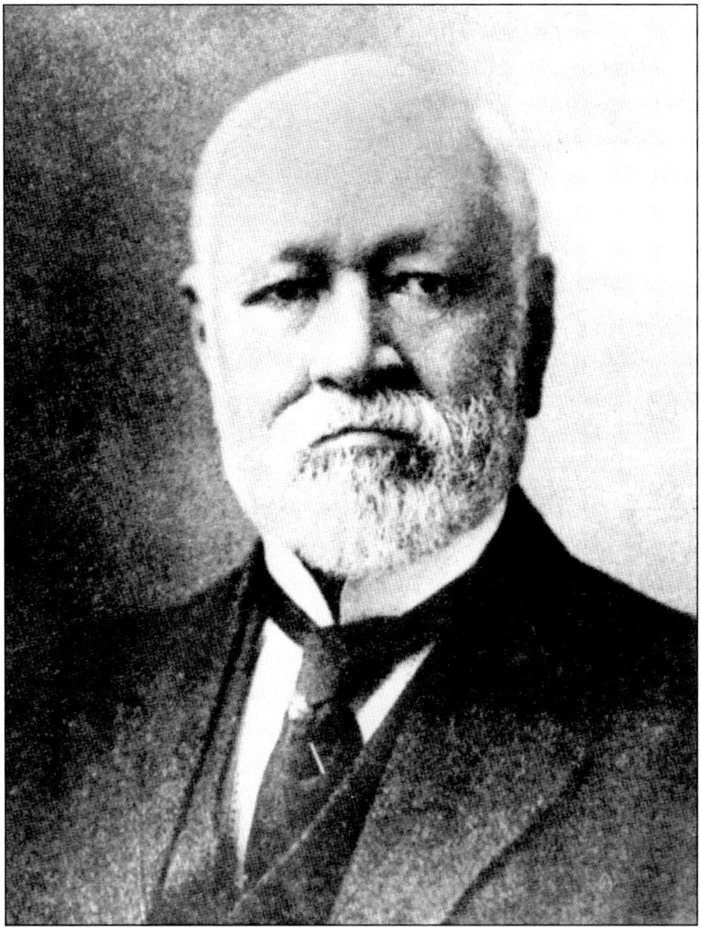

Pickney Benton Stewart Pinchback. P. B. S. Pinchback was born in May 1837 in Macon, Georgia, the son of a formerly enslaved mother who married her former slave master and bore him several children. Until his father's death, Pinchback enjoyed a privileged lifestyle. However, after his father's death, Pinchback's family was in jeopardy and his mother and siblings fled to join Pinchback, who was already in Ohio. At the outbreak of the Civil War, Pinchback traveled to New Orleans and joined the Union army, where he served as captain of Company A of the 1st Louisiana Native Guard's Corps de Afrique. Pinchback rose to political power as the lieutenant governor of Louisiana under Henry Clay Warmoth's administration during Reconstruction. Pinchback assumed this position after lieutenant governor Oscar Dunn died unexpectedly. When Governor Warmoth came under impeachment, he was temporarily removed from office, allowing Pinchback to become the first African American to serve as a U.S. state governor—and the last until 1990. Pinchback served as governor for only 35 days—from December 19, 1872, until January 13, 1873—before Warmoth's term ended. Pinchback ran successfully for legislative office twice after his term as Louisiana governor. In 1874, he won a seat to the U.S. House of Representatives, and in 1876, he won election to the U.S. Senate. Both elections were disputed by state Democrats, and in both cases, Pinchback's opponents were seated instead of him. In 1885, Pinchback attended Straight College, and the Louisiana Bar admitted him in 1886. Pinchback held leadership positions with the Louisiana State Board of Education, which he persuaded to establish Southern University in 1880. He later served on the university's board of trustees. Pinchback died in 1921 and is buried in Metairie Cemetery, which was, at the time, a segregated cemetery. (Courtesy of Moorland-Springarn Research Center, Howard University, Washington, D.C.)

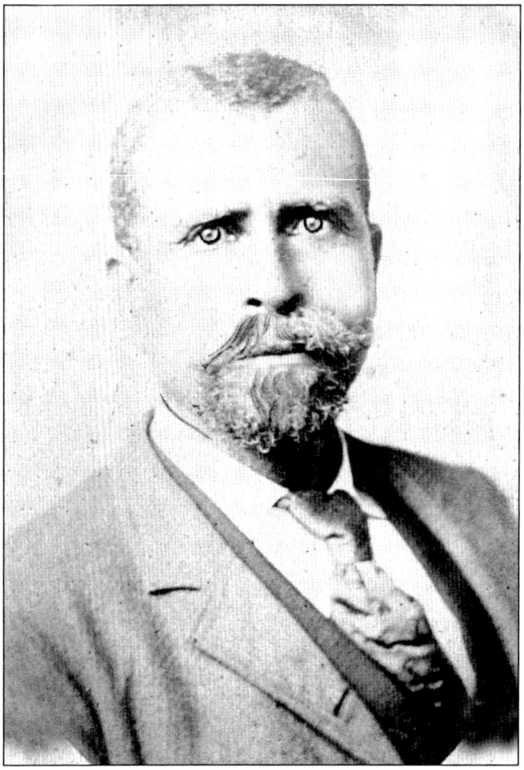

Walter Williams Sr. Born in Toronto in 1846, Williams was the child of parents who had fled to Canada via the Underground Railroad—not because of enslavement but for love. Williams' parents were breaking the miscegenation laws of the day. By 1868, however, Williams was teaching school in Vermilionville, Louisiana, and the 1870 U.S. Census records him as residing in both New Orleans and Vermilionville (present-day Lafayette). By 1889, Williams lived in Algiers, Louisiana, and had since 1886 been part of the politically powerful U. S. Customs House in New Orleans. In 1868, the American Missionary Association appointed Williams as headmaster of the Excelsior School in Lafayette, Louisiana. He operated the school until 1902. (Courtesy of Austin M. Sonnier Jr.)

Watercolor. This 19th-century watercolor painted by an unknown artist depicts a typical New Orleans street scene of African American women dressed in petticoats and carrying parasols to protect them from the sun. Note the woman third from the left; she is wearing a tignon, as opposed to a hat like the other women. This helps to date the painting, for it was during the term of Spanish New Orleans governor Don Estevan Miro (1785–1791) that a law was passed requiring women of African descent to wear head coverings when in public. Women answered this edict with stylish protest that brought just as much if not more attention to their beauty—exactly what the law intended to avoid. (Courtesy of the Louisiana State Museum.)

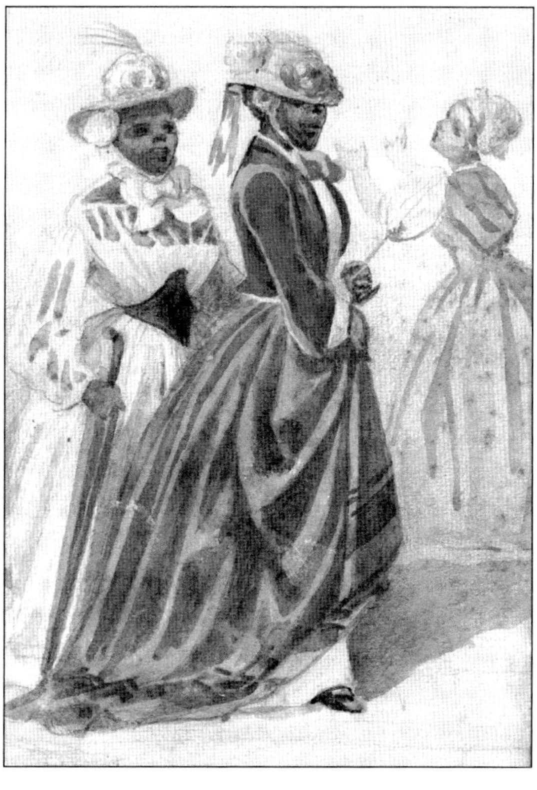

Douglas Family Servant. This 1850s portrait suggests that this unidentified woman was highly regarded. To sit for a portrait meant time away from chores as well as the ability to pay the fees of the artist. Unfortunately, little information exists regarding both the portrait's painter and its subject. (Courtesy of the Louisiana State Museum.)

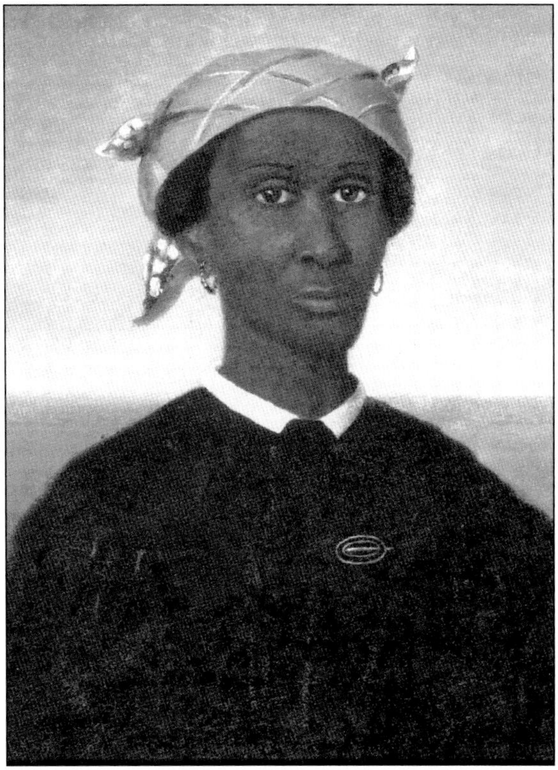

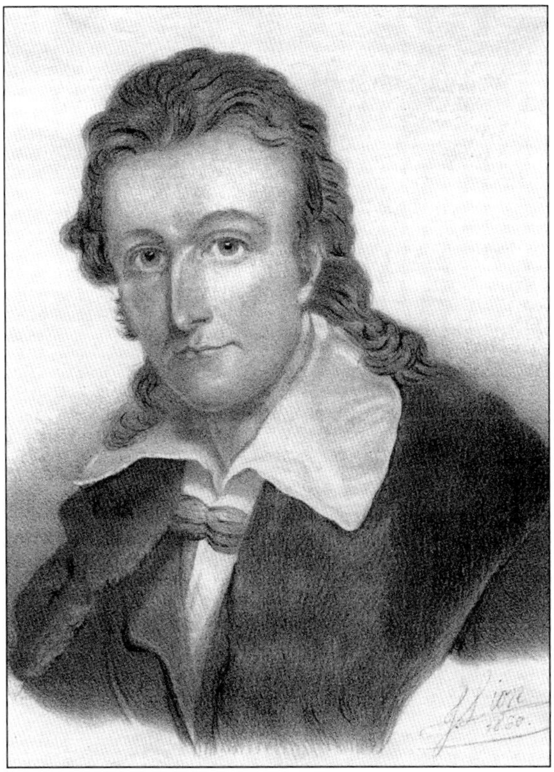

John James Audubon. The internationally known ornithologist was born in St. Domingue in 1785. His father was a French slave trader and his mother was a Creole woman of color native to the island. Audubon's mother died during the slave insurrection. After this, Audubon departed for Paris, where his father's wife saw to his upbringing. With the assistance of his Parisian family, Audubon escaped conscription into Napoleon's army by being sent to the United States outside of Philadelphia, Pennsylvania, where he lived on a familial estate. While Audubon's work painting birds offered little financial stability, he maintained residency in New Orleans in the French Quarter, where he completed his seminal work *Birds of America*, with its total of 435 life-sized prints. This image of Audubon is a lithograph done by Julies Lion, a free man of color who made his living as an artist in 19th-century New Orleans. (Courtesy of the Louisiana State Museum.)

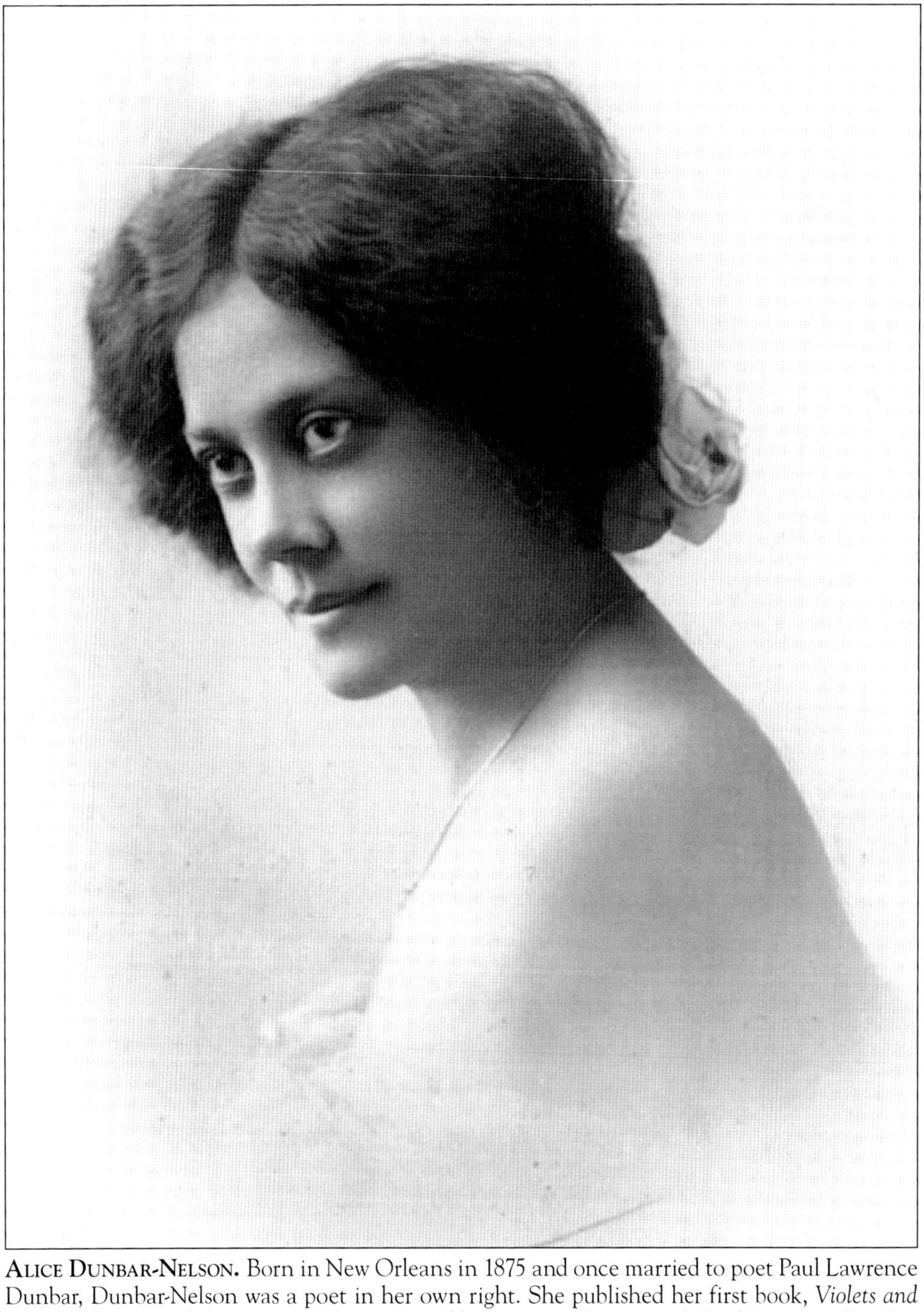

ALICE DUNBAR-NELSON. Born in New Orleans in 1875 and once married to poet Paul Lawrence Dunbar, Dunbar-Nelson was a poet in her own right. She published her first book, *Violets and Other Tales,* in 1895. Her personal diaries reveal her stormy relations with Paul Lawrence Dunbar and her own active relations with a network of black lesbians during the 1920s. In 1915, Dunbar-Nelson served as the secretary of the National Association of Colored Women; in 1922, she led efforts to pass the Dyer Federal Anti-Lynching Bill as head of the Anti-Lynching Crusaders in Delaware. (Courtesy of the University of Delaware/Alice Dunbar Nelson Collection.)

Voodoo Queen. Arguably one of the most famous citizens of New Orleans, Marie Laveau was a free woman of color—and like many women in 19th-century New Orleans, she was an entrepreneur. Though a devoted Catholic, she neither rejected nor abandoned traditional African spiritual practices. Because of her voodoo spiritual practices, the myths surrounding Laveau's life today unfortunately serve to pry dollars from the hands of tourists rather than to honor Marie Laveau's role as a conservator of African culture. While unproven, this image is frequently sited as being that of the great American "Voodoo Queen."(Courtesy of the Louisiana State Museum.)

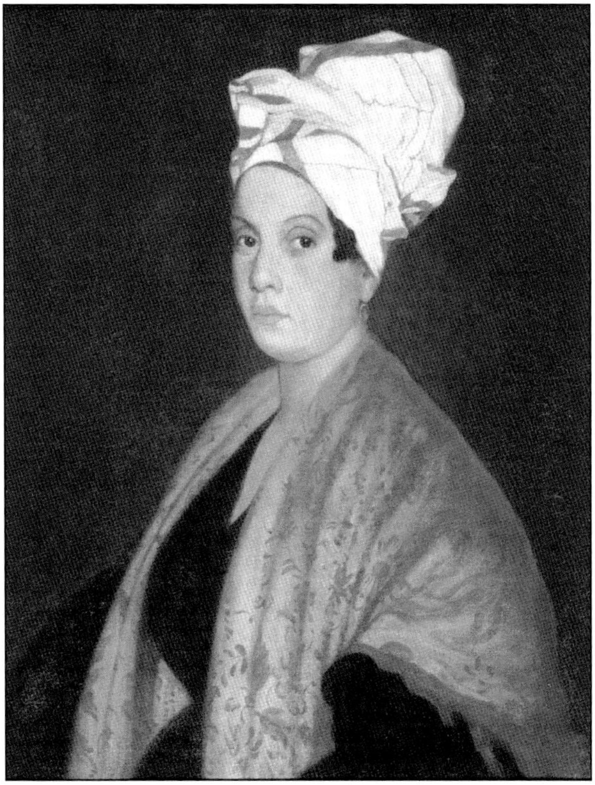

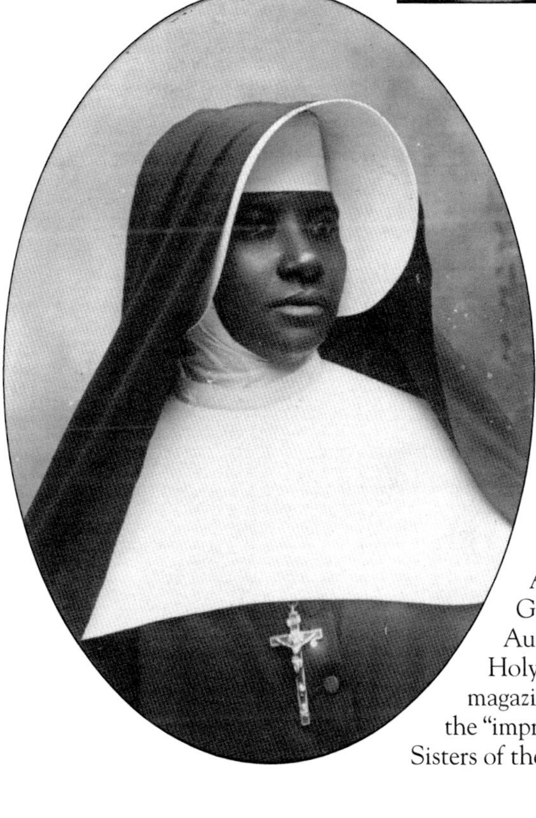

Mother Superior. Mother Mary Austin Jones served as The Sisters of the Holy Family's superior general from 1891 until her death on February 12, 1909. Serving as the sixth mother superior of the order, Mother Austin secured over 100 acres of land in the Gentilly area of New Orleans for $10 an acre. Austin authored the article "The Sisters of the Holy Family," which appeared in *Alexander*, a magazine established to share information regarding the "improvement of the Negro race." (Courtesy of the Sisters of the Holy Family.)

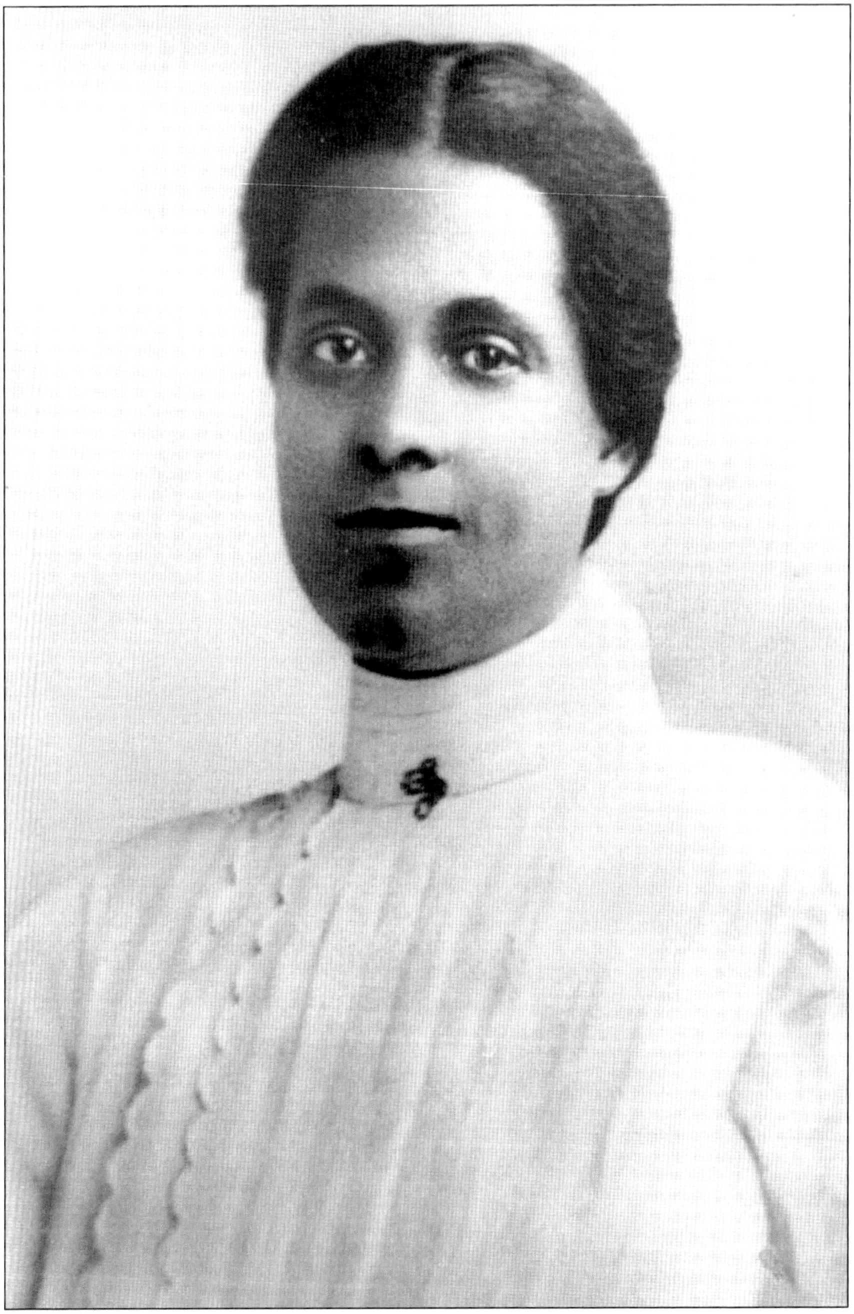

VALENA C. JONES. Valena Cecelia Mac Arthur Jones was born August 3, 1877, in Bay St. Louis, Mississippi. She began teaching school in rural Mississippi about 1890, two years before she graduated from Straight College. By 1897, Jones was teaching in New Orleans and received high acclaim as an educator. During the four years she taught in New Orleans, she was voted the "most popular colored teacher in the city." Jones died January 13, 1917. In 1918, the Valena Jones School was named in her honor. Valena C. Jones became the fourth African American for whom a New Orleans public school was named. (Courtesy of the Louisiana Division/City Archives, New Orleans Public Library.)

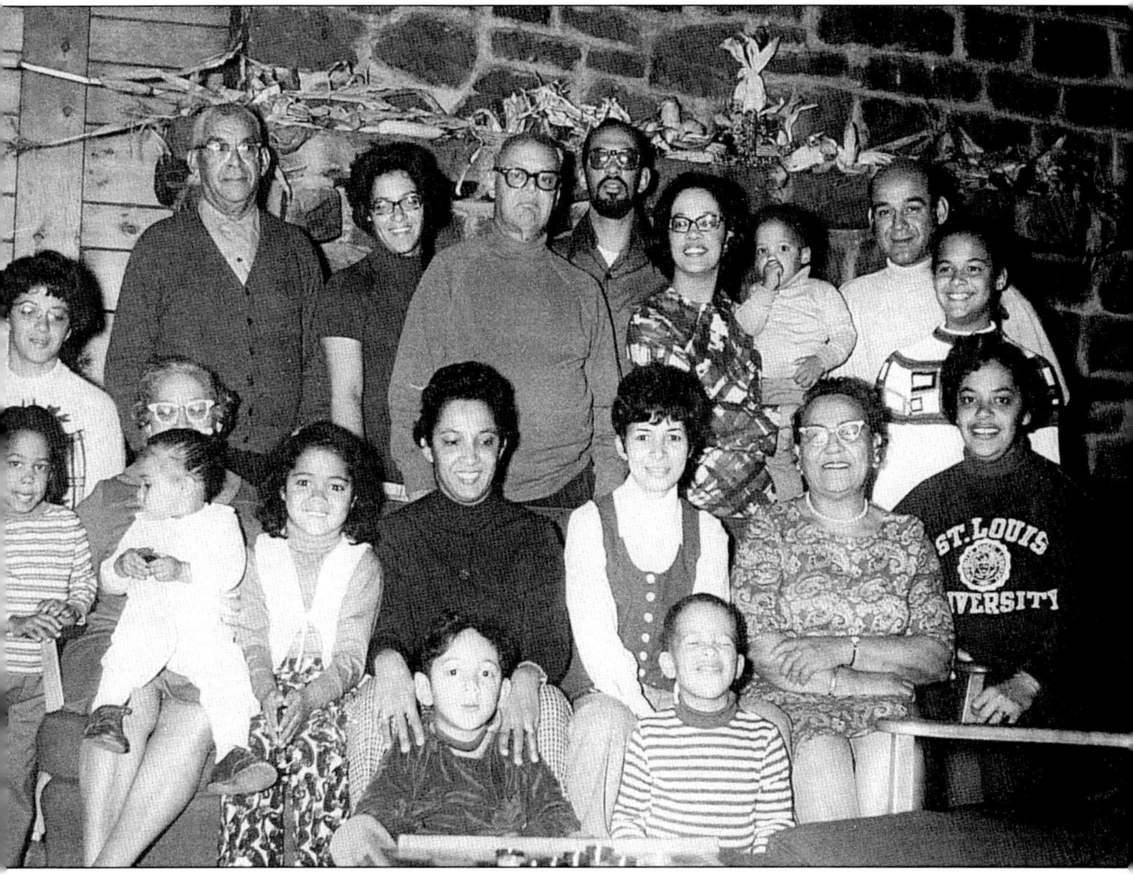

TUREAUD FAMILY. The Tureaud family is pictured here in 1968 at Split Rock Lodge in the Pocono Mountains of Pennsylvania during the Thanksgiving holiday. From left to right are (first row) Chavis Patterson and Alex Tureaud III; (second row) Vanessa Nichols, Ronda Tureaud, Lucille Tureaud, Tina Patterson, Sylvia Patterson, Fay Tureaud, Louie Patterson, and Carole Tureaud; (third row) Jane Tureaud, Doward Patterson, Janet Tureaud, A. P. Tureaud Sr., A. P. Tureaud Jr, Ellise Nicholls, Lisa Nicholls, Theodore Patterson, and Gina Patterson. (Courtesy of Alexander Pierre Tureaud Jr.)

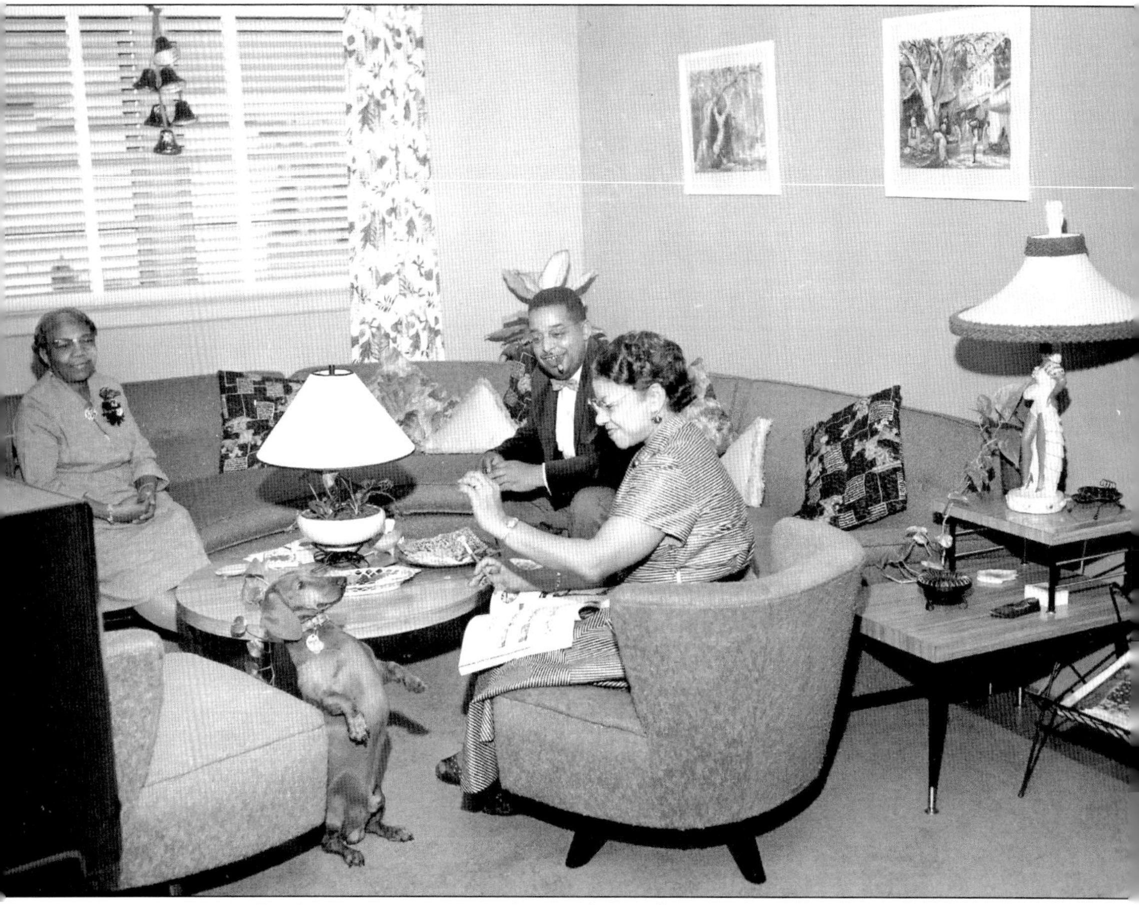

AN EVENING OF CARD PLAYING. Residents of Pontchartrain Park gather to enjoy an evening of family entertainment at the community clubhouse. (Courtesy of the Louisiana Division/City Archives, New Orleans Public Library.)

Little Keith. This is an image of Keith Weldon Medley in 1955. Medley is the author of *We as Freemen: Plessy v. Ferguson*, the acclaimed biography of the Comité des Citoyens. (Courtesy of Keith Weldon Medley.)

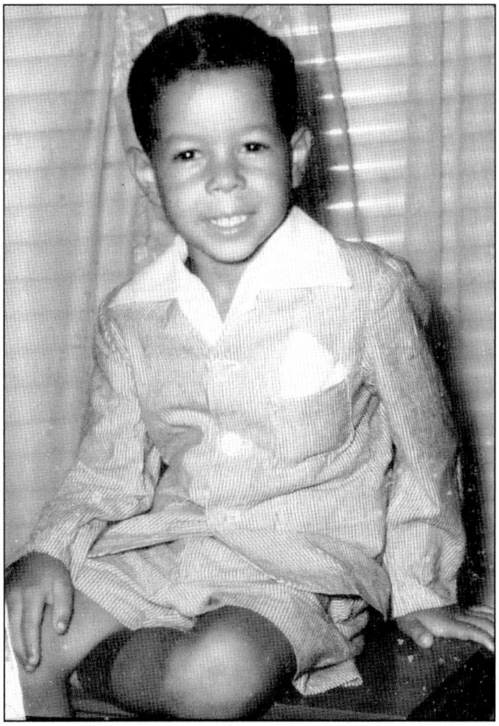

Alfred and Veronica Medley. This photograph shows the parents of Keith Weldon Medley. (Courtesy of Keith Weldon Medley.)

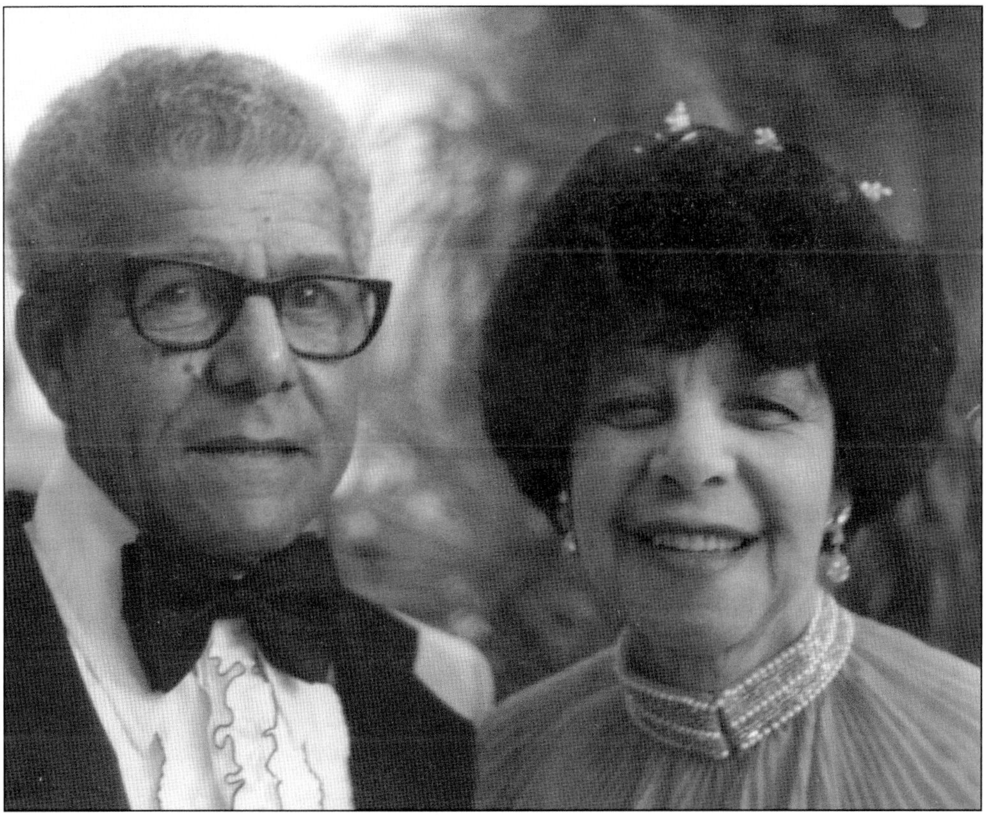

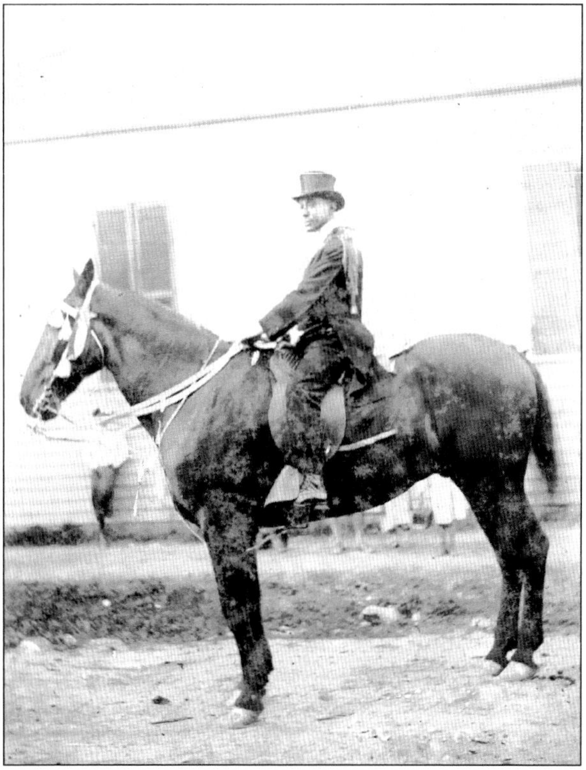

Nobility. The image of the mounted rider wearing a top hat, tuxedo, and leather boots clearly serves as visual documentation of economic transitions within the African American community of New Orleans. The rider, judging by his attire, aspires to greater heights. He is dressed formally, yet his surroundings are less than formal. The unpaved streets and the pedestrians, while not fully visible, are no less revealing. A closer look will reveal the children standing barefoot admiring the rider and his mare. (Courtesy of the Louisiana State Museum.)

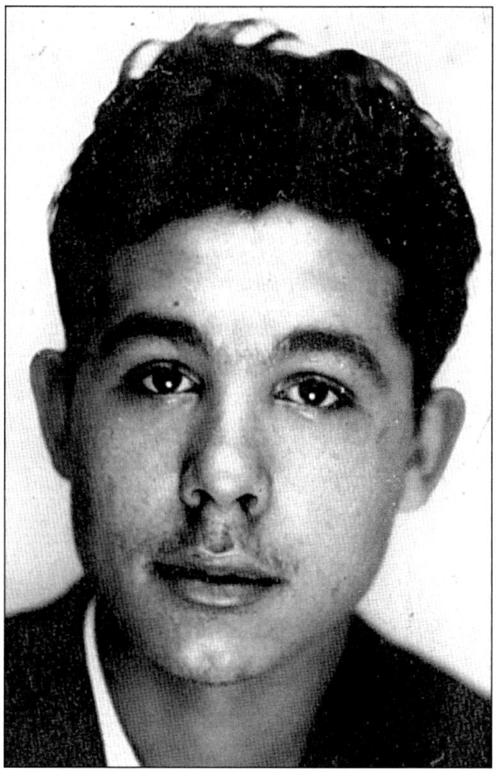

Craftsman. Pictured here is Irving Trevigne as a young sailor. Trevigne would later aspire and maintain a career as an accomplished artisan. A great many New Orleans homes bear the imprint of his craftsmanship. (Courtesy of Barbara Trevigne.)

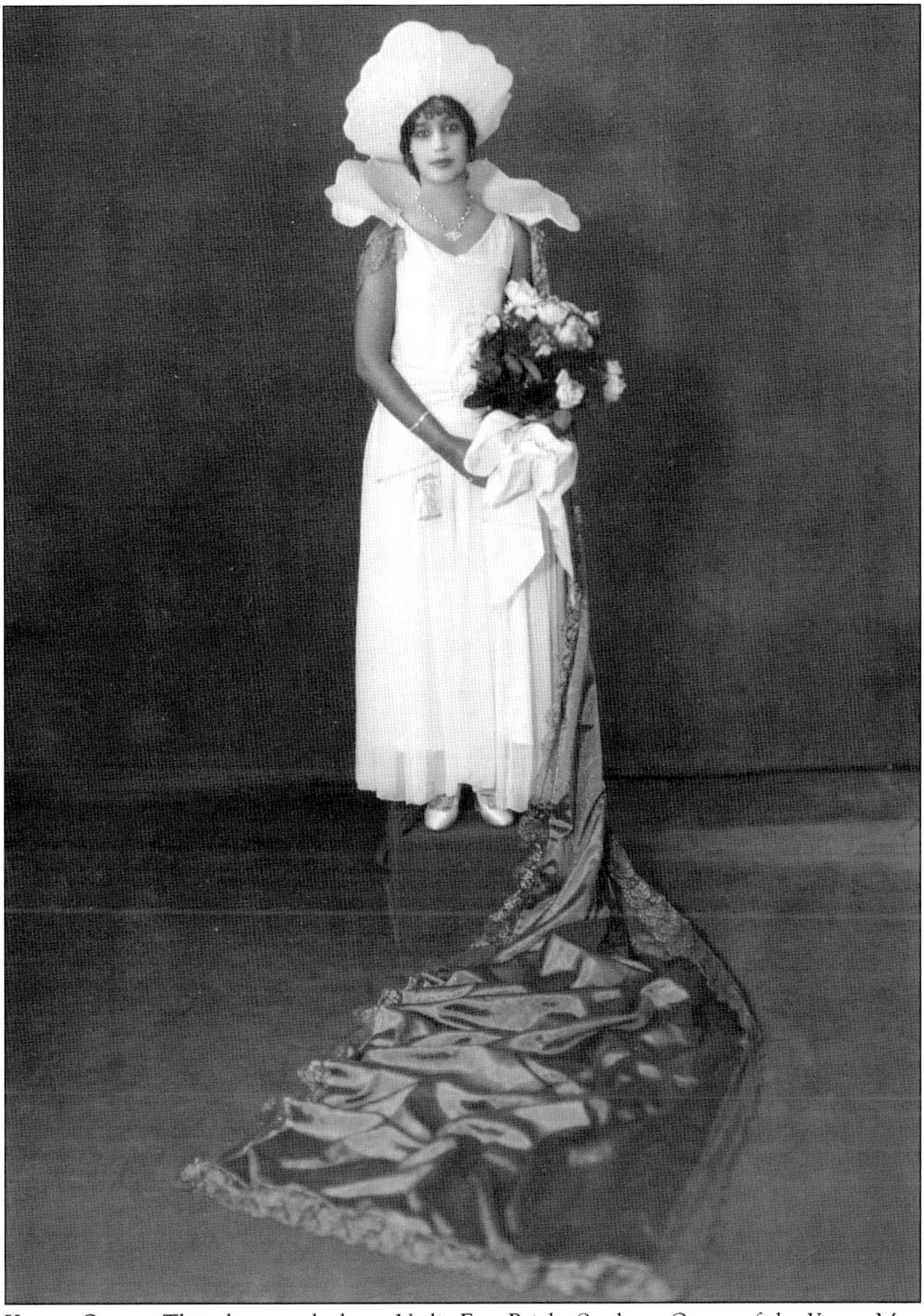

YOUNG QUEEN. This photograph shows Verlie Etta Bright Starks as Queen of the Young Men Illinois Club taken in 1930 in New Orleans. Starks is shown with a white gown sewn by her aunt Tee Bertha Dixon and a headdress. Gifted seamstresses sewed many of the gowns worn by carnival queens in the New Orleans African American community. The photograph is inscribed, "To Mother and Daddy from your daughter Verlie." (Courtesy of the Louisiana State Museum.)

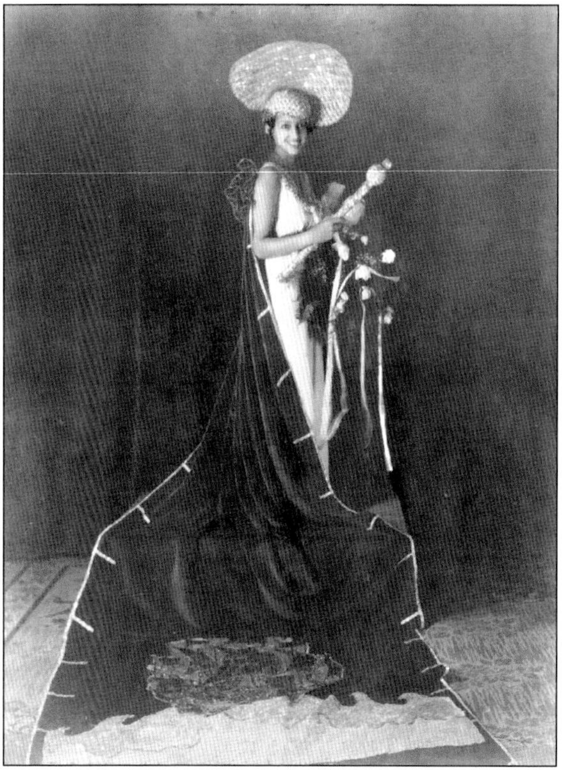

BRIGHT AS QUEEN. Shown here is Zerline Bright as the 1934 Queen of the Young Men Illinois Club, standing on a dais in a white gown with a very large headdress. Bright is holding a scepter and a bouquet of flowers. The mantle features a sailing ship with waves in sequins arranged in the foreground. (Courtesy of the Louisiana State Museum.)

ON THE WAY TO THE CAMP. Many New Orleanians had resort houses built out on various bodies of water, such as Lake Catherine. Pictured here are Irma Trevigne and her son Noel Trevigne showing his catch of the day. Vacationing families also made boats to accommodate their journey to other summer resorts. (Courtesy of Barbara Trevigne.)

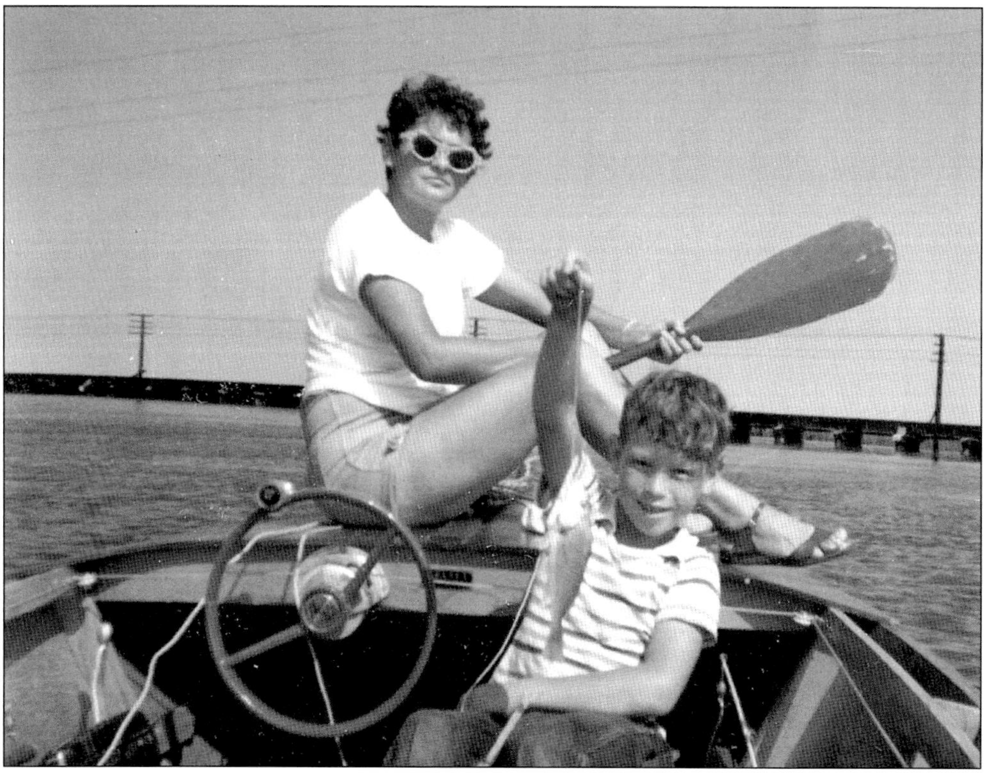

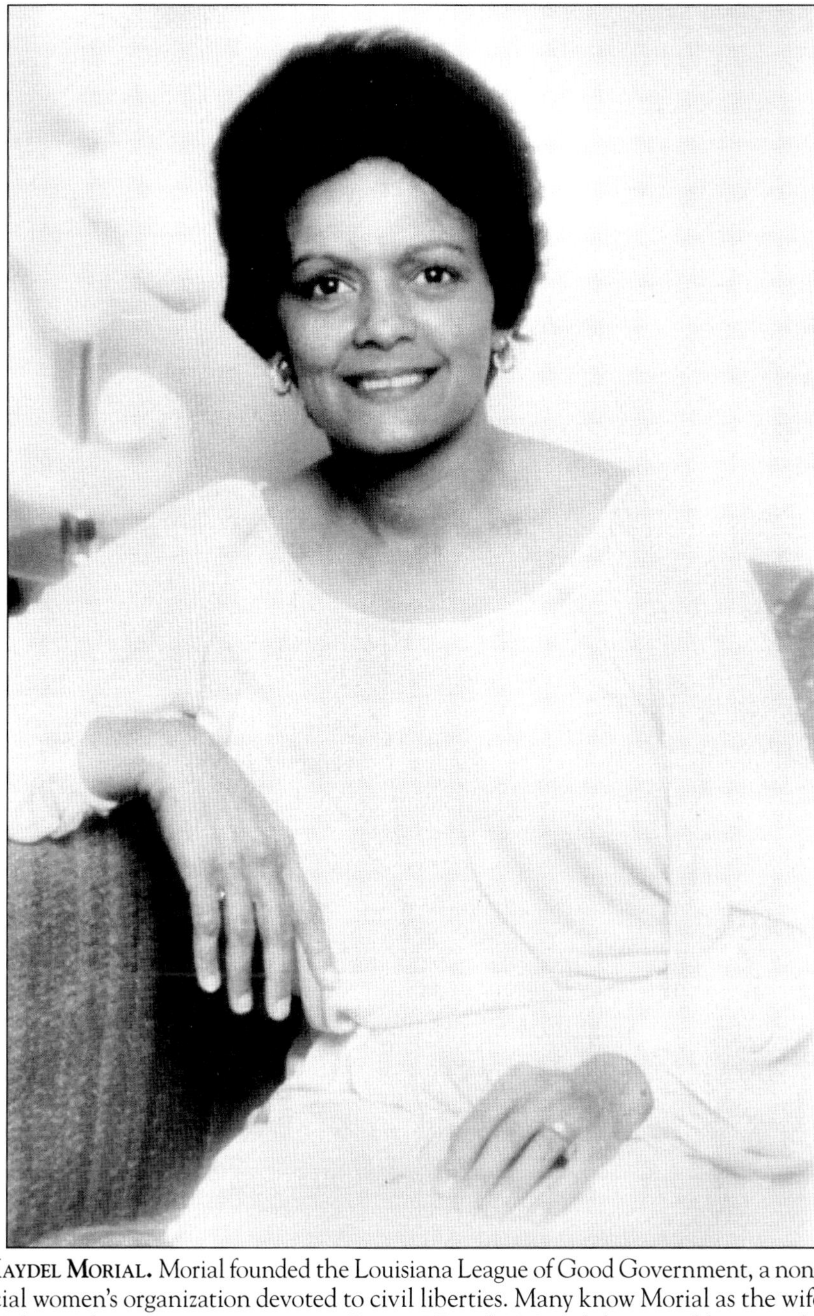

SYBIL HAYDEL MORIAL. Morial founded the Louisiana League of Good Government, a nonpartisan, interracial women's organization devoted to civil liberties. Many know Morial as the wife of New Orleans' first African American mayor, Ernest "Dutch" Morial, but in addition to being the First Lady of New Orleans and a mother of five, Haydel-Morial led an impressive life in her own right. Educated at Boston University and a classmate of Dr. Martin Luther King Jr., Sybil Morial served as the executive producer of the highly acclaimed documentary *A House Divided*, which focused on the desegregation of New Orleans. Haydel-Morial had a long career concerned with improvements for health care and education for African Americans. Haydel-Morial recently retired from Xavier University and the Board of Louisiana Blue Cross Blue Shield. (Courtesy of the Louisiana Division/City Archives, New Orleans Public Library.)

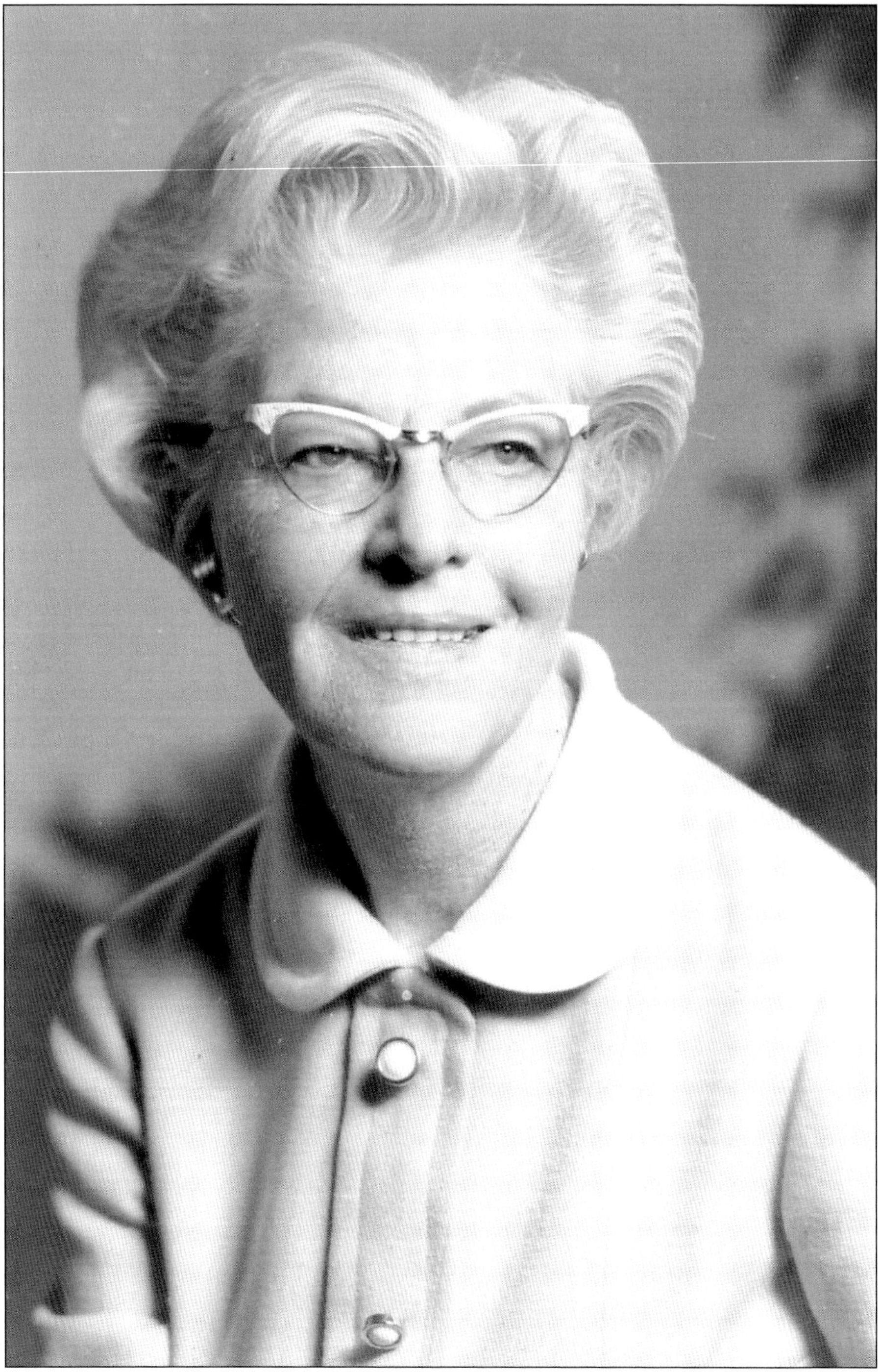

PHILANTHROPIST. Rosa Freeman Keller once served as the president of the New Orleans chapter of the National Urban League. A well-respected philanthropist, Keller applied her wealth to supporting the educational advancement of African Americans. Dillard University, Flint Goodridge Hospital, and Pontchartrain Park were all recipients of Keller's generosity. (Courtesy of the Louisiana Division/City Archives, New Orleans Public Library.)

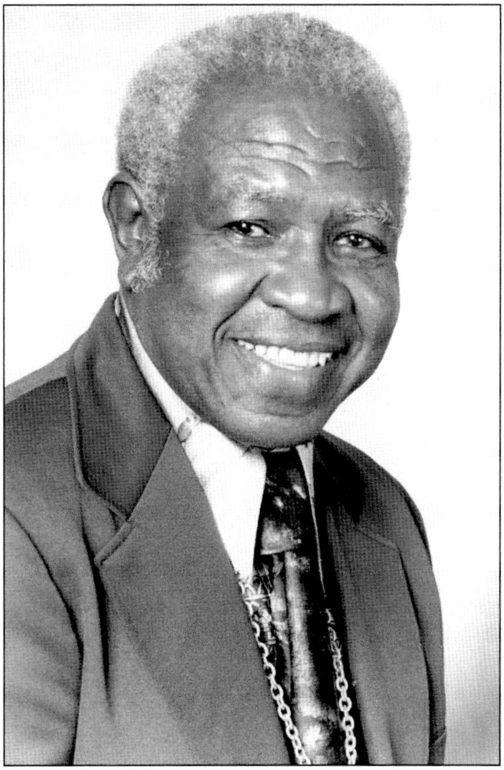

MORRIS F. X. JEFF. A pioneer for civil rights and education in New Orleans, Morris Jeff served as the director for the New Orleans Recreation Department and sat as King of the Zulu Parade in 1974. The Morris F. X. Jeff Elementary School was named in his honor. (Closed after Hurricane Katrina, the school will reopen in 2010 due to strong community support.) In addition to the school, the Morris F. X. Jeff Municipal Auditorium at 1201 St. Peter Street also honors Jeff. The building, built in 1930, hosts community events. (Courtesy of the Louisiana Division/City Archives, New Orleans Public Library.)

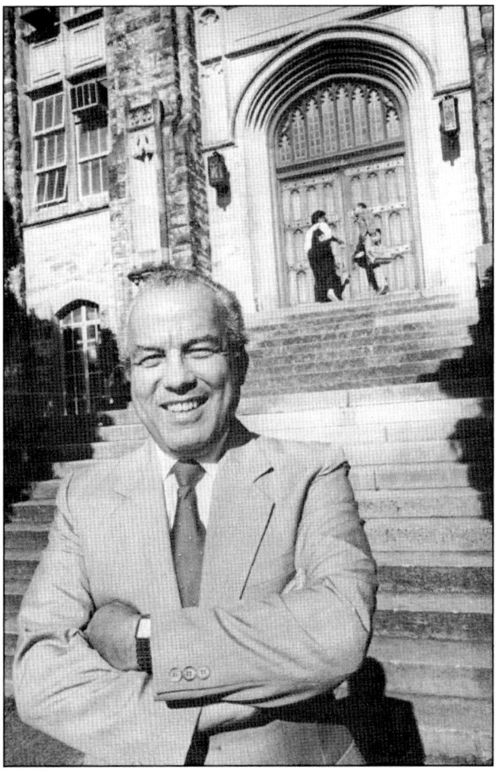

NORMAN FRANCIS. A native of Lafayette, Louisiana, Norman Francis graduated from Xavier University of Louisiana, completed a law degree from Loyola University School of Law, and then served in the military from 1955 to 1957. Afterwards he returned to New Orleans, where he began his career at Xavier University, first as director of student services and then, by 1967, as vice president of the university. Within a year, Norman Francis became the first African American to ascend to the presidency of the nation's only historically African American Catholic university. (Courtesy of Dr. Norman Francis.)

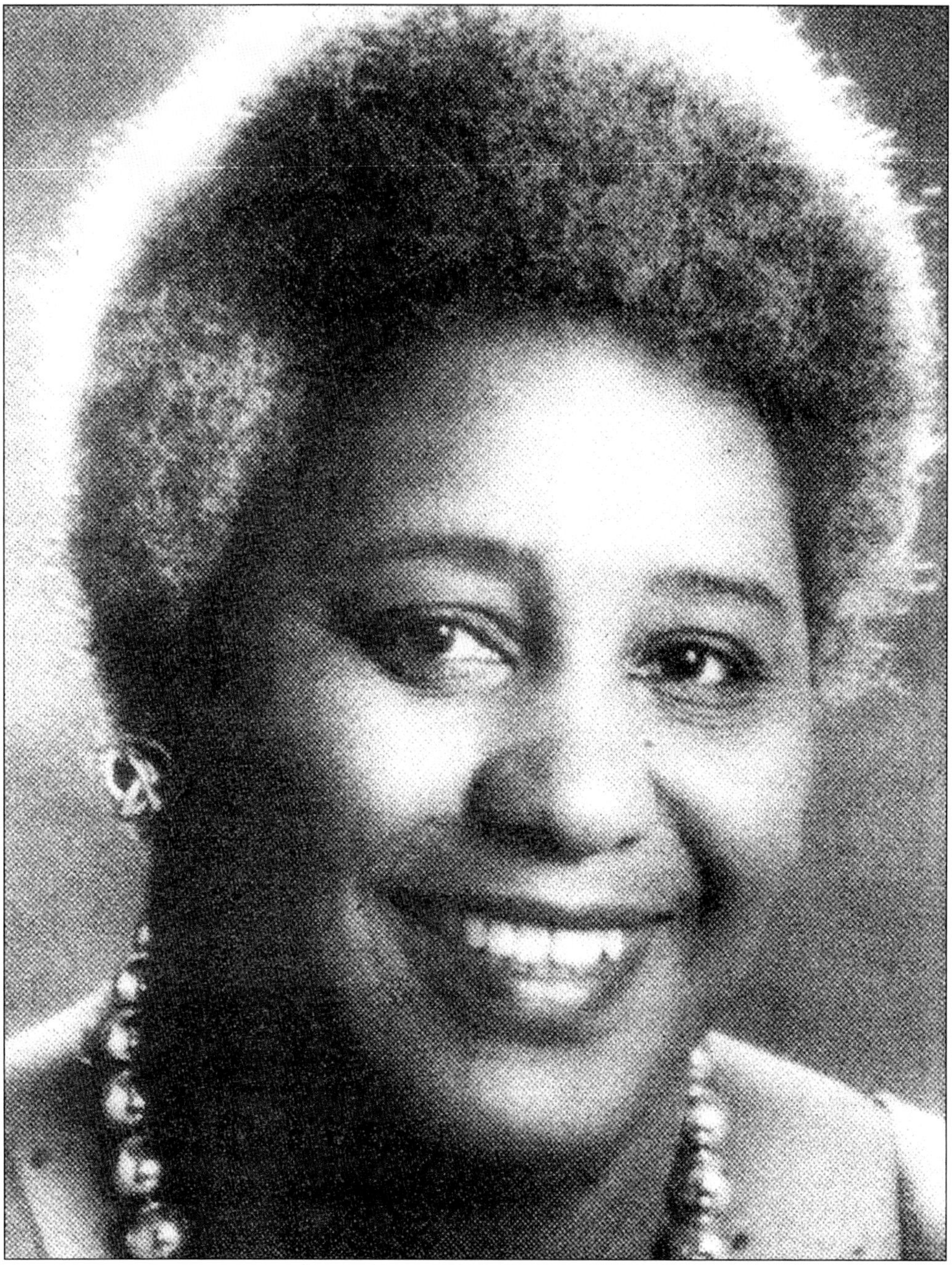

ORETHA CASTLE HAILEY. Oretha Hailey served as the chairperson of the New Orleans chapter of Congress for Racial Equality (CORE). Along with her sister Doris Jean, Carlene Smith, Sandra Nixon, and Julian Aaron, Castle was at the vanguard of civil rights activism in New Orleans during the 1960s. A well-regarded activist for human justice, she participated with Cecil W. Carter Jr., Rudolph "Rudy" Lombard, and Sidney "Lanny" Goldfinch in an act of civil disobedience when on September 12, 1960, the activists sought to integrate the lunch counter of the 1005 Canal Street McCrory Department Store. Their actions resulted in the 1963 landmark U.S. Supreme Court ruling, *Lombard v. Louisiana*. (Courtesy of Okyame Haley, J.D.)

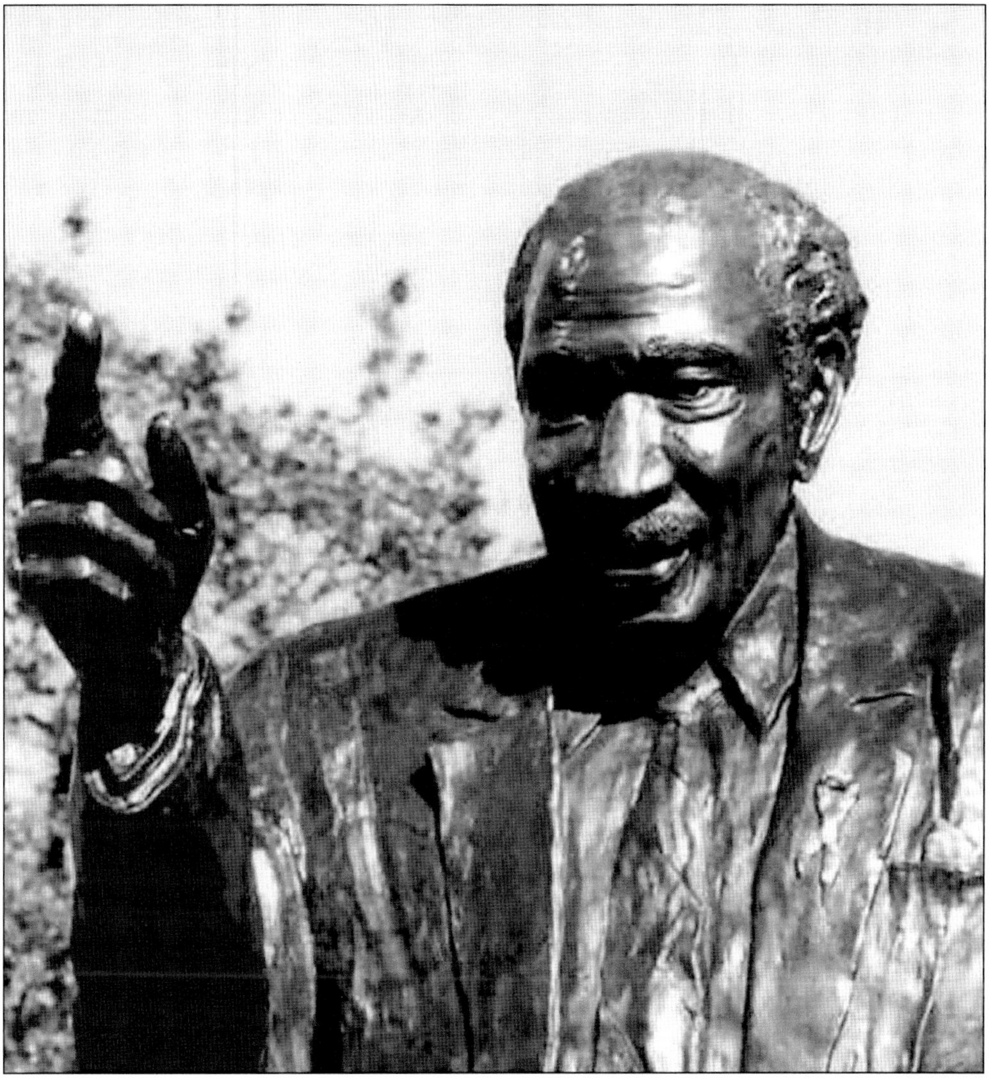

Rev. Avery Alexander. An ordained minister and an elected legislator in the Louisiana House of Representatives, Alexander was born June 29, 1910. A 1944 graduate of Union Baptist Theological Seminary, Alexander served in the Democratic Party from 1975 until his death in 1999. A fervent participant in the civil rights movement, Alexander led successful boycotts throughout New Orleans to establish racially just hiring practices by both the government and private businesses. During a 1963 sit-in at the lunch counter of the cafeteria of New Orleans City Hall, Alexander was dragged by his heels from the building. The artist Sheleen Jones-Adenle sculpted a life-sized monument honoring Alexander, which stood outside of City Hall prior to Hurricane Katrina. It is currently under renovation. The once-segregated Charity Hospital was renamed Avery C. Alexander Memorial Hospital around 2000, before its destruction by Hurricane Katrina. (Courtesy of Sheleen Jones-Adenle.)

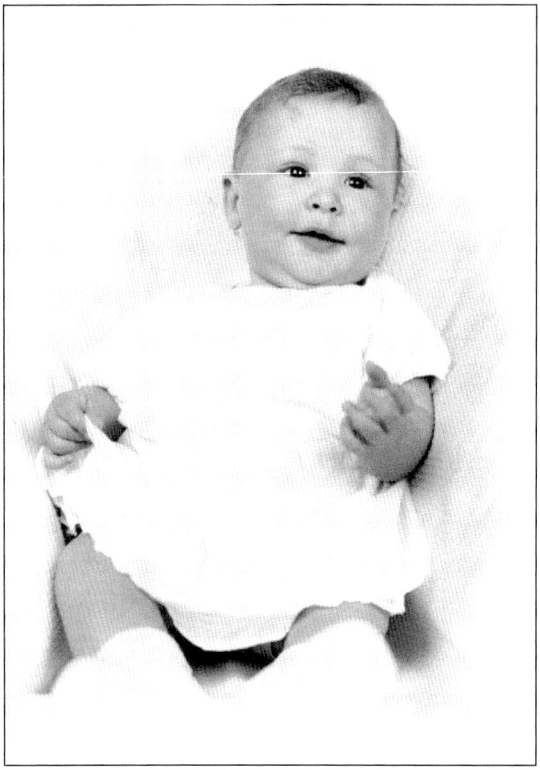

Barbara Trevigne. Seen here as an infant, Trevigne descended from the Spanish Trevino family, which made New Orleans their home when Jean Trevino settled in New Orleans and took up relations with a free woman of color, Marguerite "Gouton" Meunier. According to family history, Gouton was one of the first three women to whom Claude Treme sold property in the Faubourg Treme. Barbara Trevigne is native to New Orleans and is a leading Louisiana historian, with a special emphasis on Louisiana Creoles of Color. (Courtesy of Barbara Trevigne.)

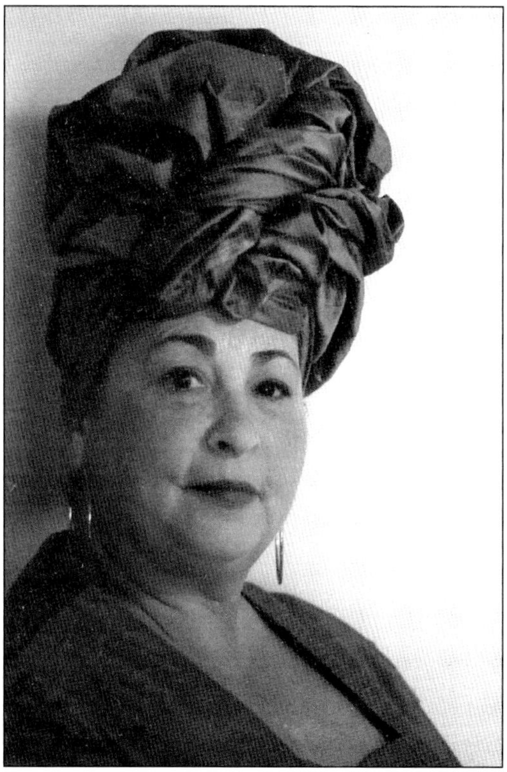

The Wearing of the Tignon. Barbara Trevigne is depicted here wearing the iconic tignon head wrapping. The public display of adorned hairstyles by women of color was outlawed in 1785. Women of the time, being familiar with the African head wrap (a *gele*), used the new restriction as an opportunity to further their stature by using beautiful fabrics and intricately wrapping their hair. Ironically, the law designed to detract attention from the beauty of these women had the opposite results—as seen here in the beauty of Barbara Trevigne, who frequently dons the attire of 18th-century women of color in her engaging historical reenactments. (Courtesy of Barbara Trevigne.)

AIMEE POTENS. This image shows Dr. Louis Roudanez's mother, Aimee Potens. (Courtesy of Marc Roudané and René Roudanez.)

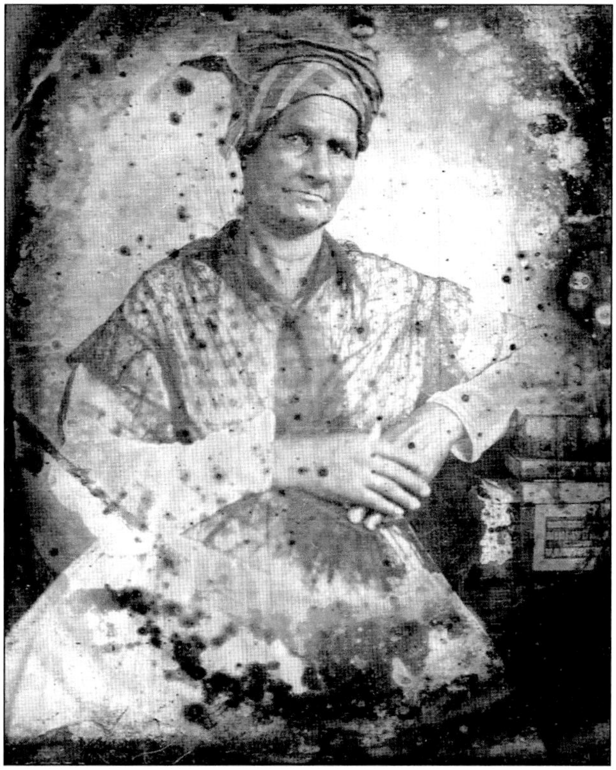

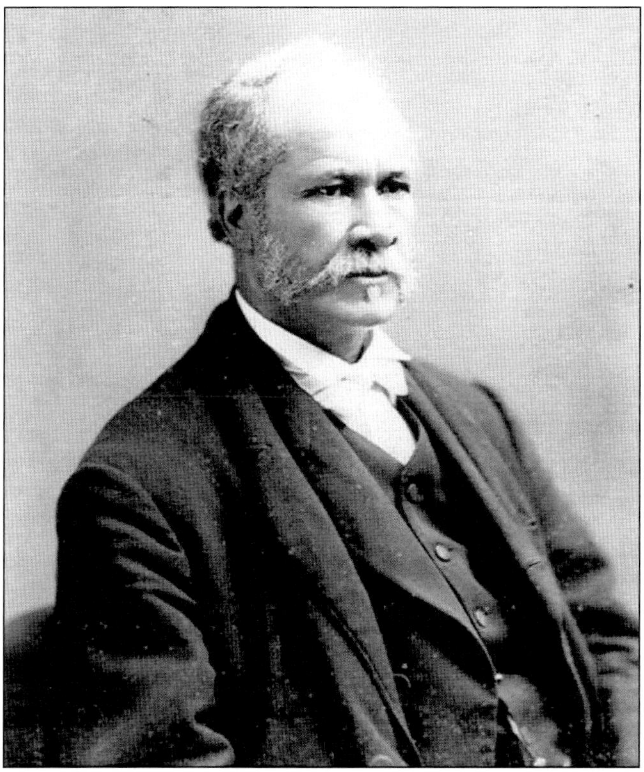

DR. LOUIS CHARLES ROUDANEZ. Born a free man of color on June 12, 1823, Roudanez lived a privileged life, first studying medicine in Paris and then at Dartmouth College. Roundanez settled in New Orleans In 1857, after college and established a lucrative private medical practice enjoying the patronage of both African Americans and whites. His clients included the Sisters of the Holy Family and the wards of their orphanage. Roudanez's interests and influence extended beyond his medical practice; he was the financial backer and editor of *L'Union* and its successor, *La Tribune*. (Courtesy of Marc Roudané and René Roudanez.)

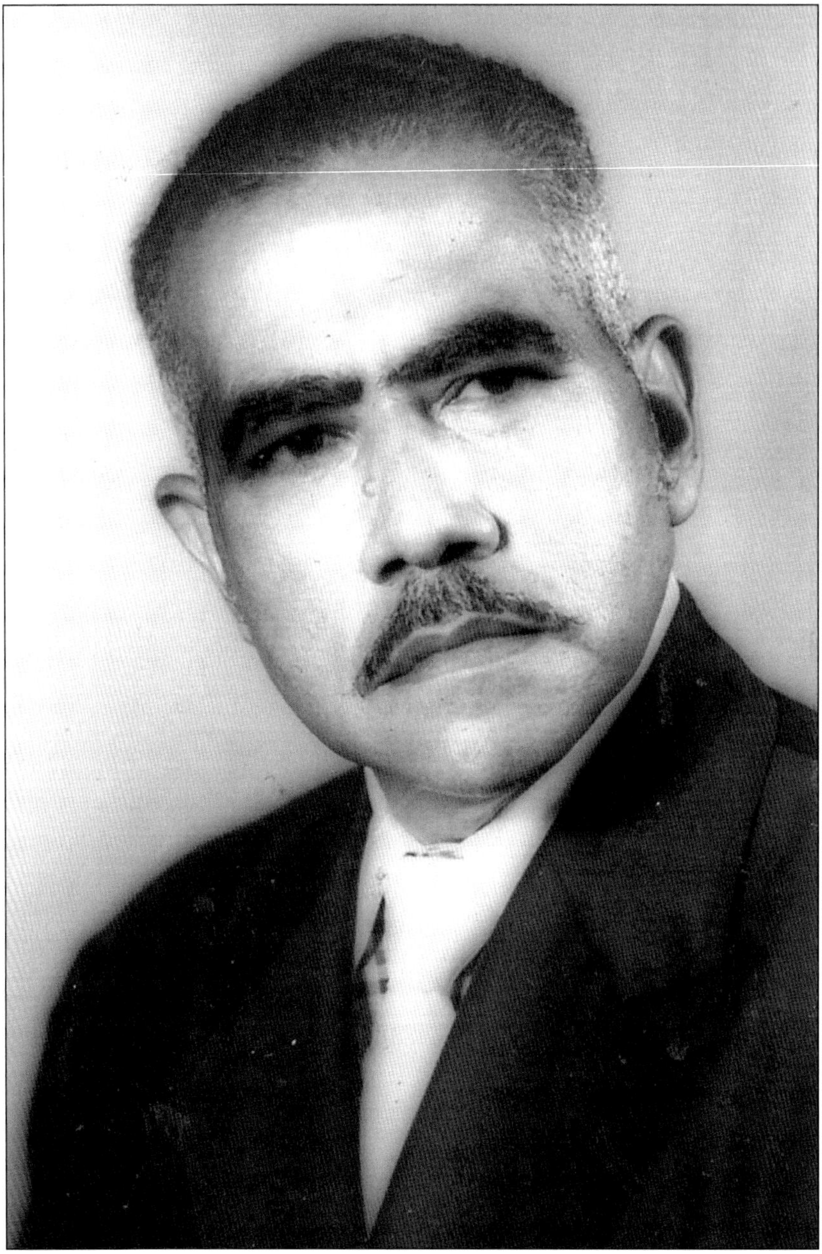

FIRST. Attorney Revius O. Ortique Jr. was the first African American elected to the Civil District Court and in 1992 and became the first African American to sit on the Louisiana Supreme Court. He retired in 1994. Ortique earned a bachelor's degree from Dillard University and a master's degree from Indiana University, and went on to earn a juris doctorate from Southern University Law Center in Baton Rouge. He contributed greatly to the civil rights movement in Louisiana in the 1950s and 1960s. Justice Ortique was appointed by five different U.S. presidents to civic positions, including being appointed by Pres. Richard Nixon to the President's Commission on Campus Unrest in the early 1970s in the wake of the violent actions that occurred on the campuses of Jackson State and Kent State Universities. (Courtesy of the Amistad Research Center, Tulane University, New Orleans, Louisiana.)

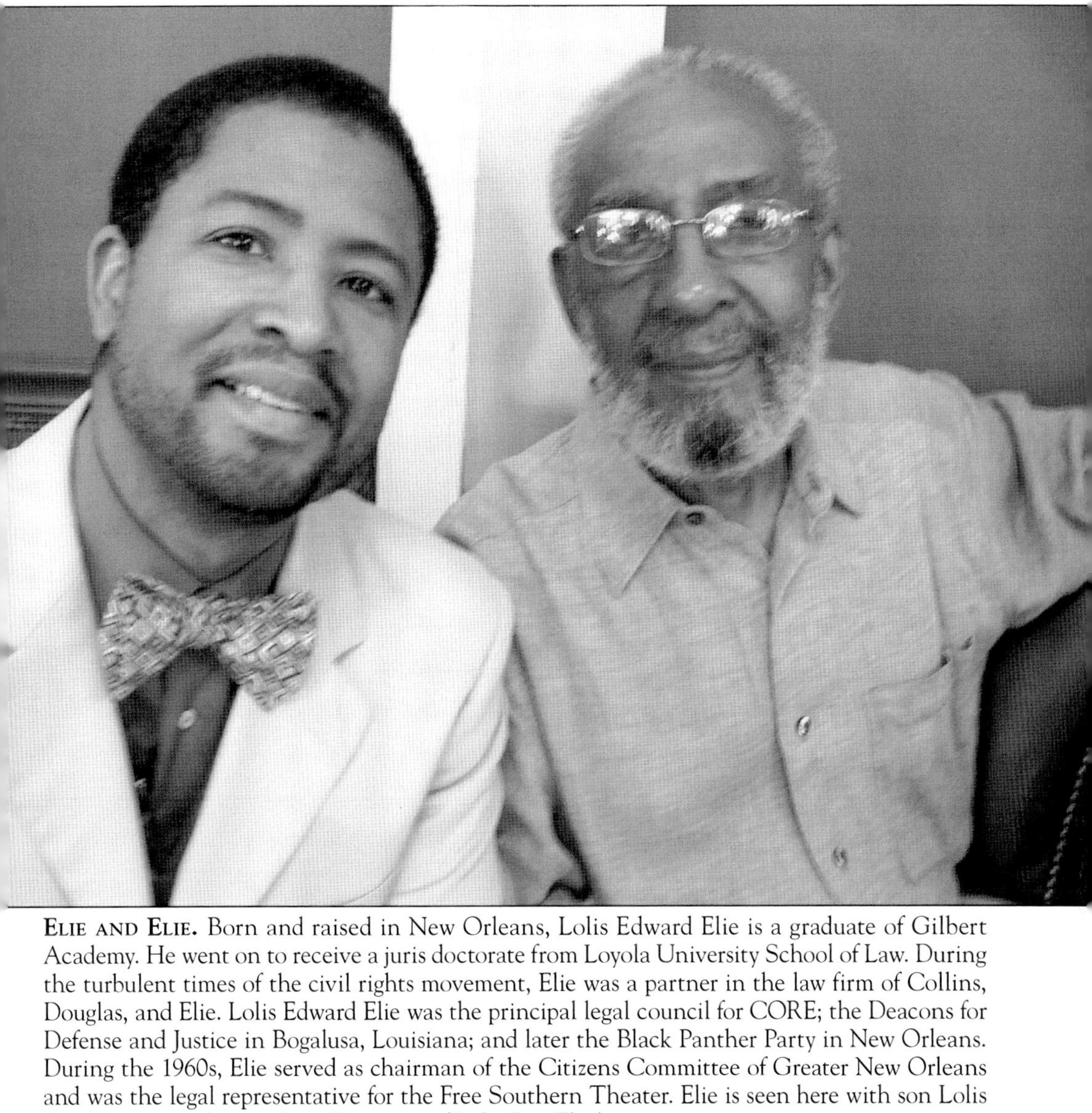

ELIE AND ELIE. Born and raised in New Orleans, Lolis Edward Elie is a graduate of Gilbert Academy. He went on to receive a juris doctorate from Loyola University School of Law. During the turbulent times of the civil rights movement, Elie was a partner in the law firm of Collins, Douglas, and Elie. Lolis Edward Elie was the principal legal council for CORE; the Deacons for Defense and Justice in Bogalusa, Louisiana; and later the Black Panther Party in New Orleans. During the 1960s, Elie served as chairman of the Citizens Committee of Greater New Orleans and was the legal representative for the Free Southern Theater. Elie is seen here with son Lolis Eric Elie, a noted journalist. (Courtesy of Lolis Eric Elie.)

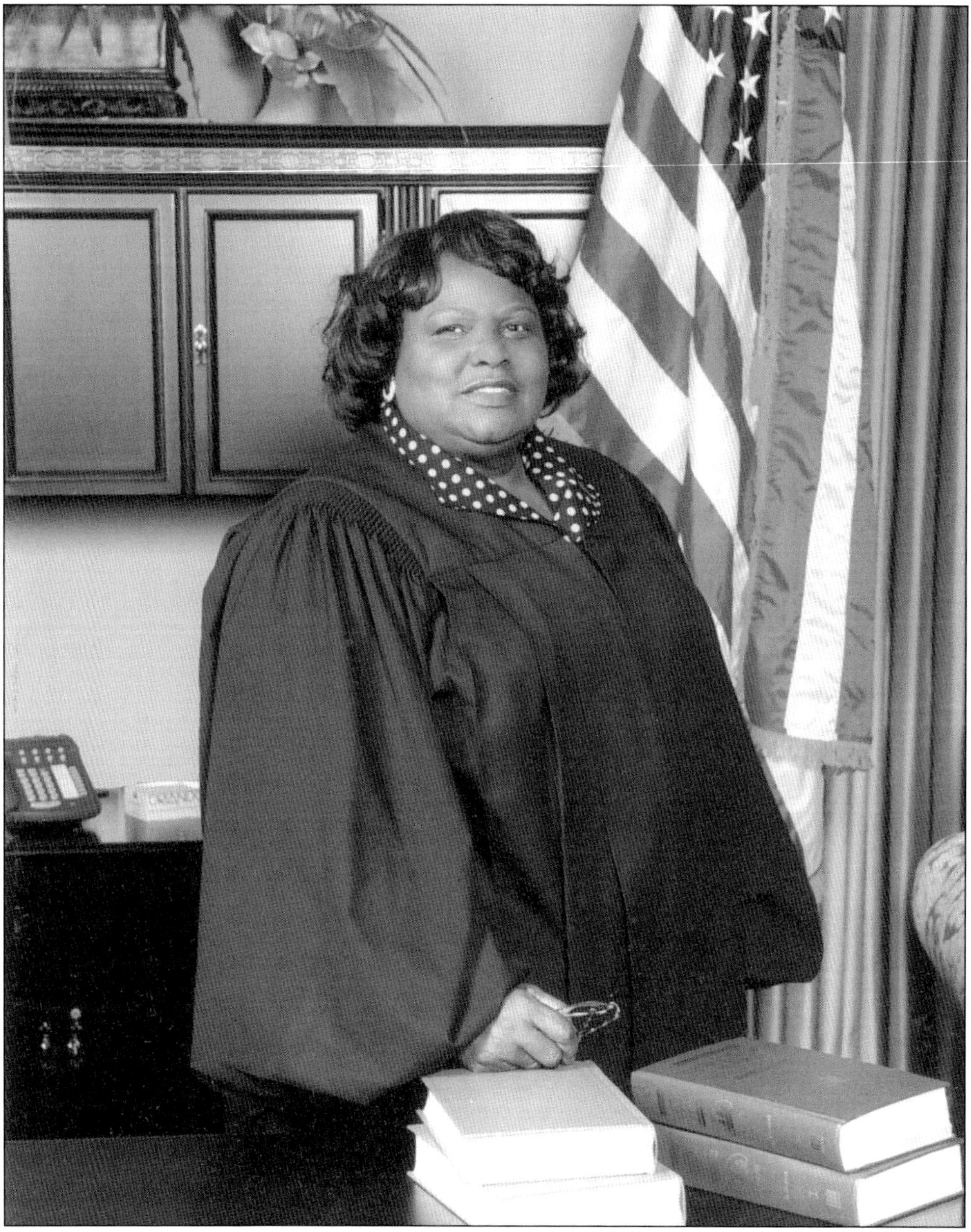

FIRST LADY. Elected in 1994, Justice Bernette Joshua Johnson was the first African American woman to serve on the Louisiana Supreme Court. Justice Johnson, a committed public servant since the 1960s, worked as a community organizer with the NAACP and the Legal Defense Fund in New York City. Justice Johnson received her bachelor of arts degree from Spelman College in Atlanta, Georgia, and after that was one of the first African American women to receive a juris doctorate degree from Louisiana State University Law School in Baton Rouge. (Courtesy of Justice Bernette Joshua Johnson.)

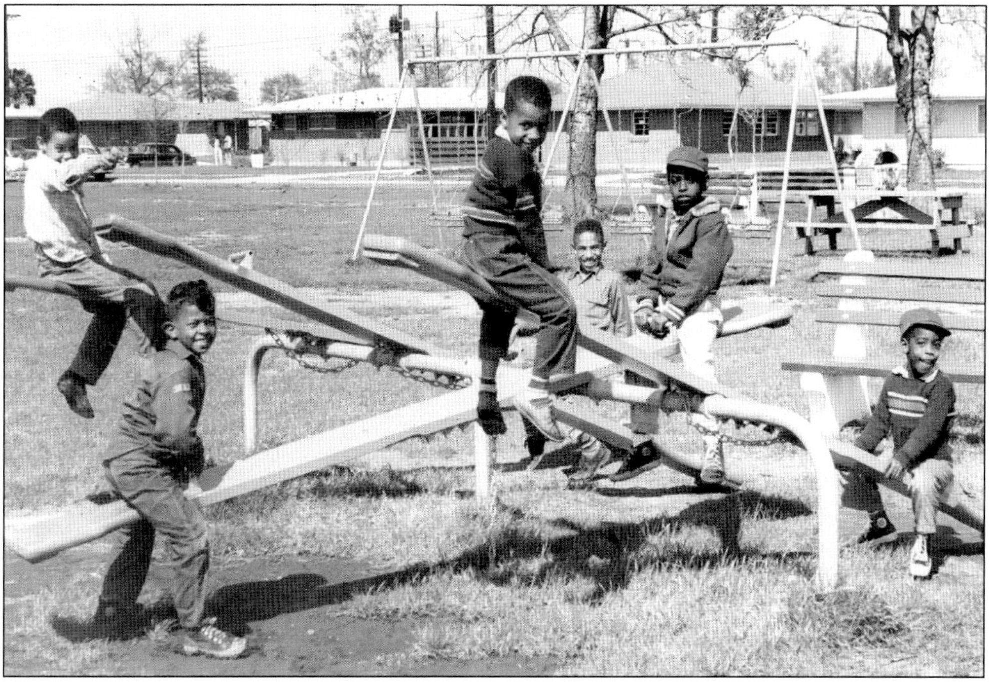

Playtime. Pontchartrain Park was complete with a playground for children to gather in and enjoy the outdoors. (Courtesy of the Louisiana Division/City Archives, New Orleans Public Library.)

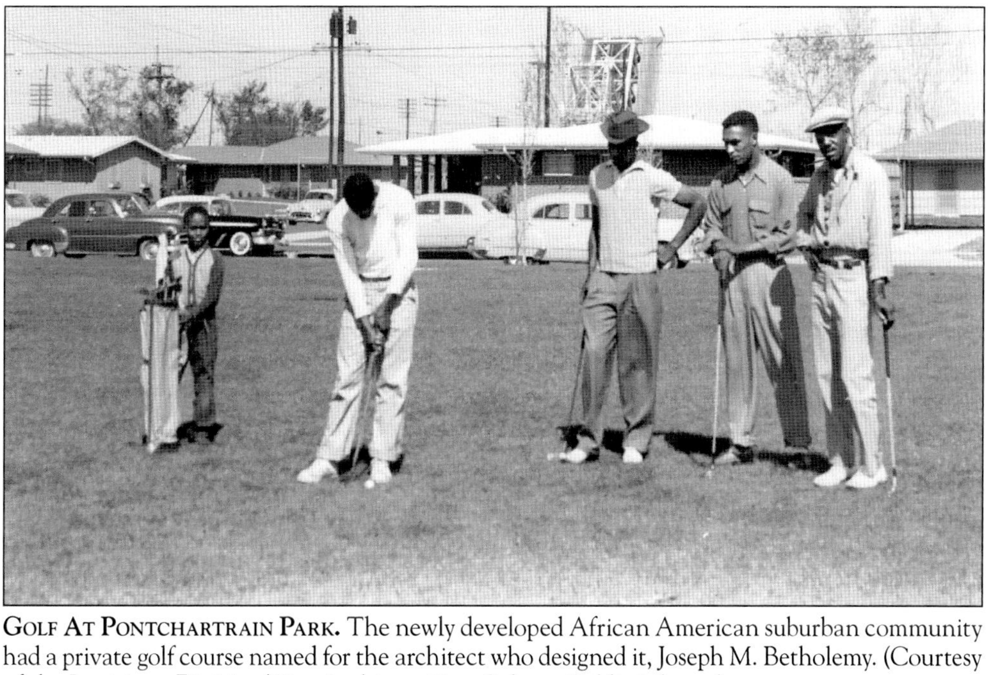

Golf At Pontchartrain Park. The newly developed African American suburban community had a private golf course named for the architect who designed it, Joseph M. Betholemy. (Courtesy of the Louisiana Division/City Archives, New Orleans Public Library.)

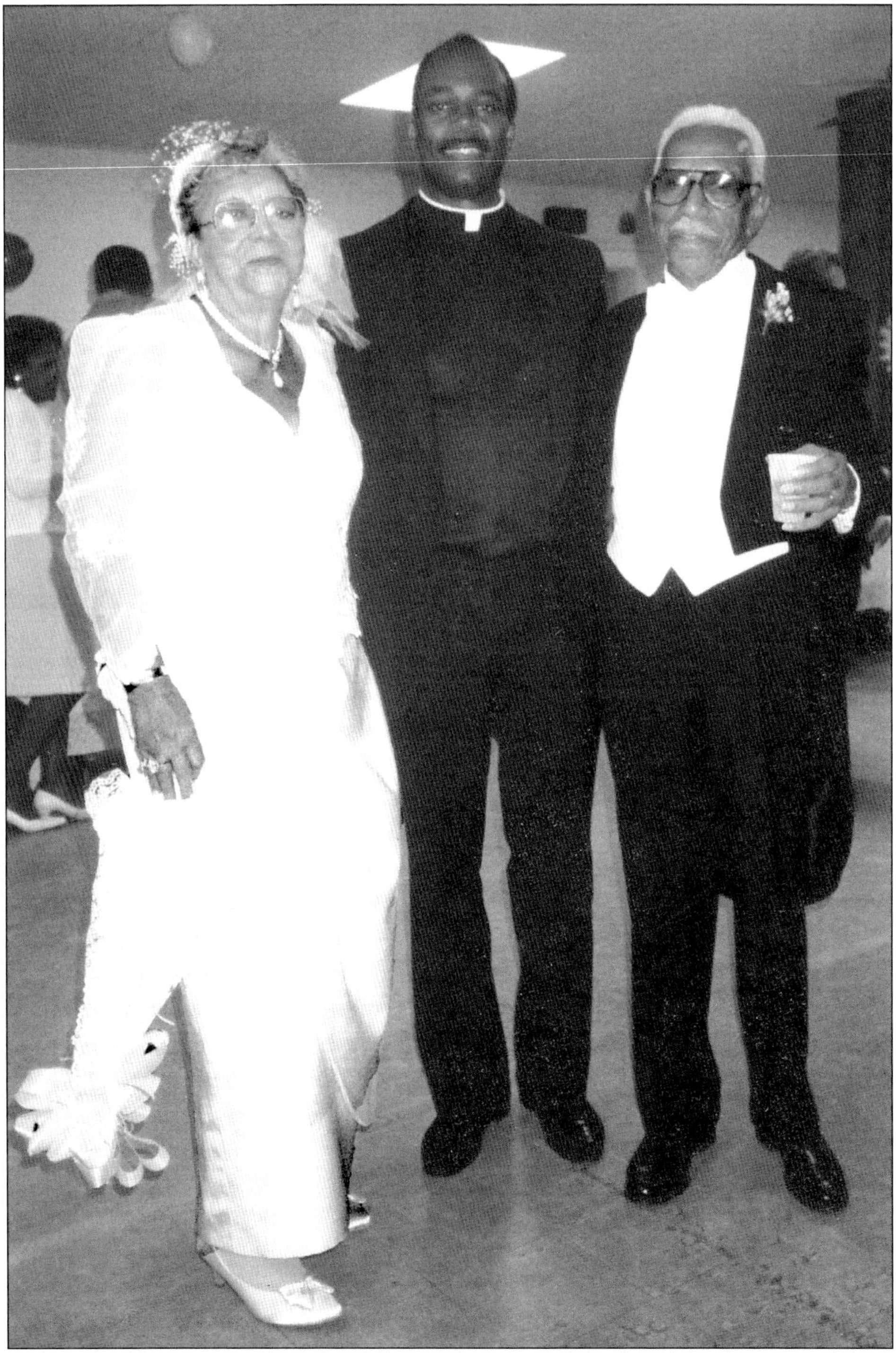

WEDDING DAY. Shown here on their wedding day posing with Father Ciprian are Yovonne Olivier and Armand Olivier, the paternal grandmother and maternal grandfather of Ron Bechet. Widowed by their previous mates, the Oliviers were each 70 years old when they wed in 1992. (Courtesy of Ron Bechet.)

Six

JAZZ

If you have to ask what Jazz is, you'll never know.

—Louis Armstrong (1901–1971)

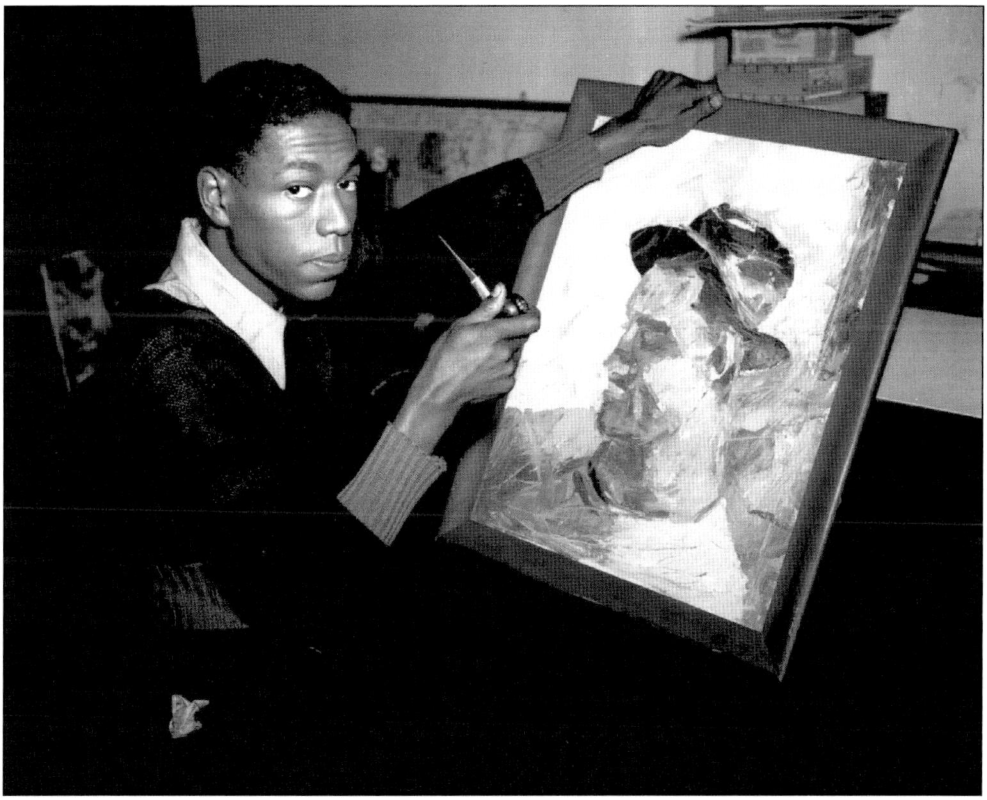

ARTIST. This image shows an unidentified visual artist in New Orleans during the 1920s. The French Quarter was a haven for many artists working for the WPA. (Courtesy of the Louisiana Division/City Archives, New Orleans Public Library.)

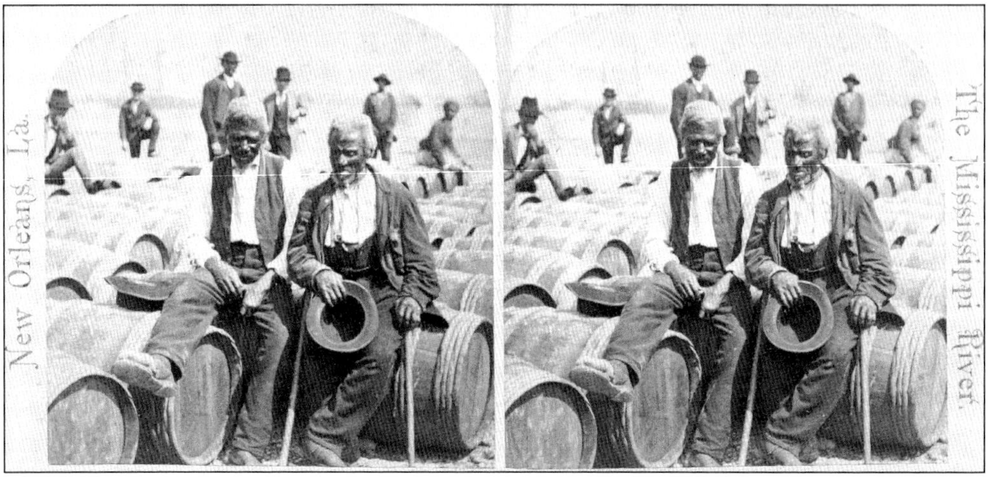

DOUBLE IMAGE. This early 1900s double image is a stereograph of a set of twins taking a break from their day labor. (Courtesy of the Louisiana State Museum.)

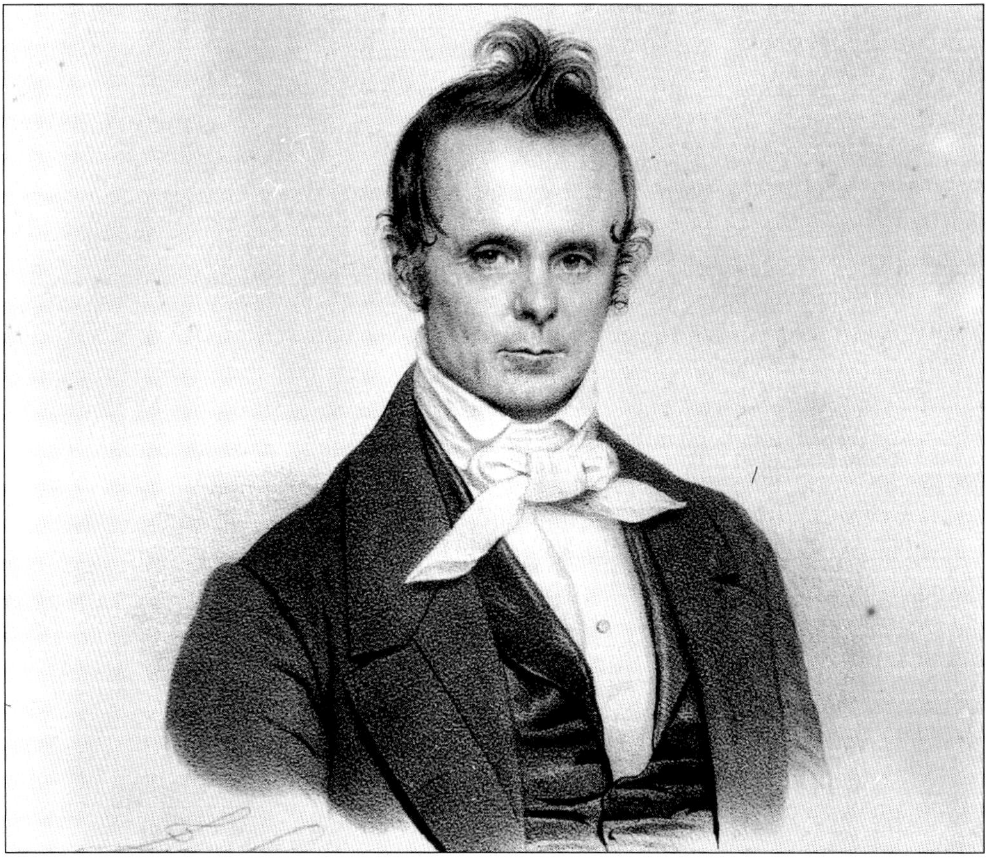

NEW ORLEANS MERCHANT. This lithograph was created by Jules Lion, a free man of color born in France who came to New Orleans to work as a visual artist. Lion produced lithographs of New Orleans street scenes, politicians, and merchants. He is credited with introducing the daguerreotype to New Orleans in 1840. Lion also opened and operated an art school and gallery. (Courtesy of the Louisiana State Museum.)

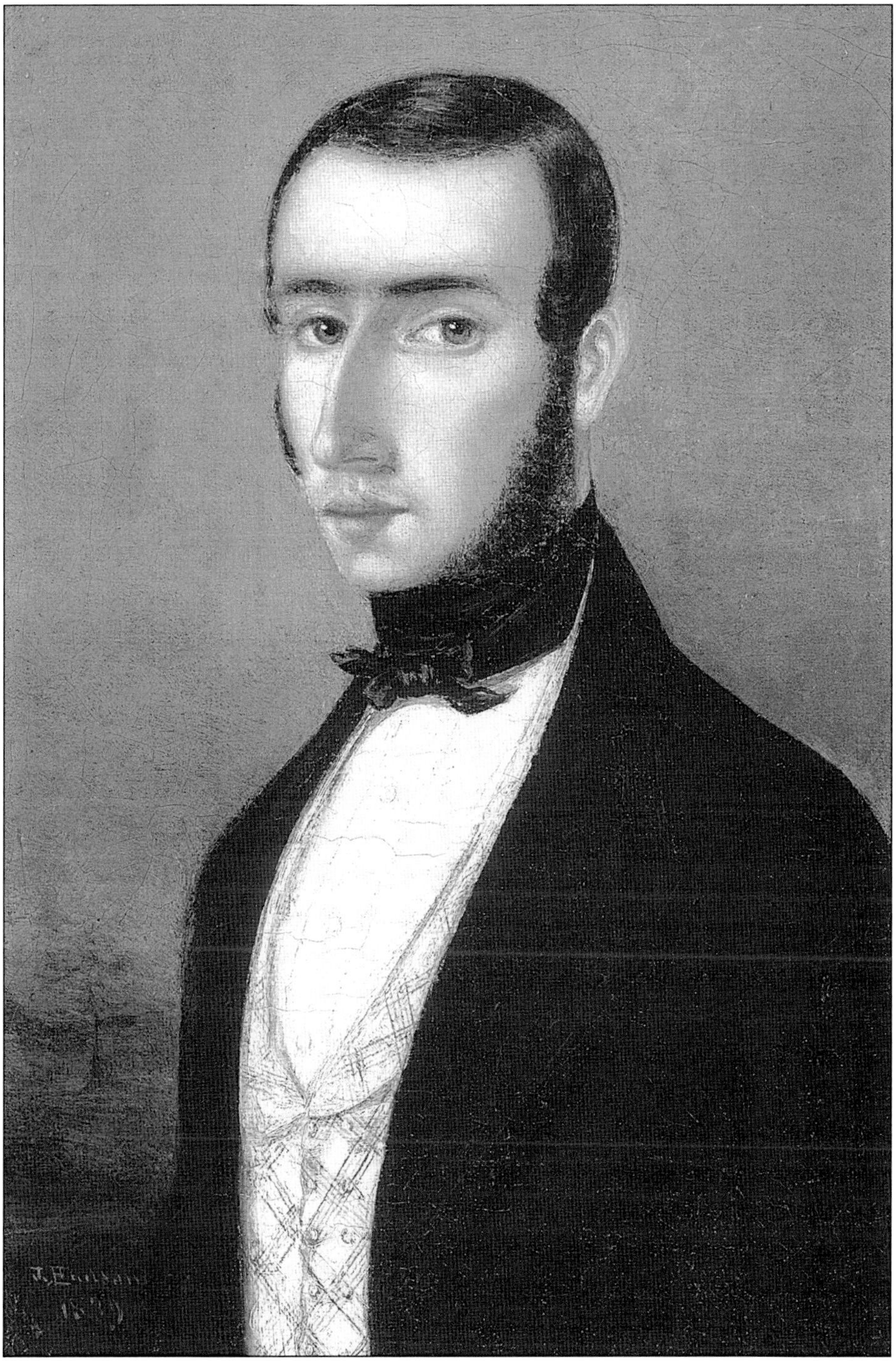

A 19TH-CENTURY MINIATURE. This miniature painting is believed to be a self-portrait of the artist Julien Hudson (1811–1844), a free man of color in New Orleans. Hudson was the son of John Thomas Hudson, an Englishman, and Suzanne Desiree Marcos, a woman of color from New Orleans. In 1831, Hudson opened a studio on Bienville Street in New Orleans. (Courtesy of the Louisiana State Museum.)

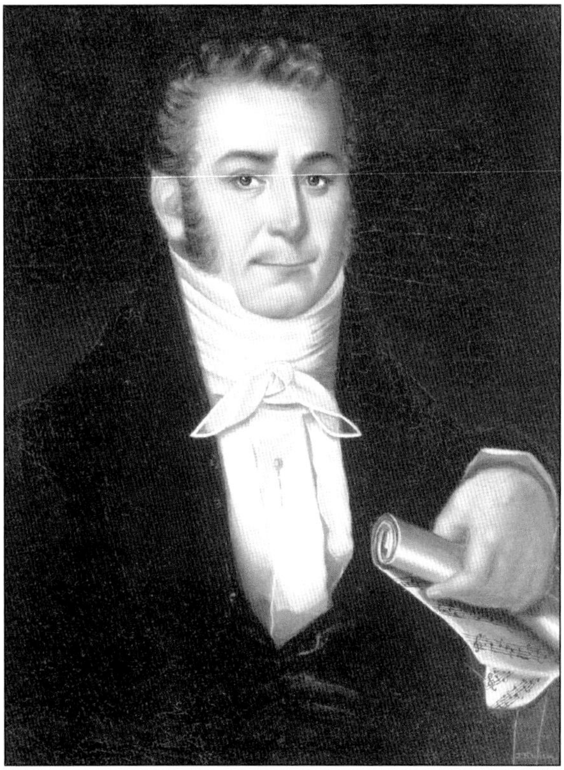

JEAN MICHEL FORTIER III. This portrait painted by Julian Hudson in 1839 is a portrait of Jean Michel Fortier III, commander of the Corps of Free Men of Color during the Battle of New Orleans. (Courtesy of the Louisiana State Museum.)

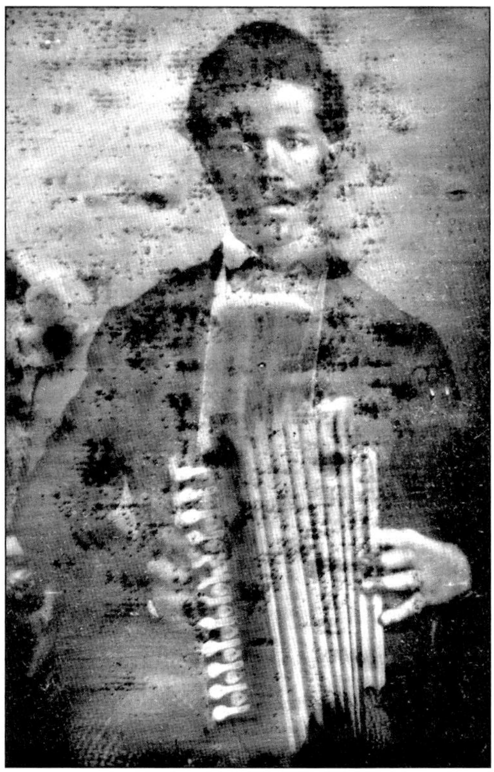

UNIDENTIFIED ACCORDION PLAYER. This c. 1850 daguerreotype of an unidentified accordion player illustrates the long relationship between African Americans, New Orleans, and music. The young man depicted in this image likely played the accordion as a street performer. (Courtesy of the Louisiana State Museum.)

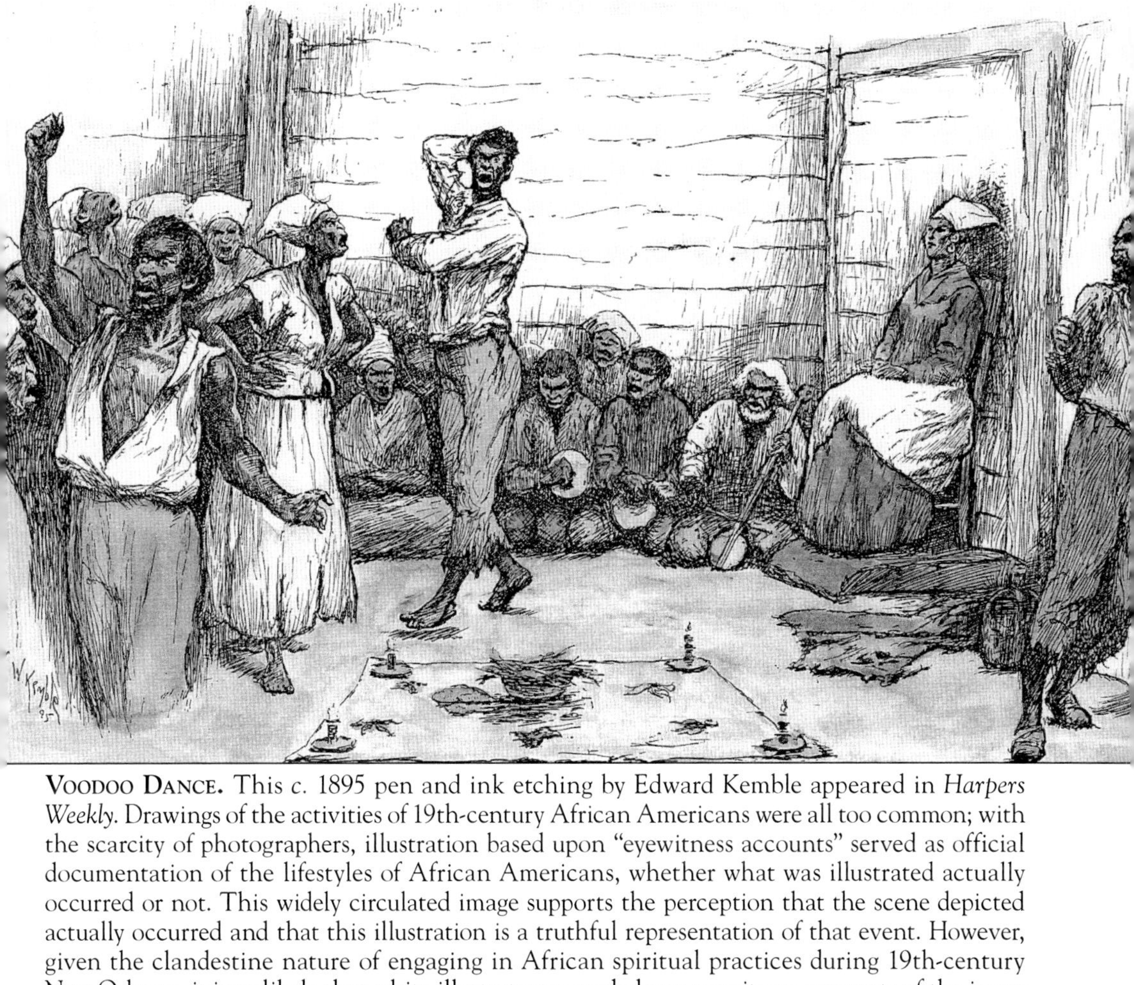

Voodoo Dance. This *c.* 1895 pen and ink etching by Edward Kemble appeared in *Harpers Weekly*. Drawings of the activities of 19th-century African Americans were all too common; with the scarcity of photographers, illustration based upon "eyewitness accounts" served as official documentation of the lifestyles of African Americans, whether what was illustrated actually occurred or not. This widely circulated image supports the perception that the scene depicted actually occurred and that this illustration is a truthful representation of that event. However, given the clandestine nature of engaging in African spiritual practices during 19th-century New Orleans, it is unlikely that white illustrators recorded any eyewitness accounts of the inner workings of African American ways of life. Images of this sort were merely the tabloid sensation of their day. (Courtesy of the Louisiana State Museum.)

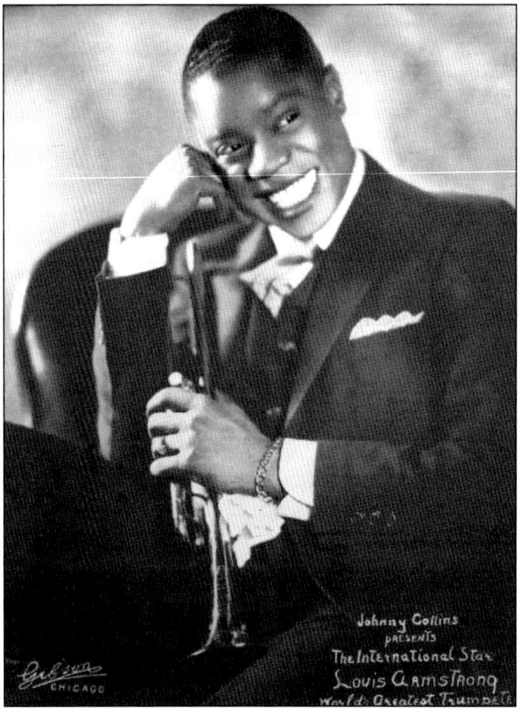

Louis Armstrong. Born in 1901 in New Orleans, Armstrong became famous for playing the cornet and for his raspy singing voice. A stint in the Waif's Home Orphanage altered the trajectory of Armstrong's life. (Courtesy of the New Orleans Jazz Club/Louisiana State Museum.)

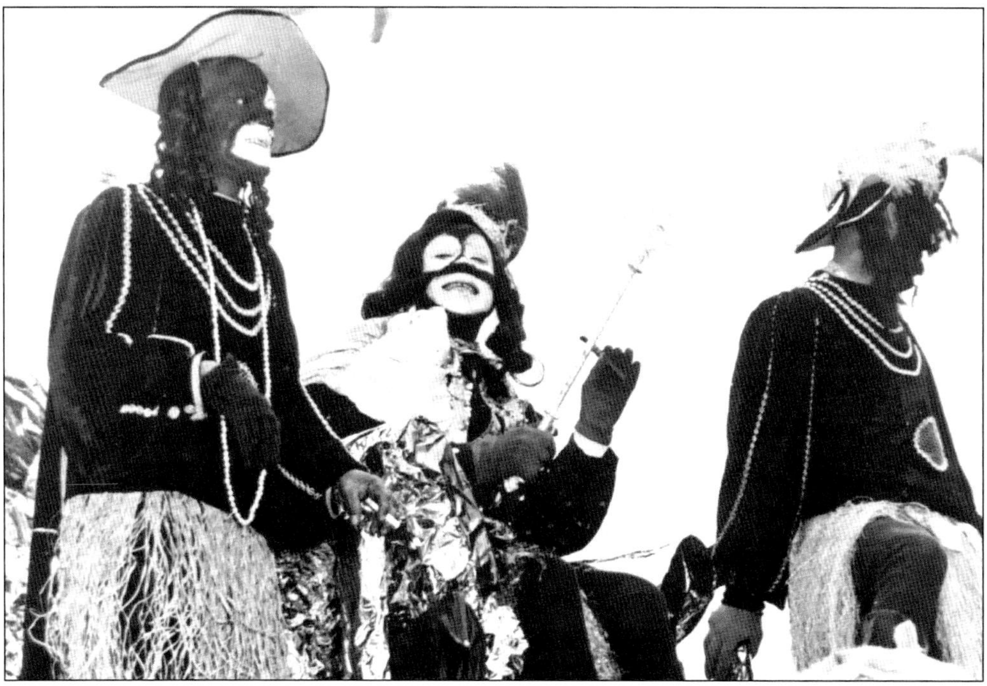

Armstrong As Zulu King. Once fame arrived, Armstrong never forgot New Orleans. Eventually, he realized his secret passion to serve as the King of the Zulu Parade, as seen here. Armstrong rides high, masked in the traditional blackface trademark of Zulu marchers. While the Zulu Social Aid and Pleasure Club still blackens the face of its king each year, the practice is not without its controversy. (Courtesy of the New Orleans Jazz Club/Louisiana State Museum.)

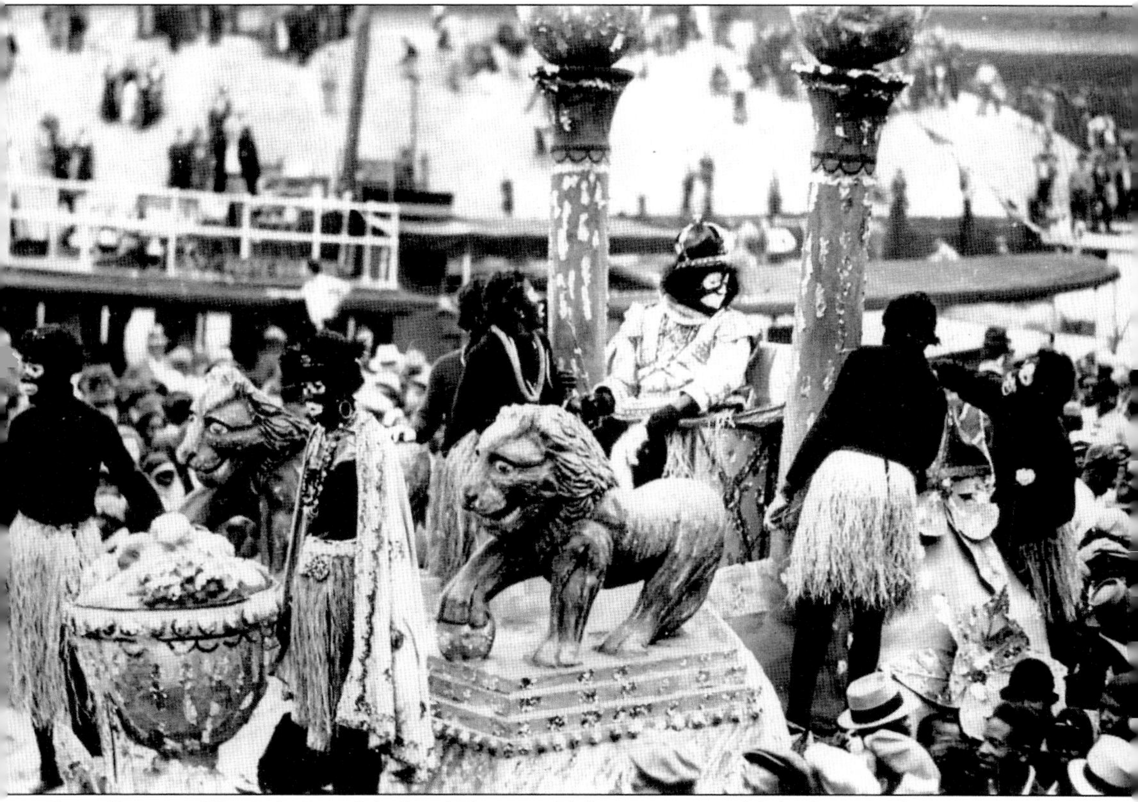

Zulu Parade. The Zulu Social Aid and Pleasure Club, Inc., was established September 20, 1916, yet Zulu marches began as early as 1909. William Story was the first king of the Zulus, wearing a lard can as a crown and a banana stalk as a scepter. Black consciences of the 1960s saw a decline in the Zulu membership over the controversial use of blackface. Historically, both white and black minstrel performers would use burnt cork as makeup to blacken their faces, creating comic African American characters whose onstage antics generally reinforced negative African American stereotypes. Historians today, however, typically view the Zulus' use of blackface more positively: as the reappropriation of a racist stereotype. (Courtesy of the State Library of Louisiana.)

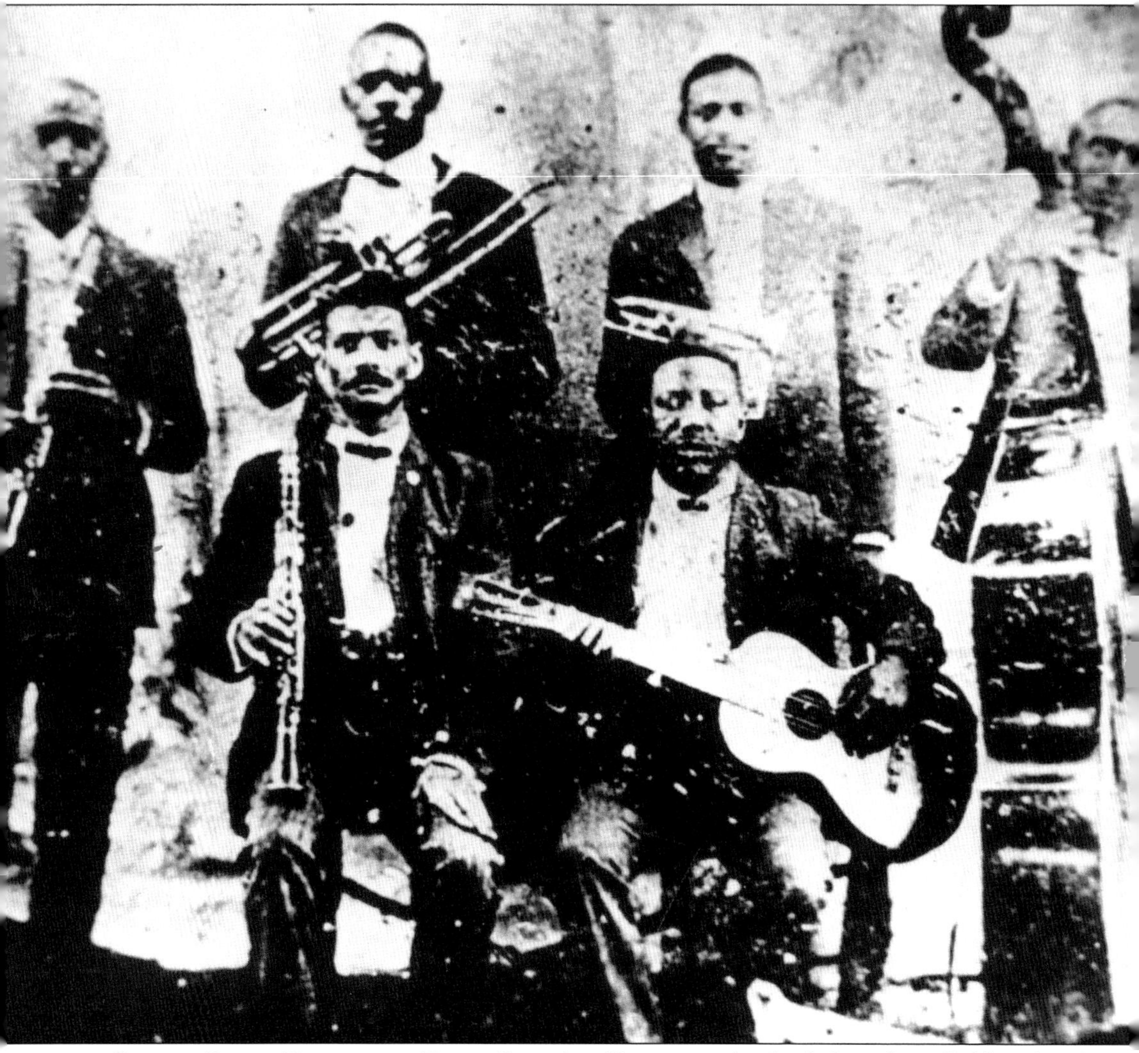

Charles Buddy Bolden and Band. Considered by some to be the father of jazz, Bolden played the cornet and was instrumental in developing music that transitioned from ragtime to jazz. His band was a top draw in New Orleans from 1900 to 1907. Bolden was known for his inventive improvisational sounds (and sheer loudness), but there are no known recordings of his music. He died on November 4, 1931, in the Louisiana State Mental Asylum in Jackson. The instruments employed by his band in this photograph speak to the transitional period between blues/ragtime and the newly emerging sounds of jazz. From left to right are (first row) Frank Lewis and Jeff "Brock" Mumford; (second row) William Warner, William Cornish, Charlie "Buddy" Bolden, and James Johnson. (Courtesy of the New Orleans Jazz Club/Louisiana State Museum.)

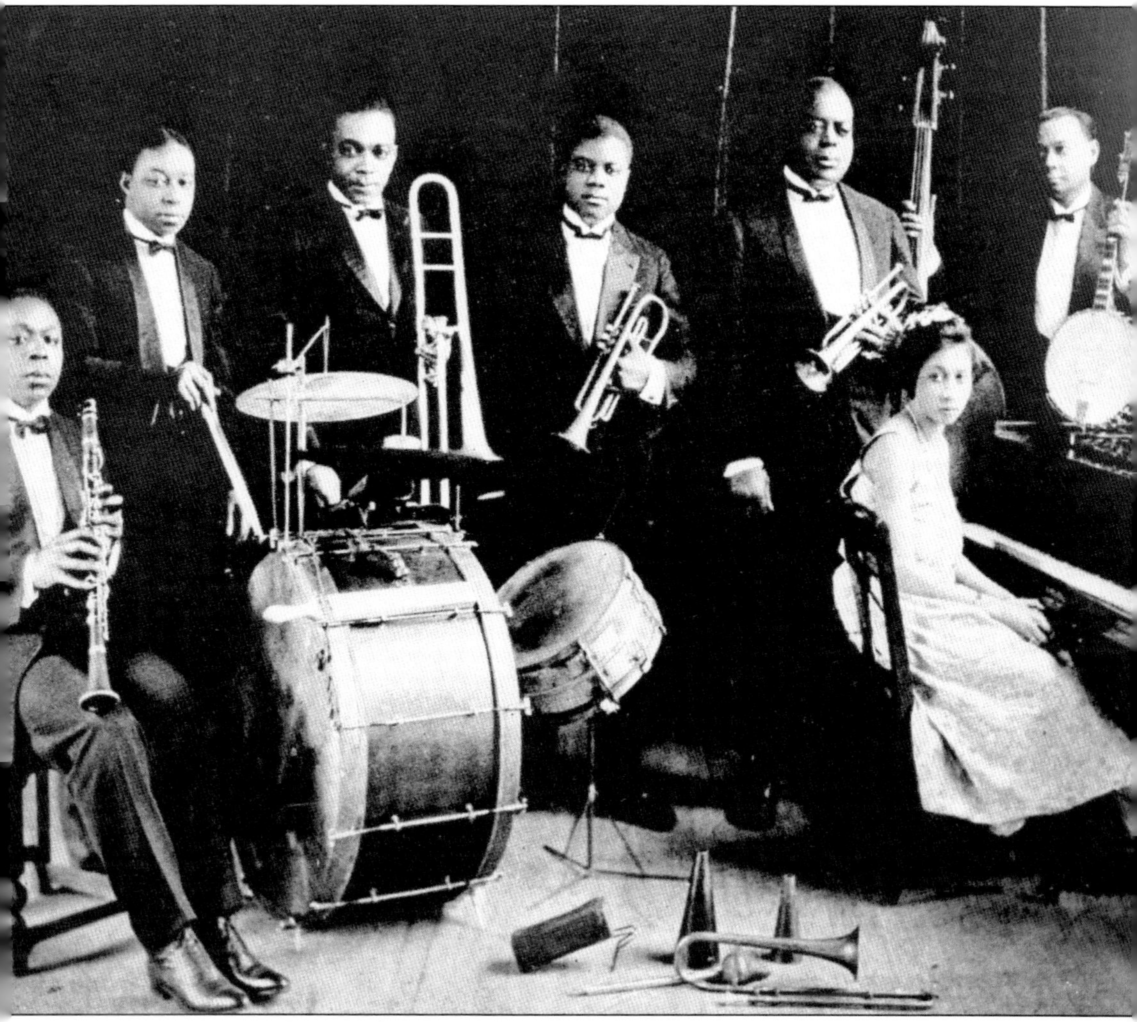

Joe "King" Oliver's Band. The New Orleans bandleader and cornet-player Joseph Nathan Oliver was born December 19, 1885. He mentored Louis Armstrong and provided him with one of his first cornets. His unique playing style originated the mute with the use of unusual instrumentations such as derby hats and a plumber's plunger. Oliver composed a number of popular tunes, including "Canal Street Blues" and "Doctor Jazz." King Oliver and his Creole Jazz Band introduced New Orleans jazz (often called Dixieland) to a larger audience once the band began touring beyond the South. Oliver never reached anything like Louis Armstrong's success, however, and died in poverty on April 10, 1938, at the age of 52. (Courtesy of the New Orleans Jazz Club/Louisiana State Museum.)

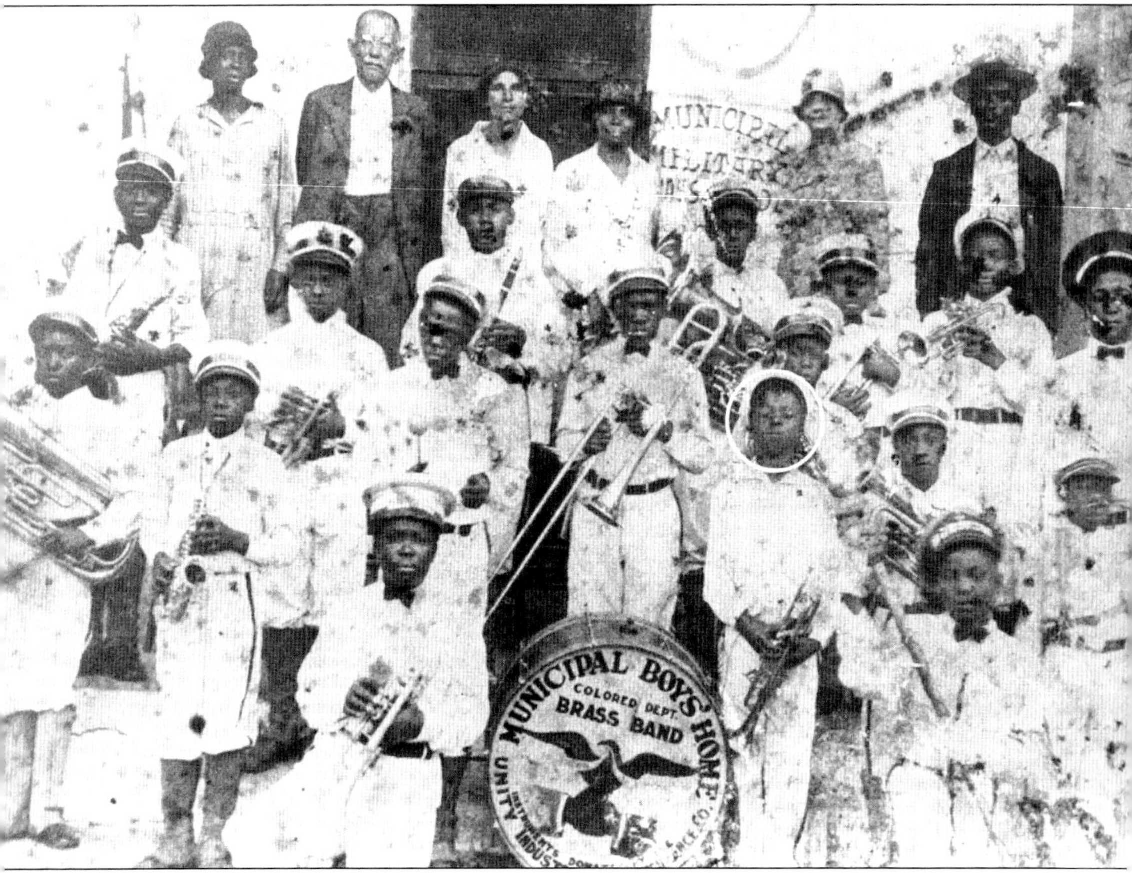

YOUNG ARMSTRONG. This image of the Brass Band of the Municipal Boys home depicts Louis Armstrong (standing adjacent to the drum) well on his way to becoming an excellent musician. (Courtesy of the New Orleans Jazz Club/Louisiana State Museum.)

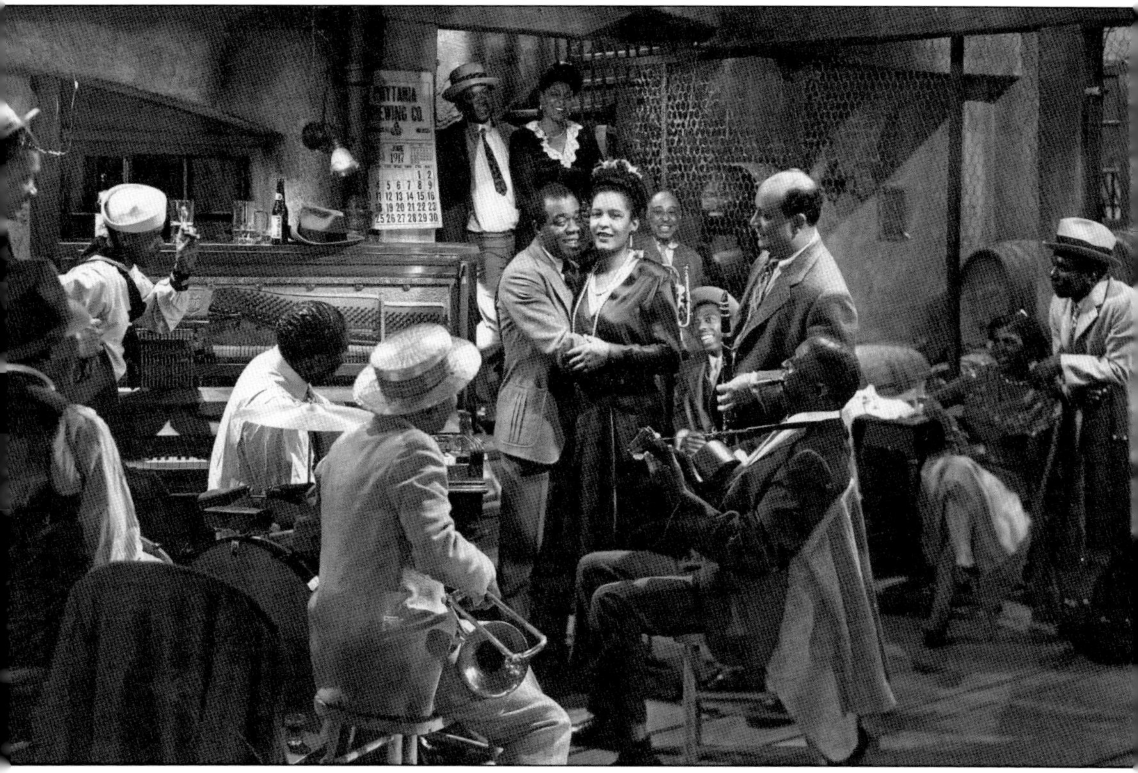

New Orleans. This still, taken from the 1947 film *New Orleans*, fictionalizes the demise of Storyville. Starring Louis Armstrong, Billie Holiday, and Sidney Bechet (seen here standing next to Holiday), the film is set in a sporting house, or bordello, located in the now-gone Storyville red-light district of New Orleans. This area was named after city alderman Sidney Story, who suggested that a designated section of New Orleans be set aside for the explicit operation of sporting houses, where one was guaranteed to find prostitution and live music. (Courtesy of the New Orleans Jazz Club/Louisiana State Museum.)

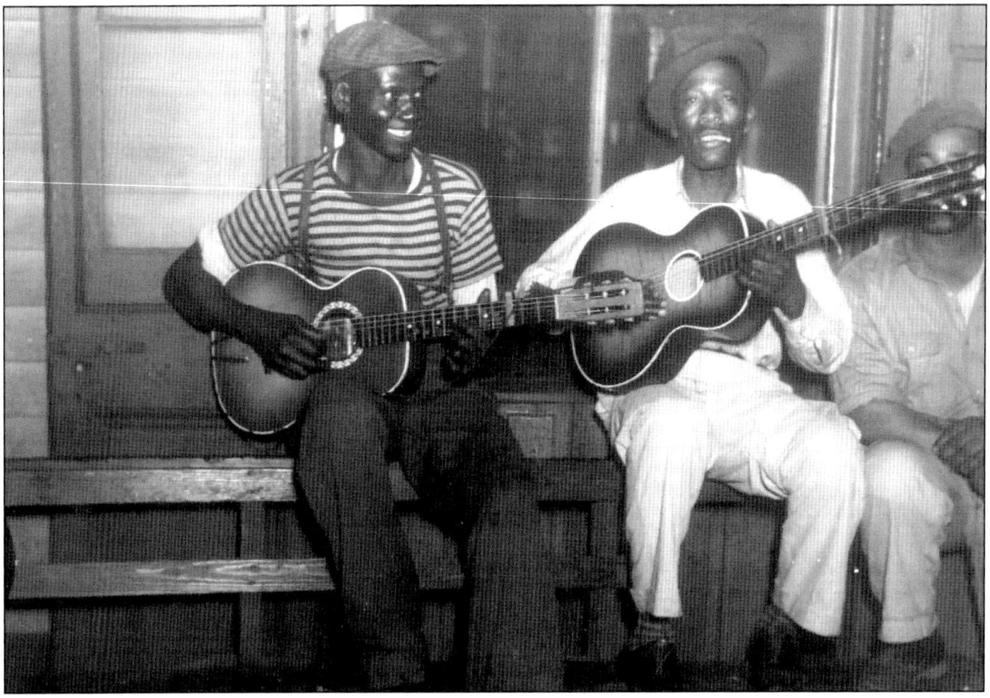

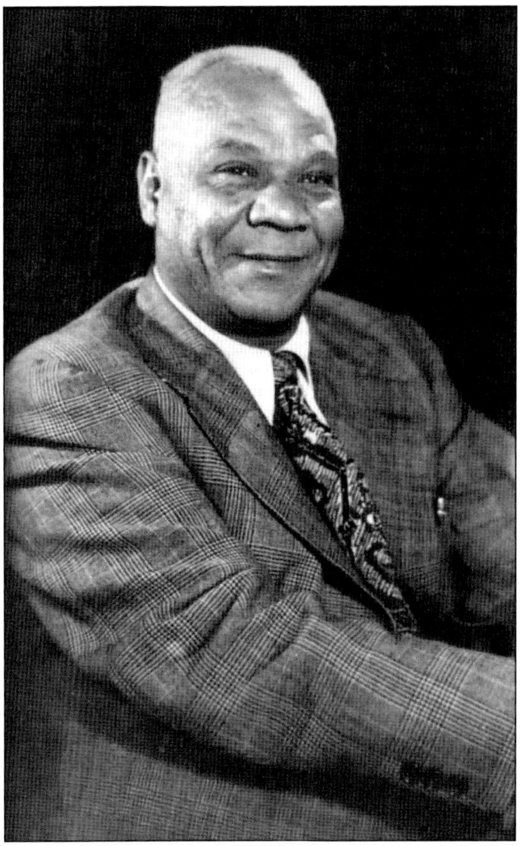

STREET MUSICIANS. These unidentified street performers are maintaining a New Orleans tradition: music and song. This *c.* 1930 image of men sitting on a front stoop with guitars suggests that they are playing the blues, traditionally associated with acoustic guitars and African American men. Jazz, conversely, is traditionally associated with brass instruments. (Courtesy of the State Library of Louisiana.)

SIDNEY BECHET. Jazz great Sidney Bechet (1897–1959) was born in New Orleans on May 14, 1897. He was a master jazz musician and composer. Bechet played a variety of musical instruments but decided to make the clarinet his main instrument. However, Bechet is best known for his musical mastery of the soprano saxophone. In 1950, Bechet relocated to France, becoming a mentor to other American expatriate artists, such as Josephine Baker (1906–1975). Bechet died in Paris in 1959. (Courtesy of the New Orleans Jazz Club/Louisiana State Museum.)

Slow Drag. This image shows Alcide "Slow Drag" Pavageau, part of a second line in front of the St. Louis Cathedral in the French Quarter c. 1980. Those who follow the band and members of a Social Aide and Pleasure Club during a parade are referred to as the "second line." Their style of parading with waving handkerchiefs and twirling parasols is called "second lining." (Courtesy of the New Orleans Jazz Club/ Louisiana State Museum.)

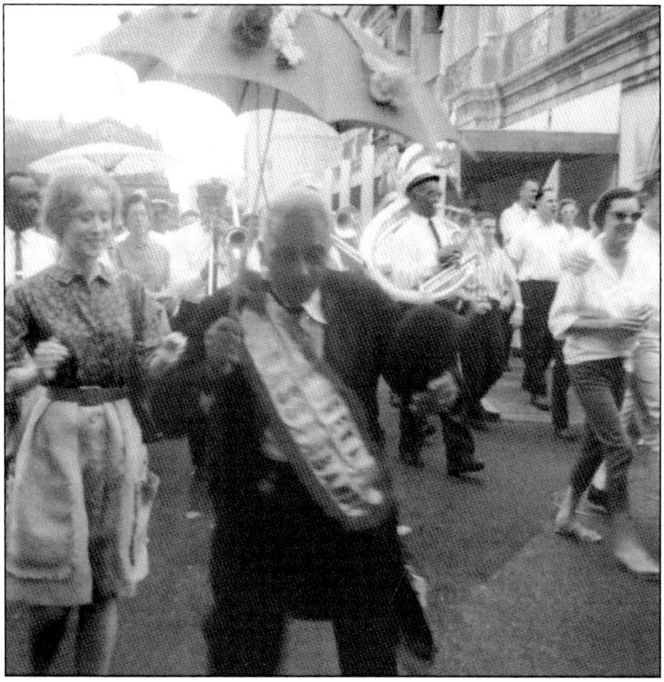

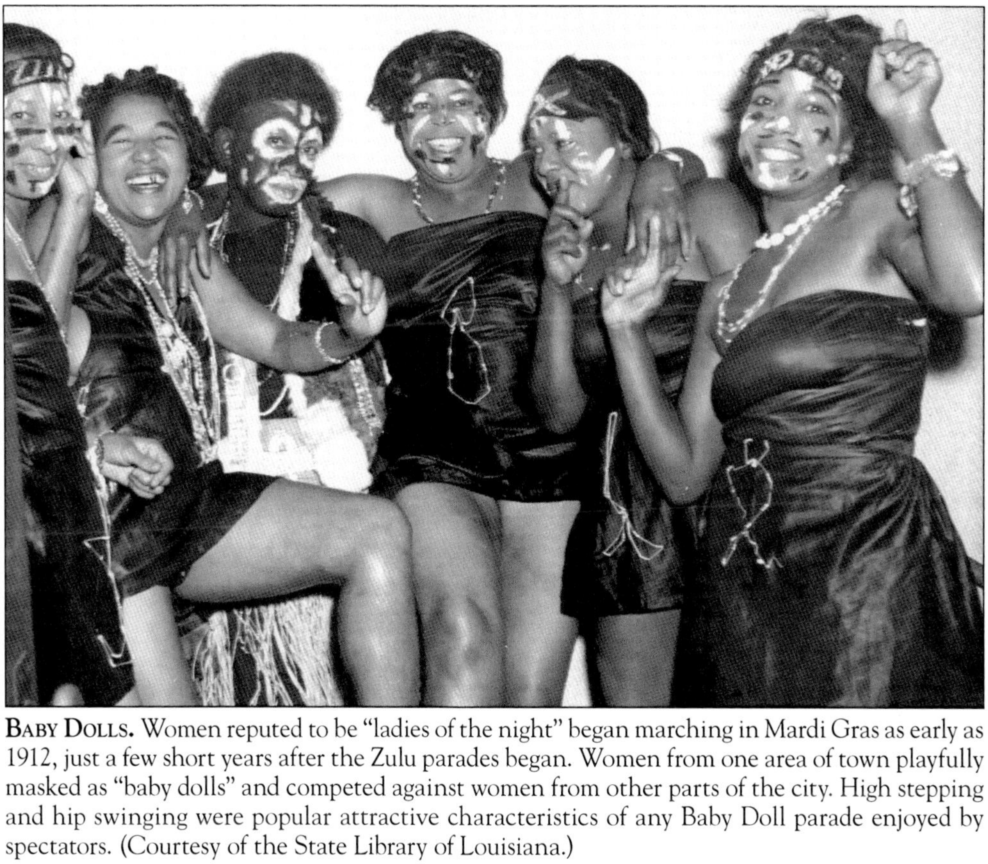

Baby Dolls. Women reputed to be "ladies of the night" began marching in Mardi Gras as early as 1912, just a few short years after the Zulu parades began. Women from one area of town playfully masked as "baby dolls" and competed against women from other parts of the city. High stepping and hip swinging were popular attractive characteristics of any Baby Doll parade enjoyed by spectators. (Courtesy of the State Library of Louisiana.)

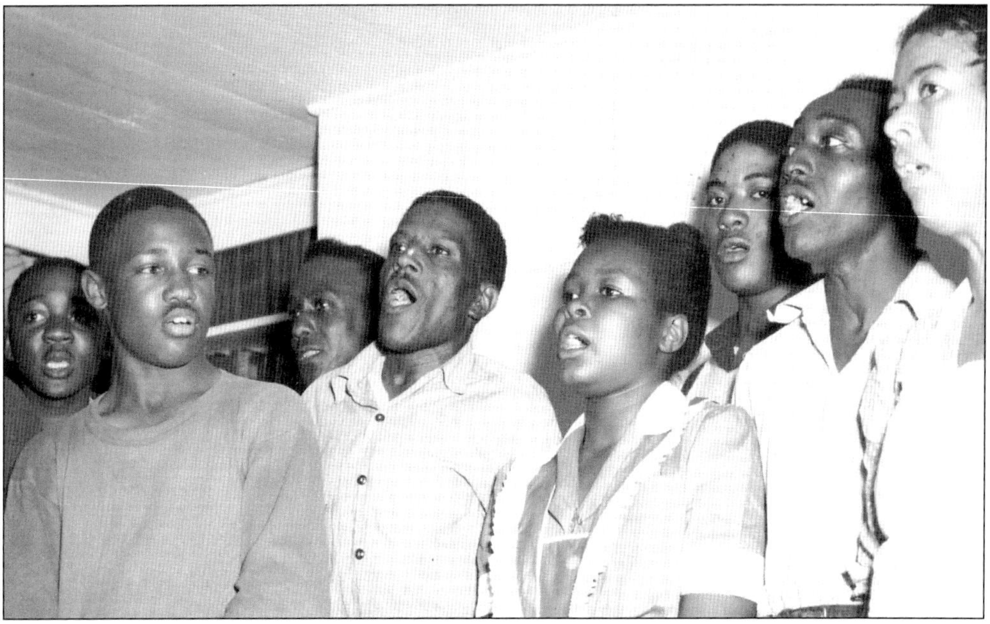

SINGERS. Photographers from other parts of the United States would come and document the cultural ways of African Americans in the South. Often they would capture the musical tradition in churches and performance halls. Shown here are groups of African American singers in a New Orleans church. (Courtesy of the State Library of Louisiana.)

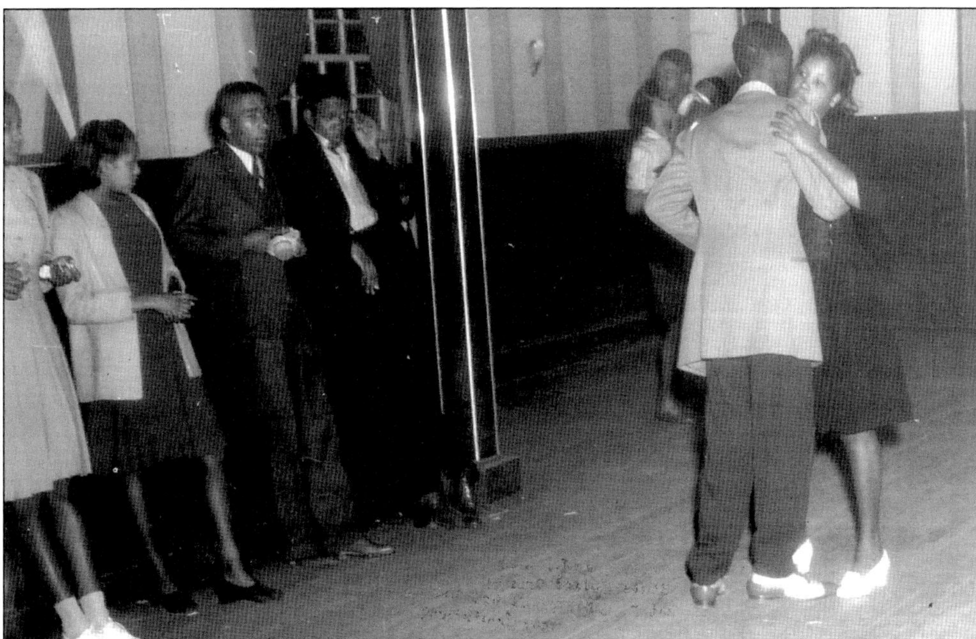

SLOW DANCE. This 1940s image of unidentified dancers at a dance hall was most likely taken during the days of the WPA, when a cadre of artists, photographers, and unskilled laborers were put to use documenting and building America. This government-sponsored program greatly added to the documentation of African Americans in the public sphere, as this image depicts. (Courtesy of the State Library of Louisiana.)

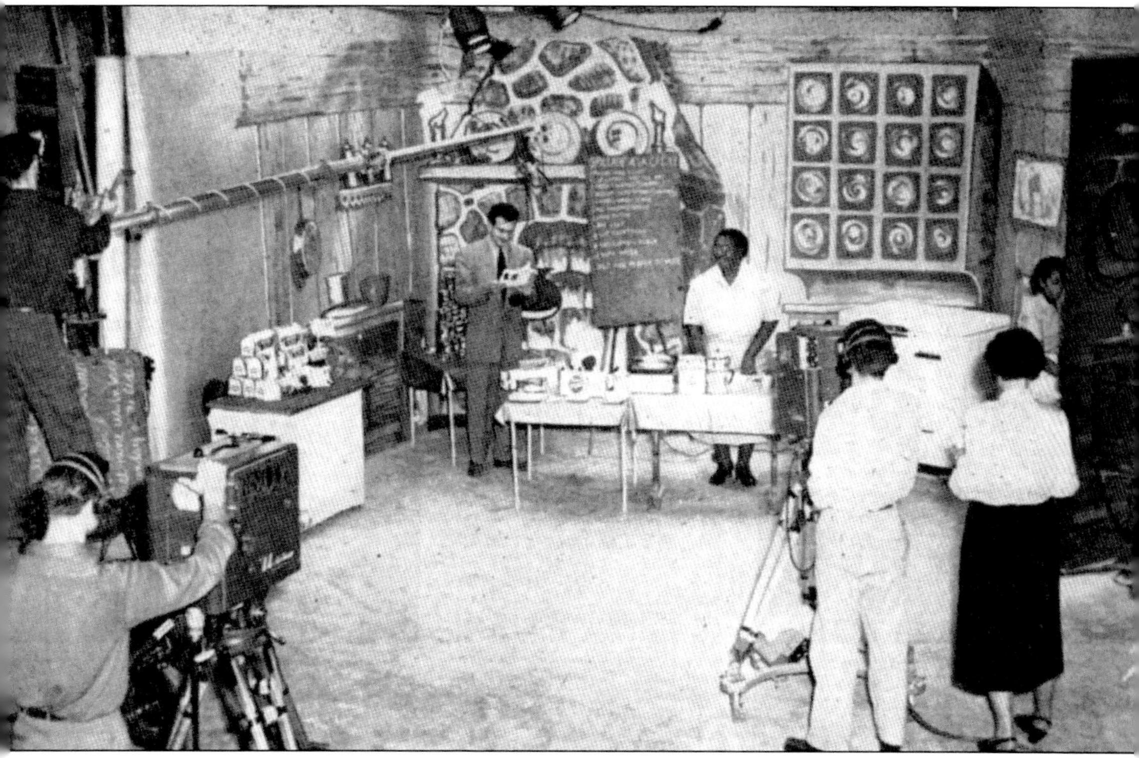

Culinary Pioneer. Shown here on the set of her television show in the 1940s, Lena Richard was the first African American woman in New Orleans to become an on-air television personality. Airing on WDSU in New Orleans, Richard hosted a weekly cooking show that ran from 1947 to 1949. Lena Richard was born in New Roads, Louisiana, and grew up in New Orleans. Richard worked as a cook for a local family who sent her to an area cooking school. She ultimately traveled to Boston to continue her culinary training. She graduated from the Fannie Farmer Cooking School in 1918. (Courtesy of the Louisiana Division/City Archives, New Orleans Public Library.)

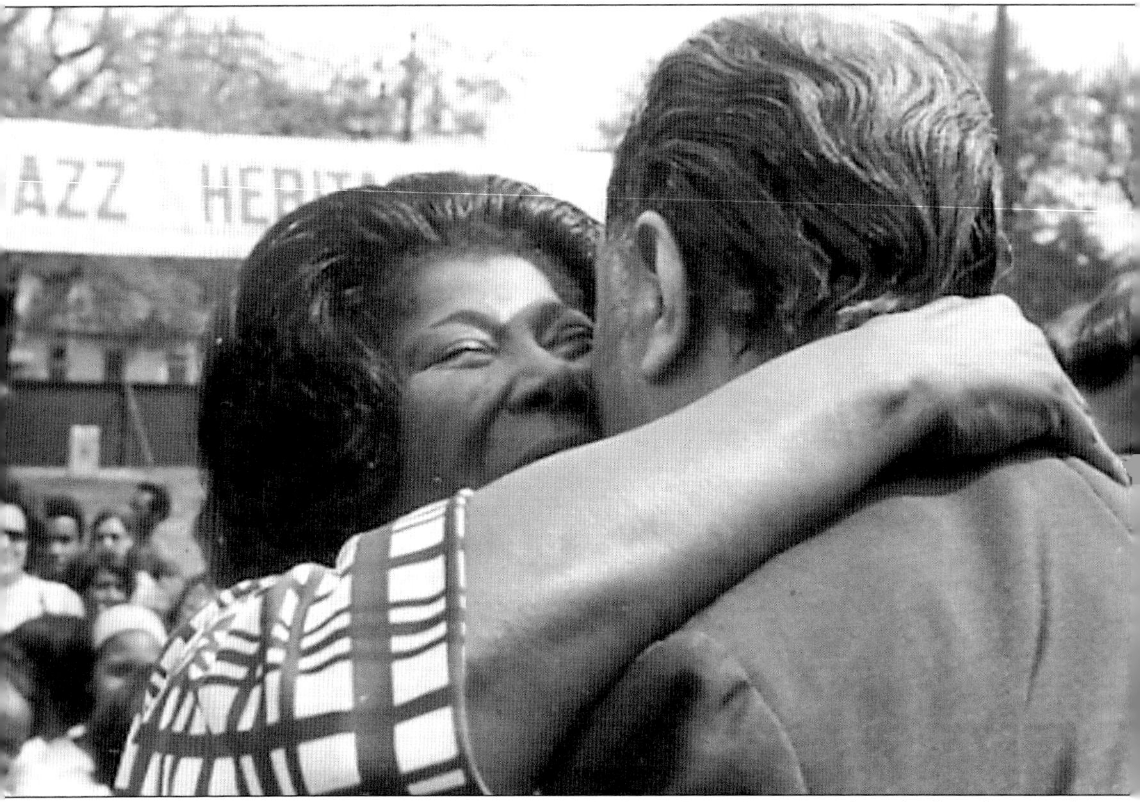

JAZZ FEST IS BORN. This photograph shows Mahalia Jackson (1911–1972) and Edward Kennedy "Duke" Ellington (1899–1974) embracing at the first New Orleans Jazz and Heritage Festival held in Congo Square (then called Beauregard Park). During the festival, Ellington led the Eureka Brass Band second lining through the festival grounds. Festival producer George Wein handed Mahalia Jackson a microphone, and she joined the procession. Mahalia Jackson was born in the Black Pearl section of the Carrollton neighborhood on Pitt Street in New Orleans and is commonly referred to as the Queen of Gospel Music. (Courtesy of the State Library of Louisiana.)

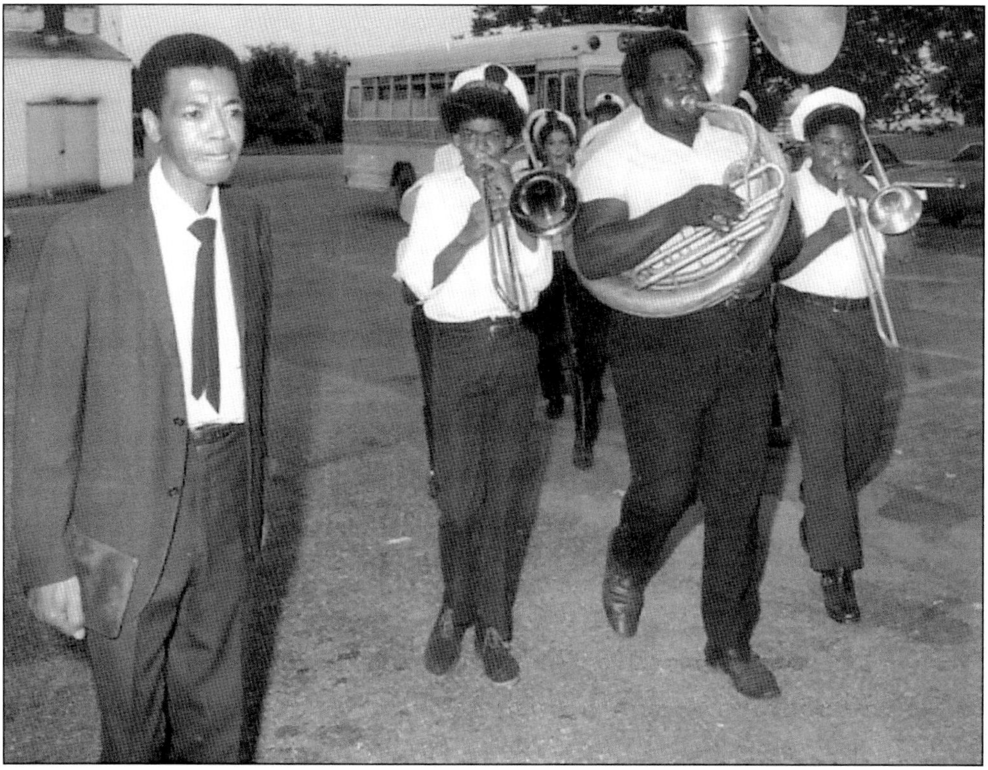

Horns. Brass band music is as much a part of New Orleans culture as red beans and rice on Mondays. Shown here are three brass band musicians with a music teacher leading in the front. (Courtesy of the State Library of Louisiana.)

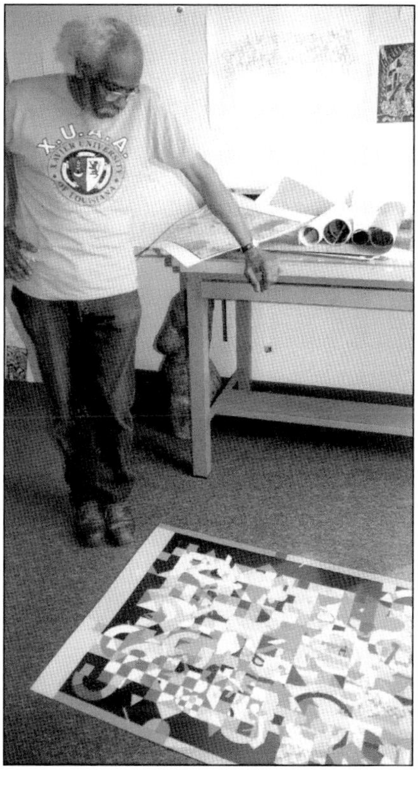

Master Artist. This photograph shows visual artist John T. Scott (1940–2007). Scott was born in the Gentilly section of New Orleans and was raised in the Lower Ninth Ward. Scott is a graduate of Xavier and Michigan State Universities. While at Michigan State, he studied with Charles Pollack, brother of artist Jackson Pollack (1912–1956). In 1992, Scott was awarded the John D. and Catherine T. MacArthur Foundation Genius Award. (Courtesy of Ron Bechet.)

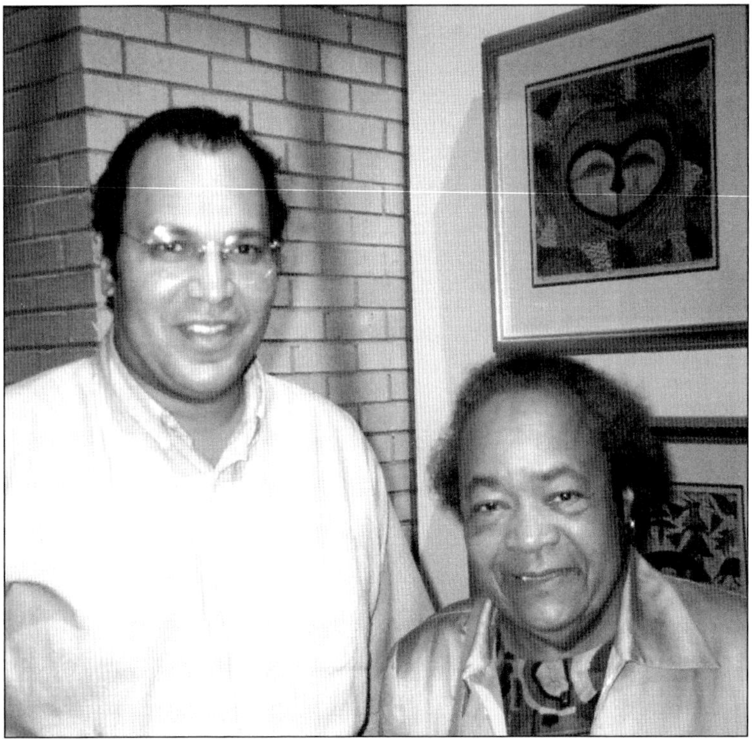

ART HISTORIAN. Seen here are artist and professor of Art at Xavier University of Louisiana standing with noted art historian and New Orleans native Samella Lewis. Dr. Lewis is best known for her writings on African American artists and her staunch support for collecting their works. (Courtesy of Ron Bechet.)

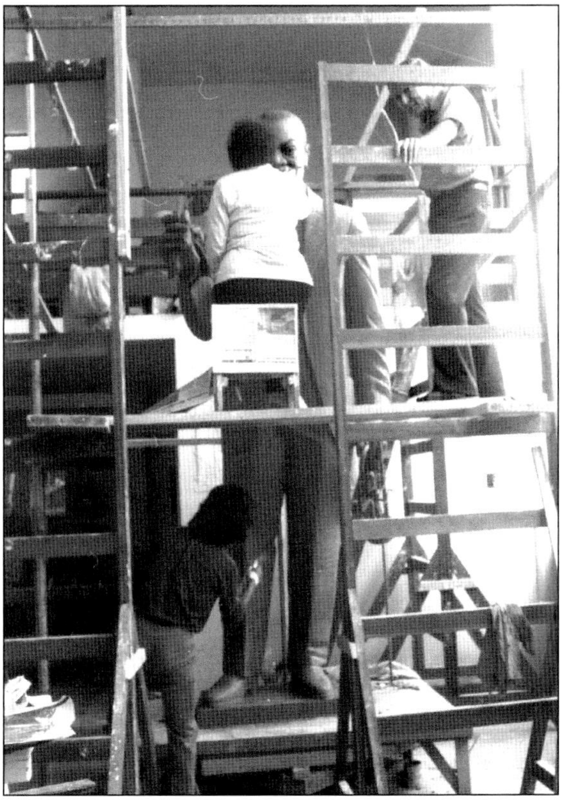

SCULPTING A NEW ORLEANS GREAT. American-Mexican sculptress and printmaker Elizabeth Catlett (1911–) is shown here on scaffolding in a studio working on a statue of jazz master Louis Armstrong. Floyd Levin is also shown on the scaffolding. The completed sculpture is currently in Louis Armstrong Park in New Orleans. (Courtesy of the New Orleans Jazz Club/ Louisiana State Museum.)

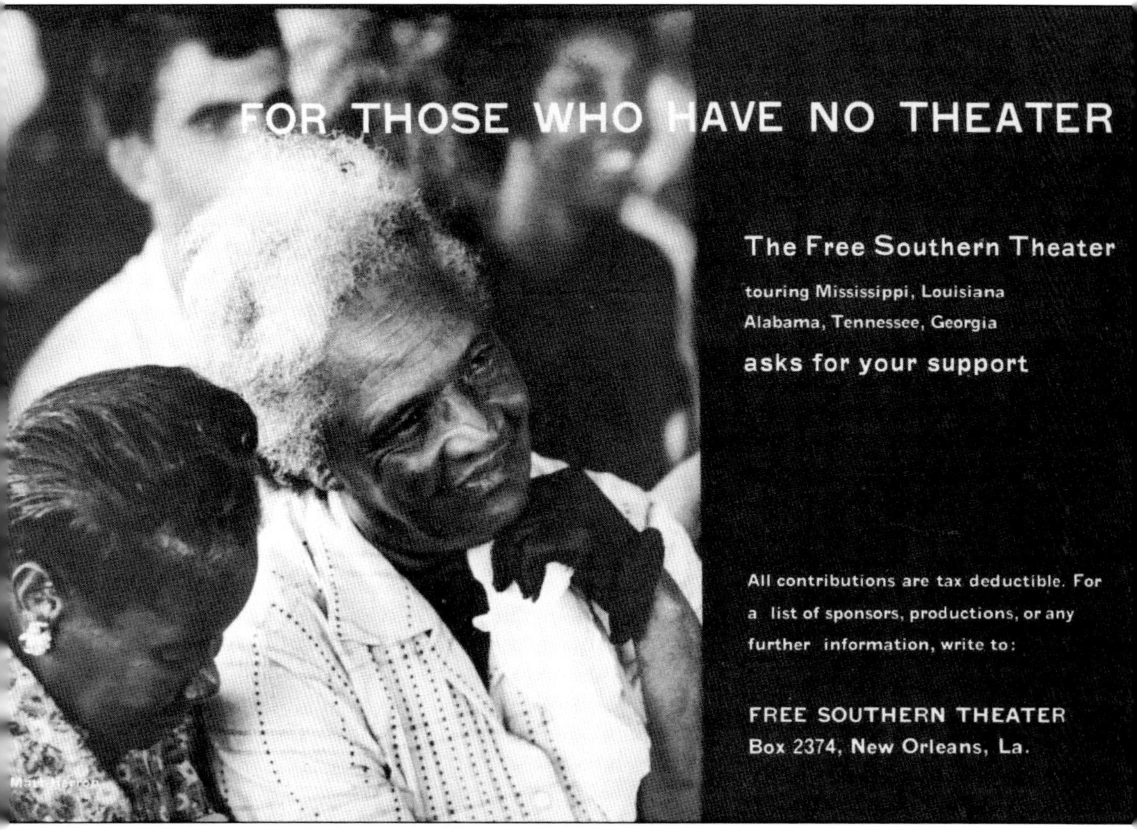

For Those Who Have No Theater. One of the most important components of the American civil rights movement was the Black Arts Movement that took shape in the late 1960s and early 1970s. The Free Southern Theater was founded by John O'Neal and Gilbert Moses at Tougaloo College in Jackson, Mississippi, in 1963. The theater company took shape and moved to New Orleans. The purpose of the company was "to use theater as an instrument to stimulate the development of critical and reflective thought among black people in the South." (Courtesy of the Amistad Research Center, Tulane University, New Orleans, Louisiana, Free Southern Theater Collection.)

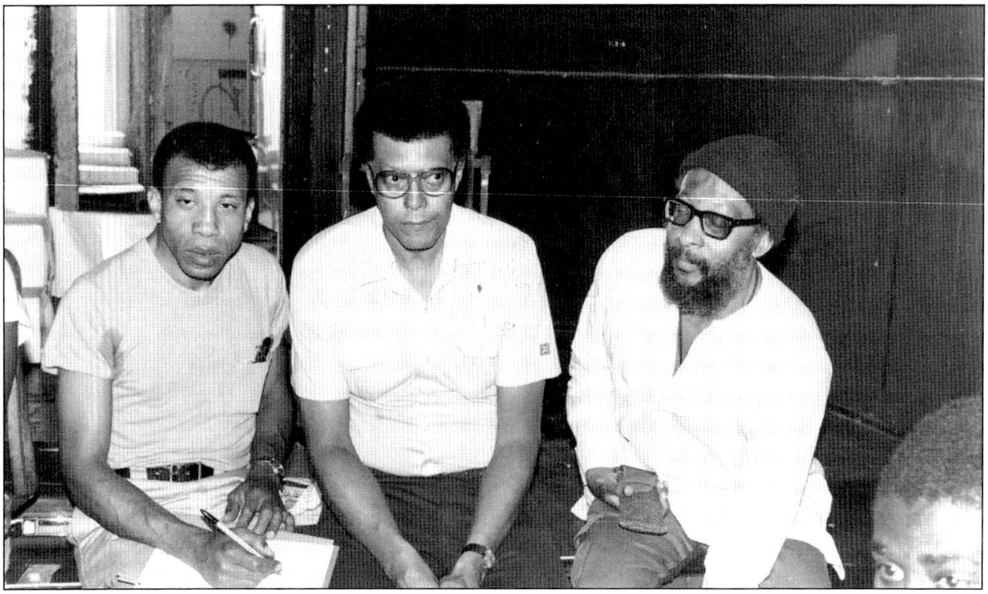

Noted Authors. From left to right are Jerry Ward Jr., Ph.D.; Tom Dent; and Kalamu ya Salaam. Salaam and Dent are native New Orleanians and have written many articles, poems, and books about the African American experience in New Orleans. Ward is a distinguished professor and writer who taught at Tougaloo College in Jackson, Mississippi, and now teaches at Dillard University, Tougaloo's sister institution. (Courtesy of Cosmo-D Productions.)

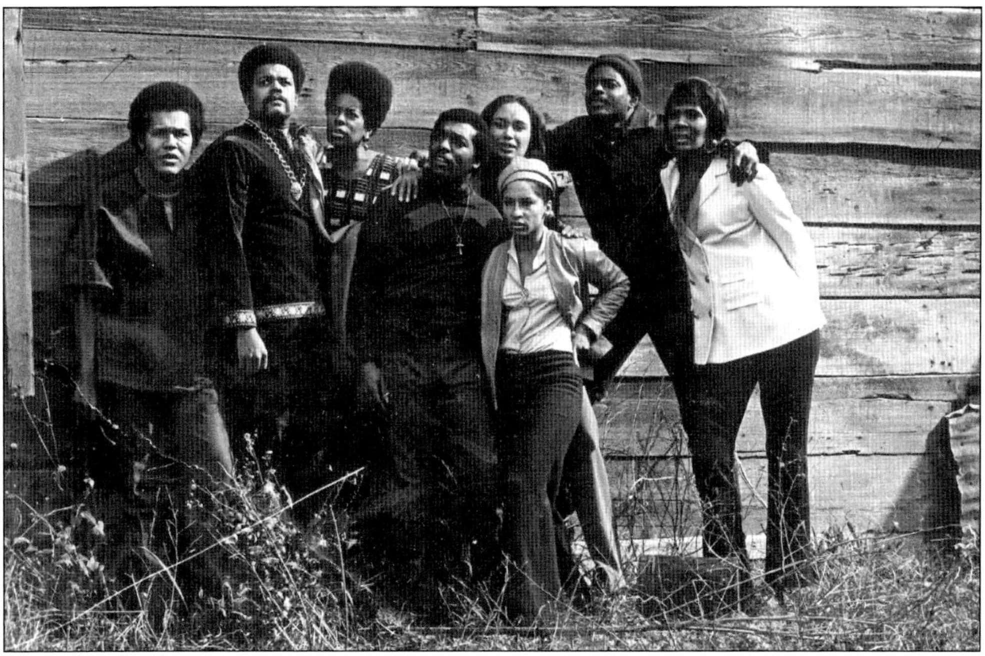

Members of the Company. This image shows members of the Free Southern Theater. Pictured here from left to right are Gil Moses, Cordell Reagan, Kelley-Marie Berry, Richard Fels, Barbara Clark, Ann Smith, Leroy Giles, and Sarah Allen. Morris Jones took this photograph. (Courtesy of the Amistad Research Center, Tulane University, New Orleans, Louisiana, Free Southern Theater Collection.)

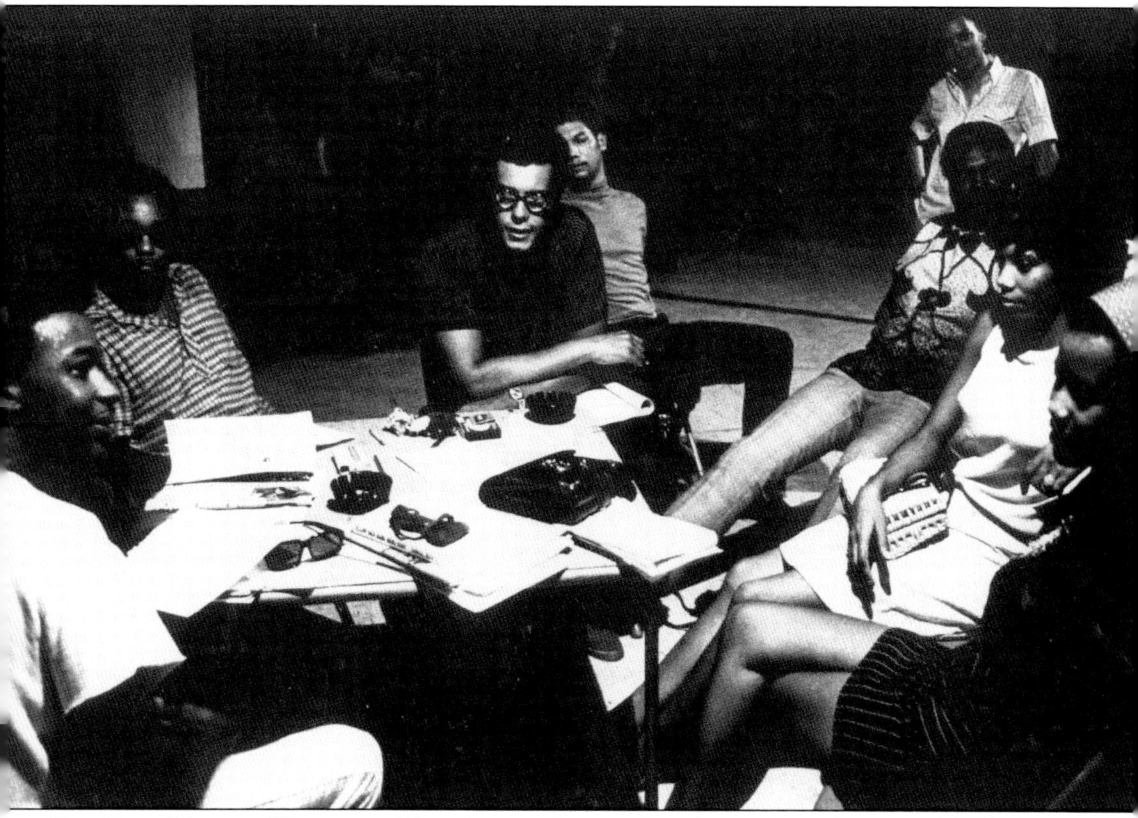

Tom Dent Writing Workshop. This photograph was taken during the early years of the Free Southern Theater and shows Dent (center) conducting a writing workshop. Tom Dent (1932–1998) was a major cultural activist in New Orleans. He was the oldest of three sons born to Dr. Albert Dent and Ernestine Jessie Covington Dent. Dent attended Morehouse College in Atlanta, Georgia, and while there, he served as editor of the literary journal *The Maroon Tiger.* Dent was a significant figure during the early years of the Free Southern Theater. In 1969, he and Gilbert Moses, cofounder of the group, edited the book *The Free Southern Theater.* Dent was also instrumental in founding the Southern Black Cultural Alliance. He served as Executive Director of the New Orleans Jazz and Heritage Festival Foundation from 1987 to 1990. (Courtesy of the Amistad Research Center, Tulane University, New Orleans, Louisiana, Free Southern Theater Collection.)

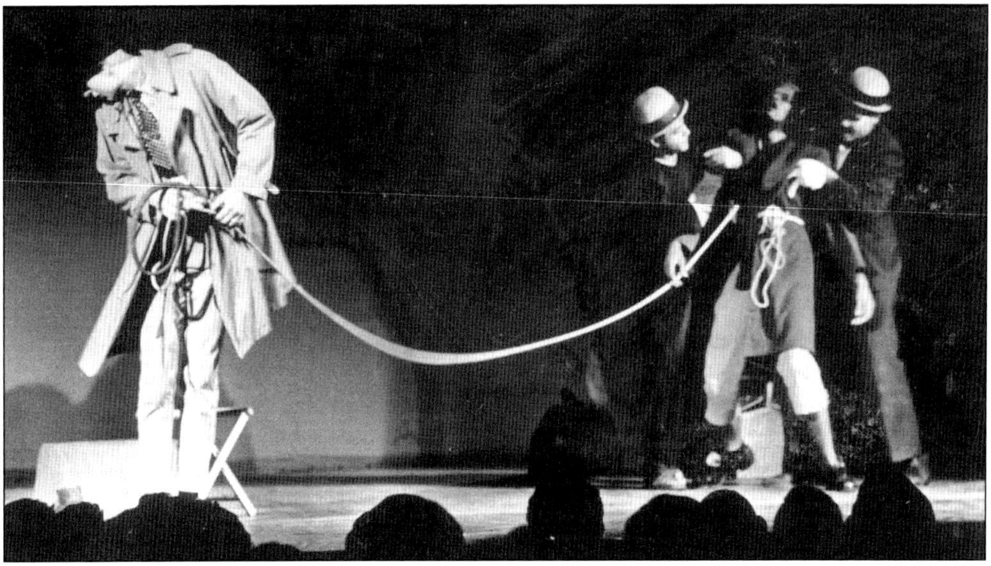

WAITING FOR GODOT. This image shows a production of *Waiting for Godot* performed by members of Free Southern Theater. (Courtesy of the Amistad Research Center, Tulane University, New Orleans, Louisiana, Free Southern Theater Collection.)

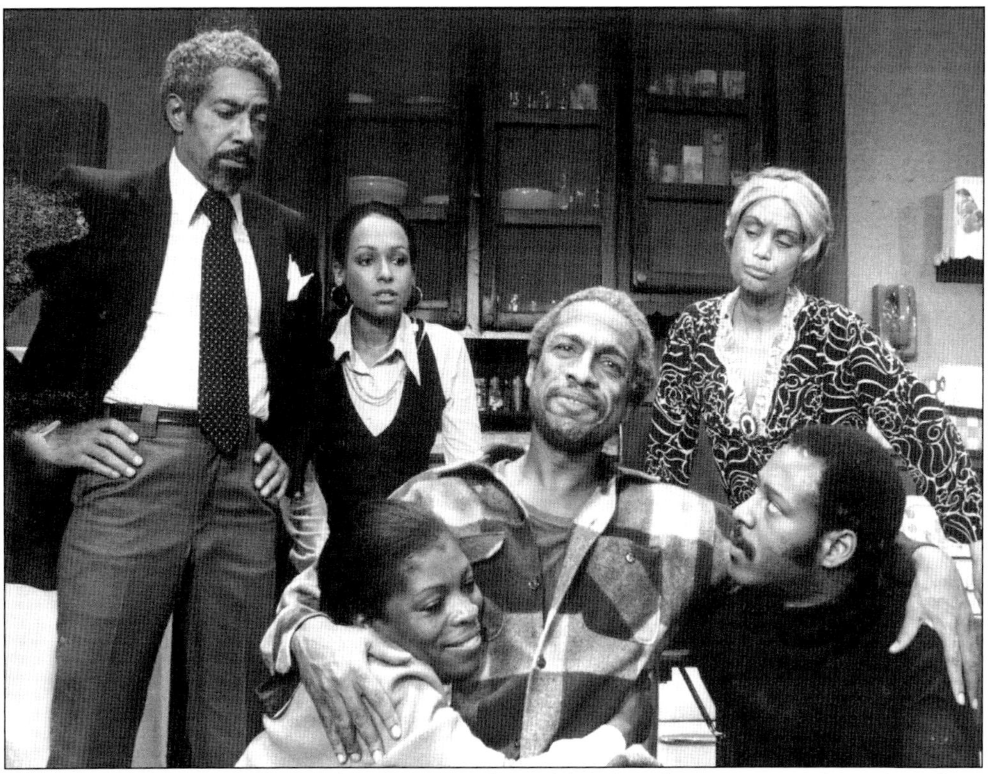

THE RIVER NIGER. This images shows cast members of the play *The River Niger.* Shown here from left to right are (first row) Roxie Roker, Arthur French, and Dean Irby; (second row) Charles Brown, Louise Heath, and Barbara Clarke. (Courtesy of the Amistad Research Center, Tulane University, New Orleans, Louisiana, Free Southern Theater Collection.)

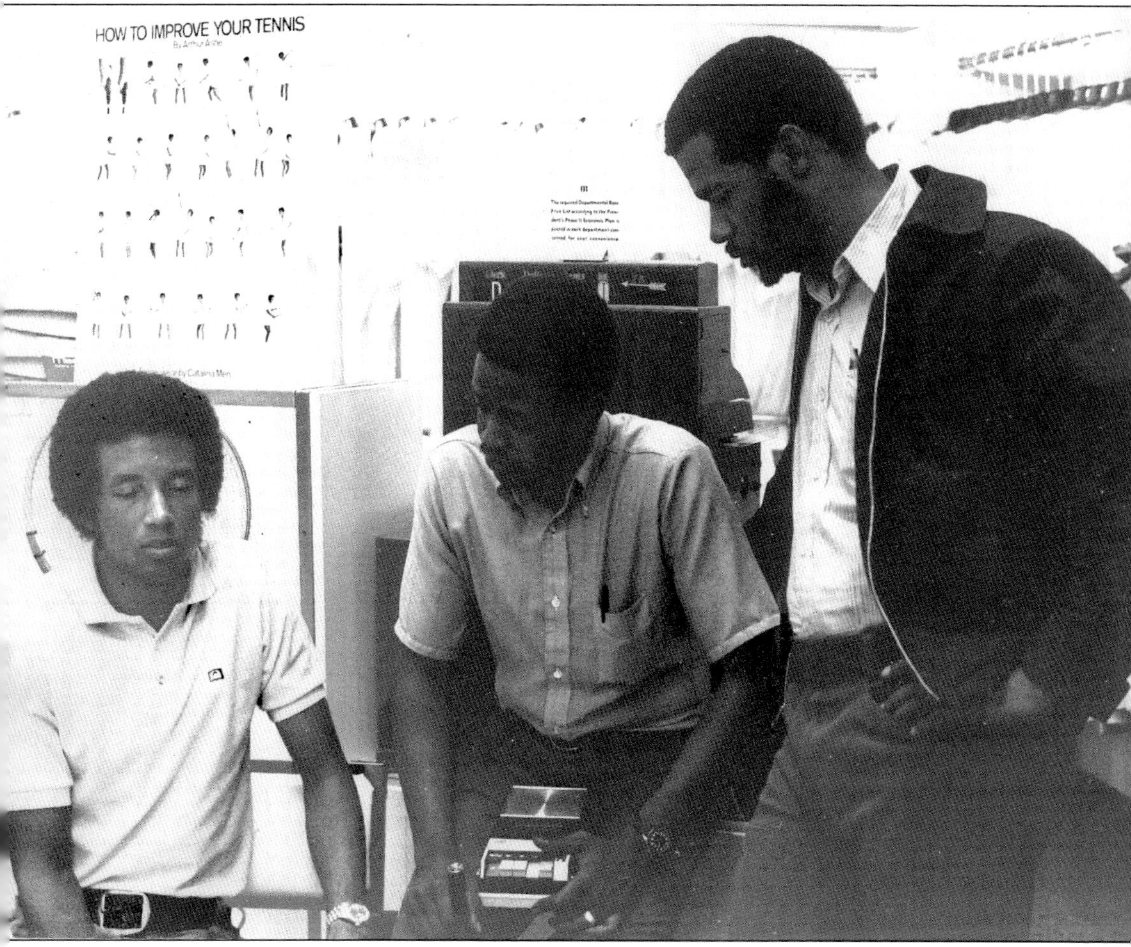

FUND-RAISING. This photograph taken in 1974 shows Arthur Ashe, Bill Rouselle, and John O'Neal. Ashe, a leading supporter, orchestrated many fund-raisers for the Free Southern Theater. (Courtesy of the Amistad Research Center, Tulane University, New Orleans, Louisiana, Free Southern Theater Collection.)

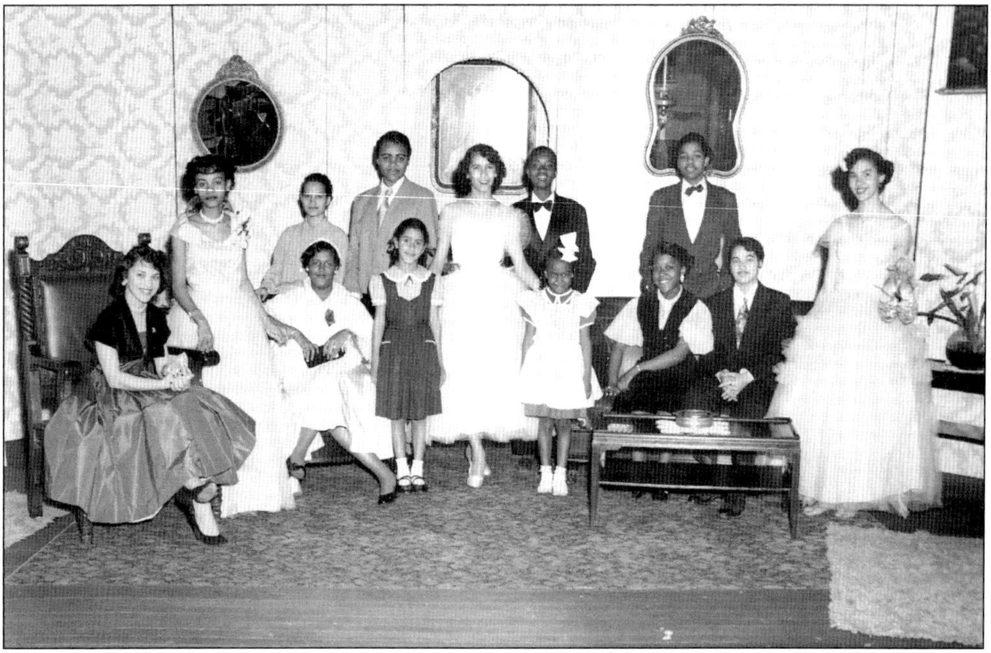

THE WORLD'S A STAGE. This image shows students at St. Mary's Academy posing on stage after performing a play. St. Mary's Academy being an all-girls school would often have male characters played by the female students, as seen here. (Courtesy of the Sisters of the Holy Family.)

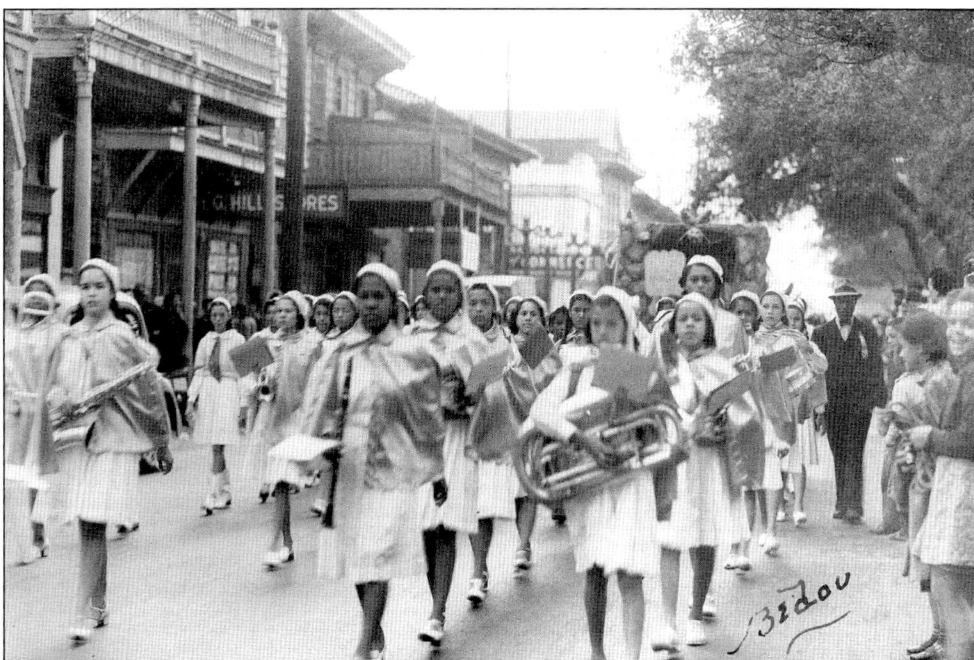

A. P. BEDOU. St. Mary's Academy students are captured on film here in 1930 as they march through the French Quarter. A. P. Bedou served as a photographer for the Sisters of the Holy Family. (Courtesy of the Sisters of the Holy Family.)

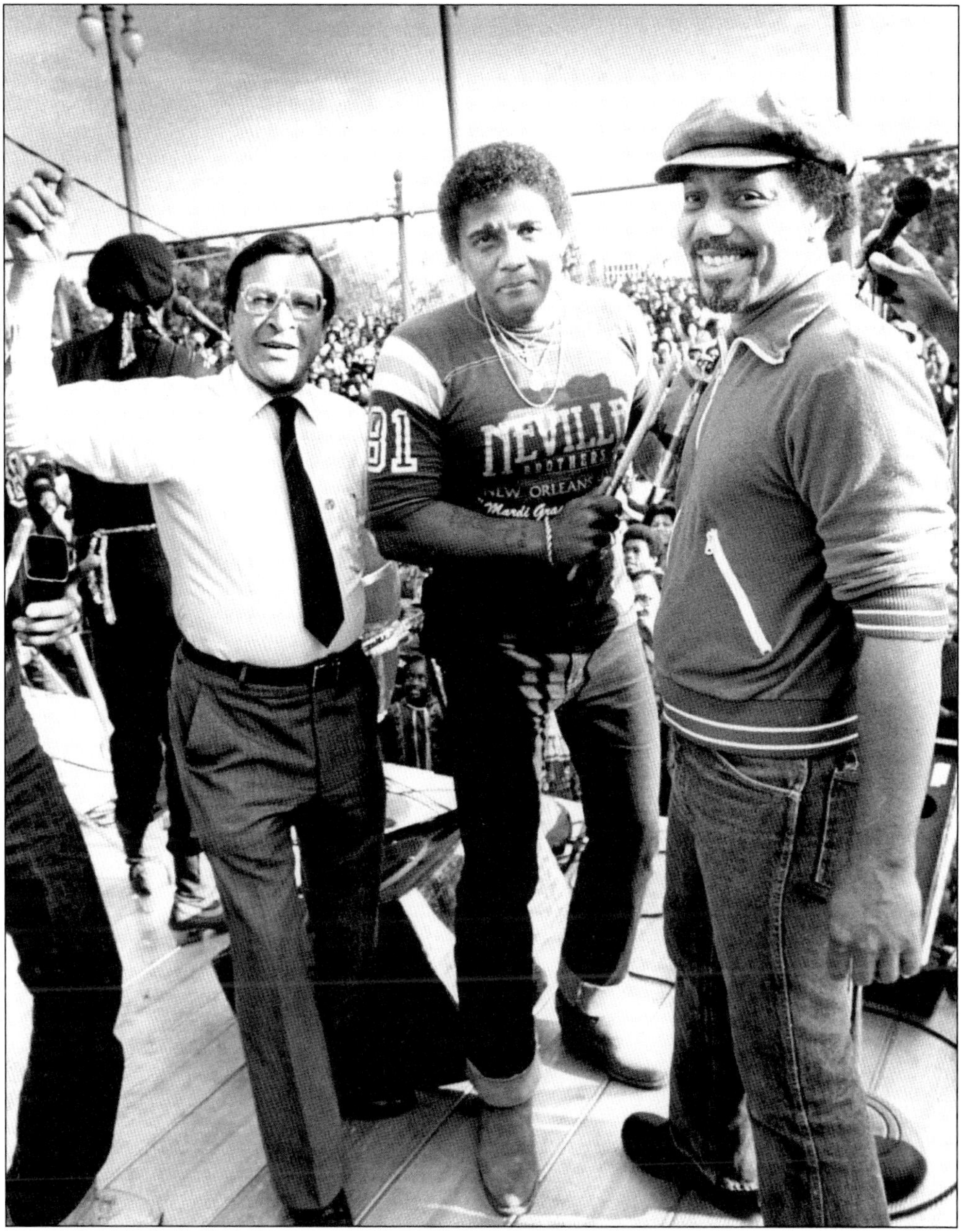

THREE GREATS. Mayor Morial added soul to city politics, and the Grammy Award-winning Neville Brothers added their own brand of New Orleans soul to their popular music. Mayor Morial is pictured on the left with music greats and New Orleans natives Aaron (center) and Art Neville. The Neville Brothers—Art, Charles, Cyril, and Aaron—began their professional careers at a 1976 recording session with the Mardi Gras Indian crew The Wild Tchoupitoulas, led by their uncle, Big Chief Jolly. (Courtesy of the Louisiana Division/City Archives, New Orleans Public Library.)

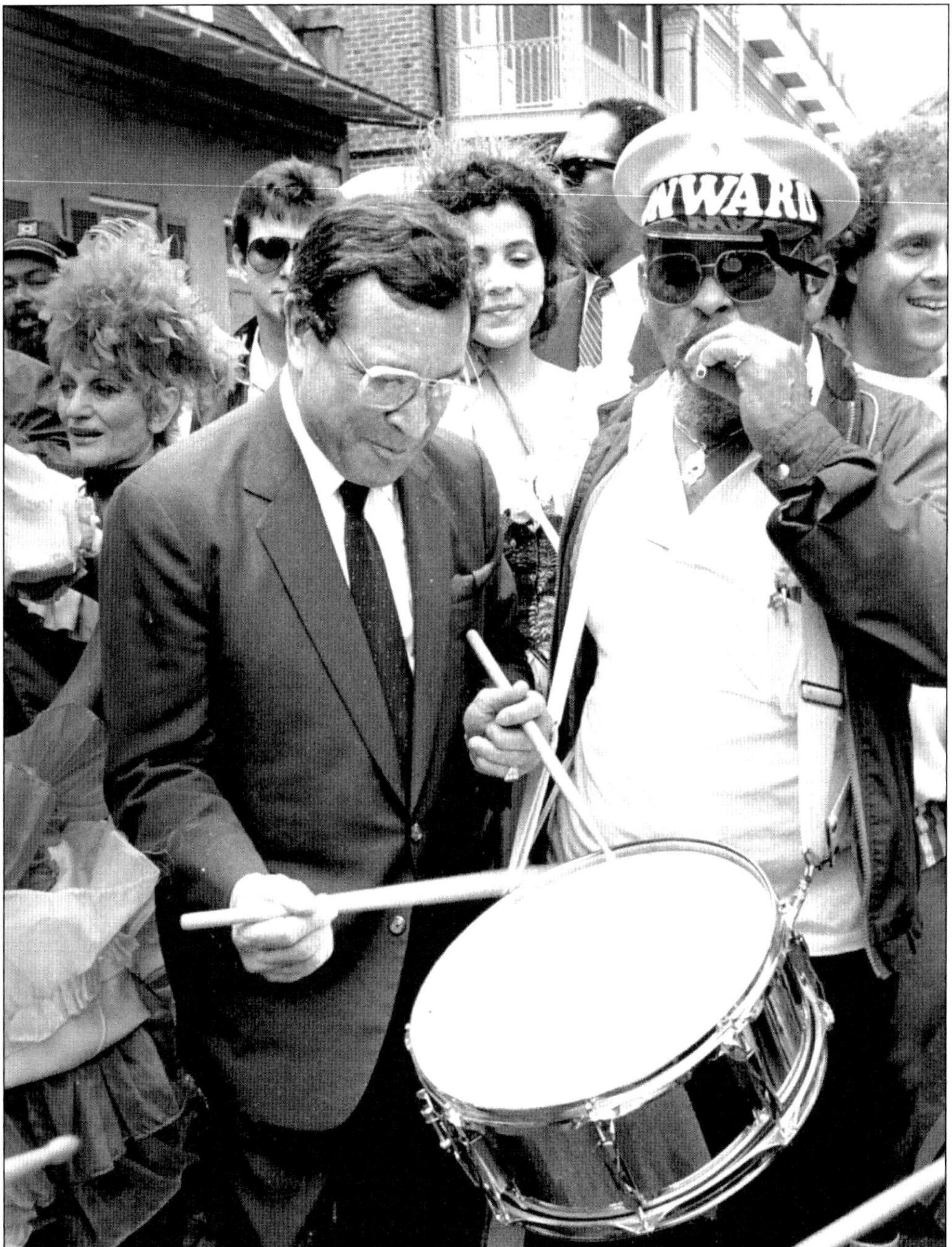

Having Fun with a Band. Arguably one of the most charismatic mayors the city has had, Ernest "Dutch" Morial is shown here having fun with a band in the French Quarter. (Courtesy of the Louisiana Division/City Archives, New Orleans Public Library.)

MURAL. Located on the exterior wall of the Ashé Cultural Arts Center, this mural depicts the arts and culture of New Orleans. Under the direction of New Orleans artist Douglass Redd, the mural was designed and painted by Shakor, Ivan Watkins, Jamar Pierre, Terrance Osborne, Lidya Araya, and Lionel Miltone. (Courtesy of Phoenix Savage.)

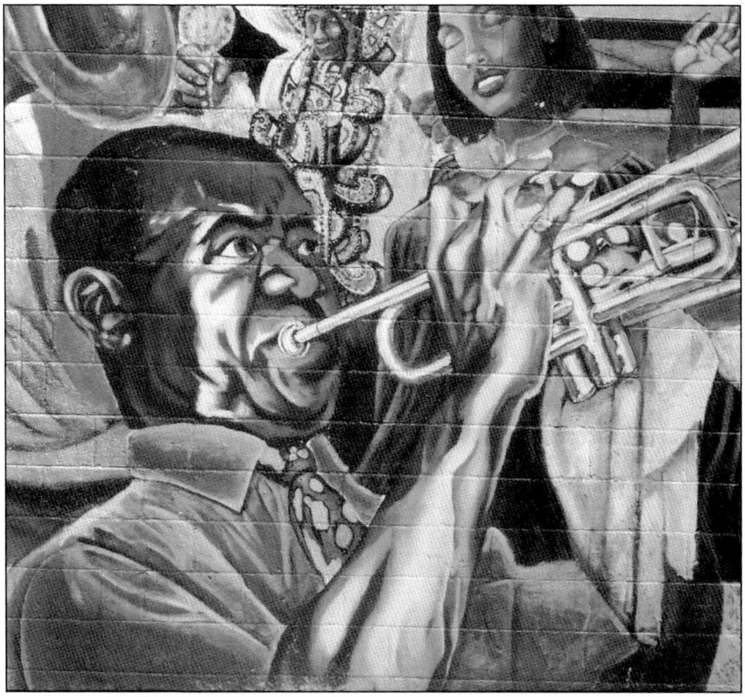

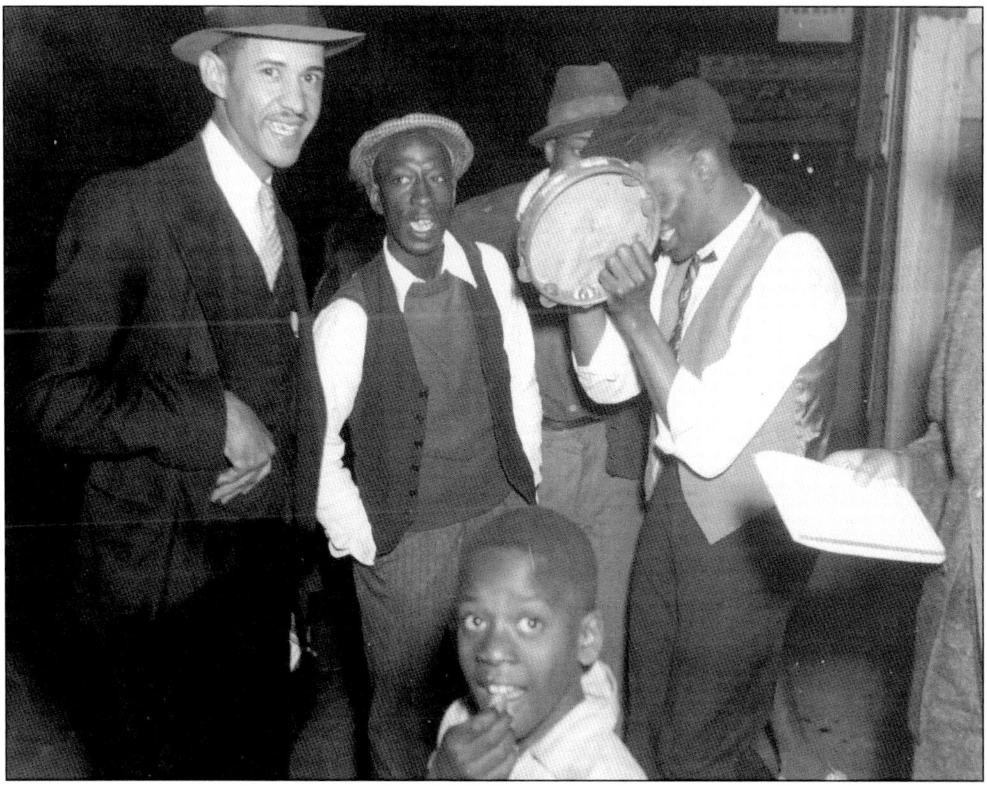

CELEBRATION. Four men and a child have fun during a Mardi Gras celebration in New Orleans in the 1930s. (Courtesy of the State Library of Louisiana.)

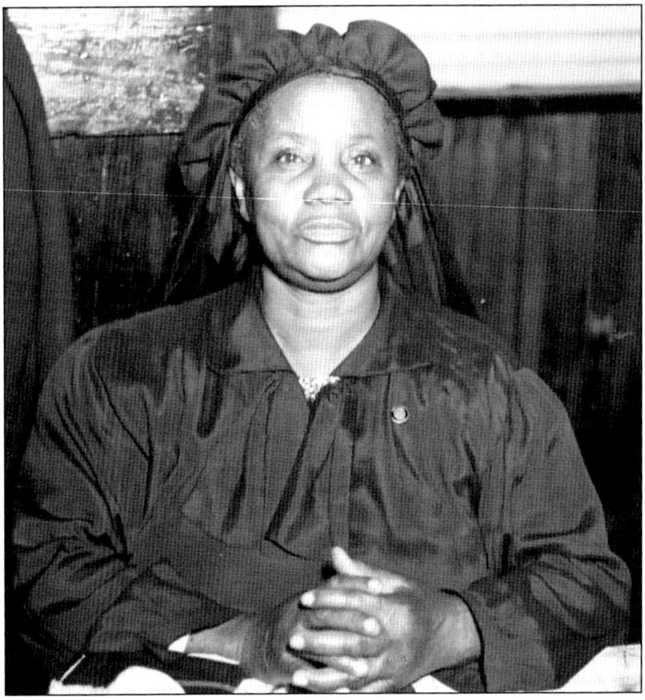

COGIC MEMBER. This is an unidentified member of the Church of God in Christ (COGIC). Founded in 1897 by Baptist ministers, COGIC has its origins outside of New Orleans, but this 1930s photograph documents that there was a COGIC community in New Orleans at that time. (Courtesy of the State Library of Louisiana.)

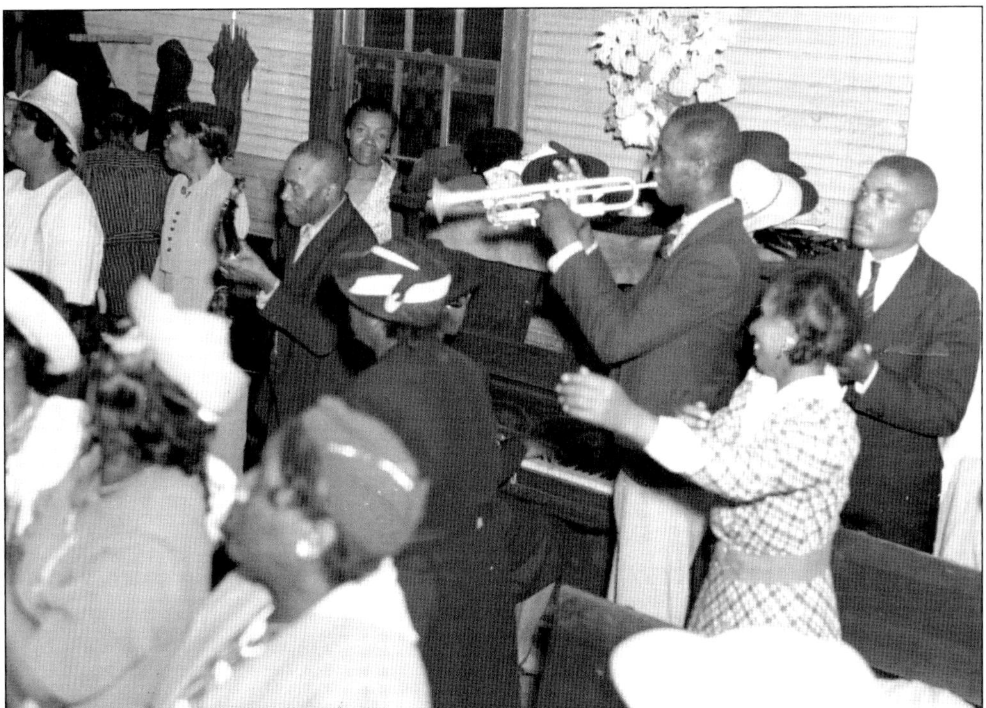

LIVELY SERVICES. This photograph shows a typical worship service at a COGIC church. Members of this faith are known for including musical instruments other than a piano and organ during worship celebrations; shown here is a member playing a trumpet. (Courtesy of the State Library of Louisiana.)

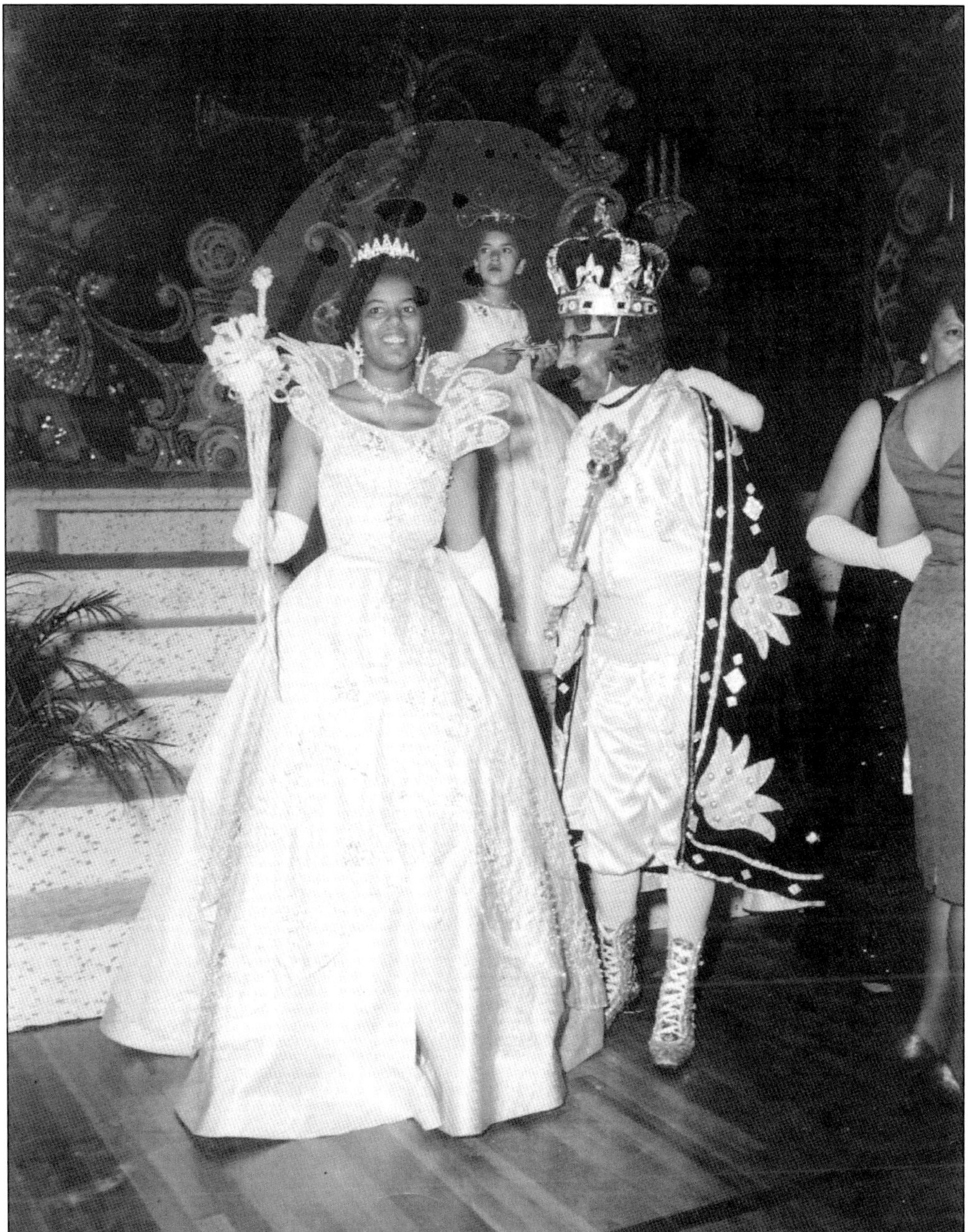

THE ORIGINAL ILLINOIS CLUB. Shown here is the reigning Queen of the Original Illinois Club, Vivian-Miranda Baranco, in 1962. The Original Illinois Club is the oldest African American carnival krewe in New Orleans. Established in 1895 as the Illinois Club, the krewe split into two separate krewes in 1926. One club was called the Original Illinois Club and the other was called the Young Men Illinois Club. Both of the clubs are still active. (Courtesy of the Louisiana State Museum.)

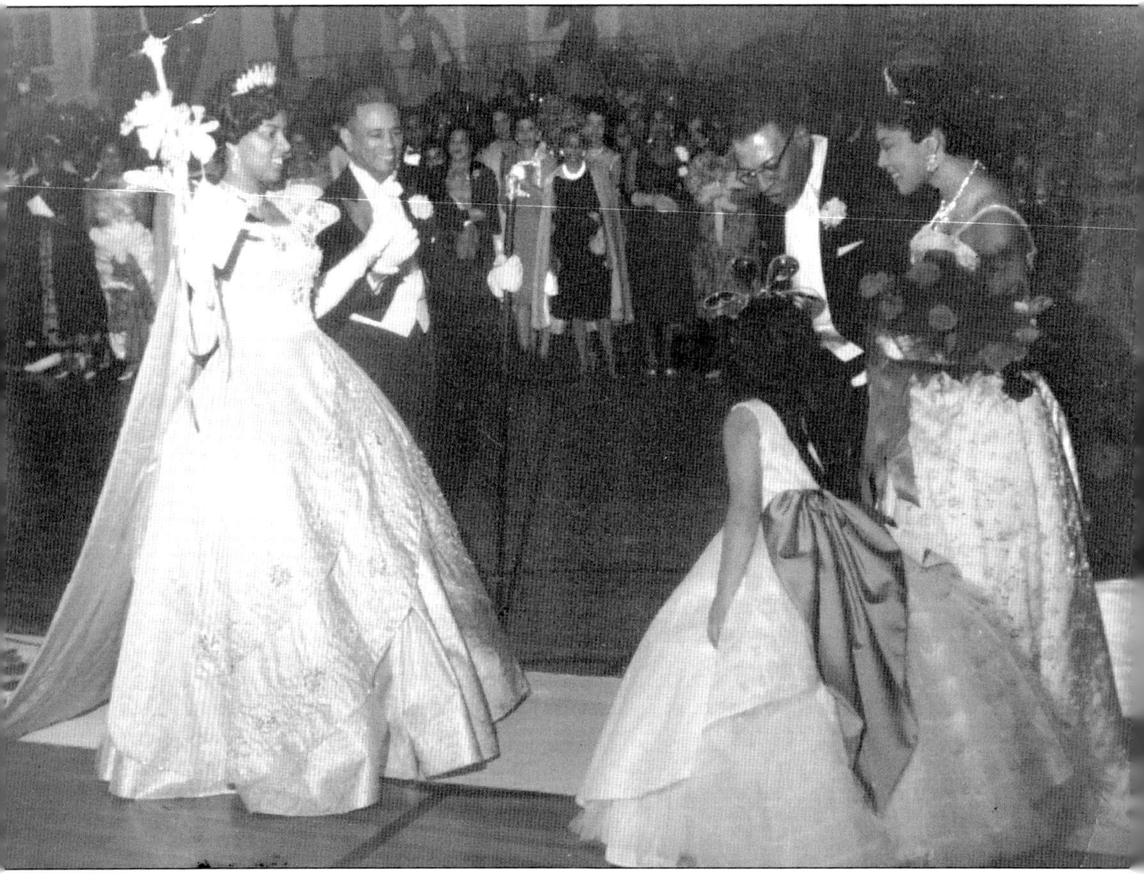

QUEEN. This photograph shows Vivian-Miranda Baranco during the ceremony presented by the Original Illinois Club in New Orleans. The Barancos were prominent residents in Baton Rouge during the mid-20th century. Dr. Baranco was a successful dentist in Baton Rouge and a longstanding member of the Original Illinois Club in New Orleans. (Courtesy of the Louisiana State Museum.)

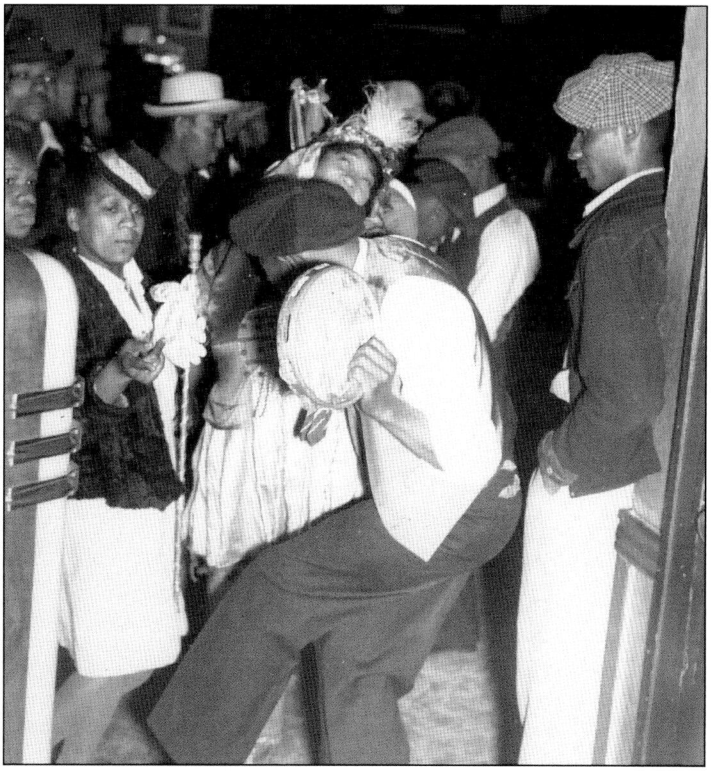

REVELRY. Shown here in this *c.* 1935 photograph are Mardi Gras revelers in New Orleans. This image was most likely taken by WPA documentarians. (Courtesy of the State Library of Louisiana.)

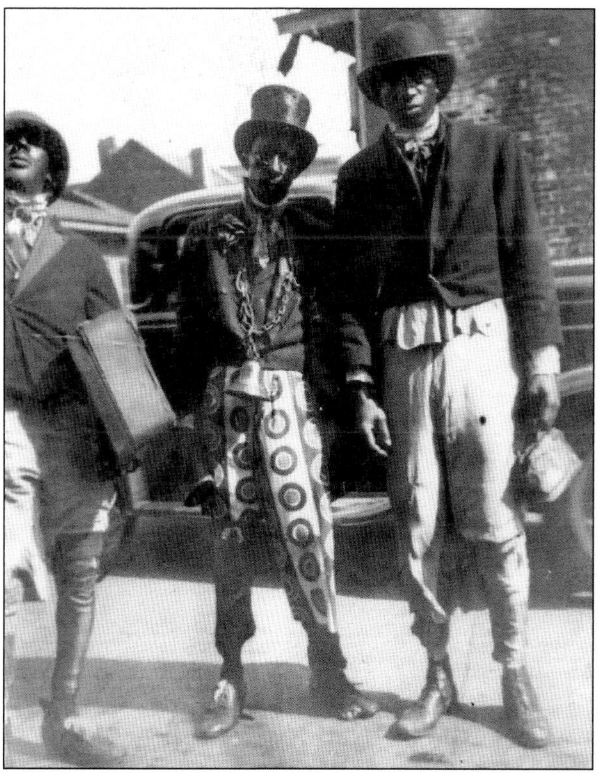

MARDI GRAS DAY. This image shows three men masking for carnival in the 1930s. (Courtesy of the State Library of Louisiana.)

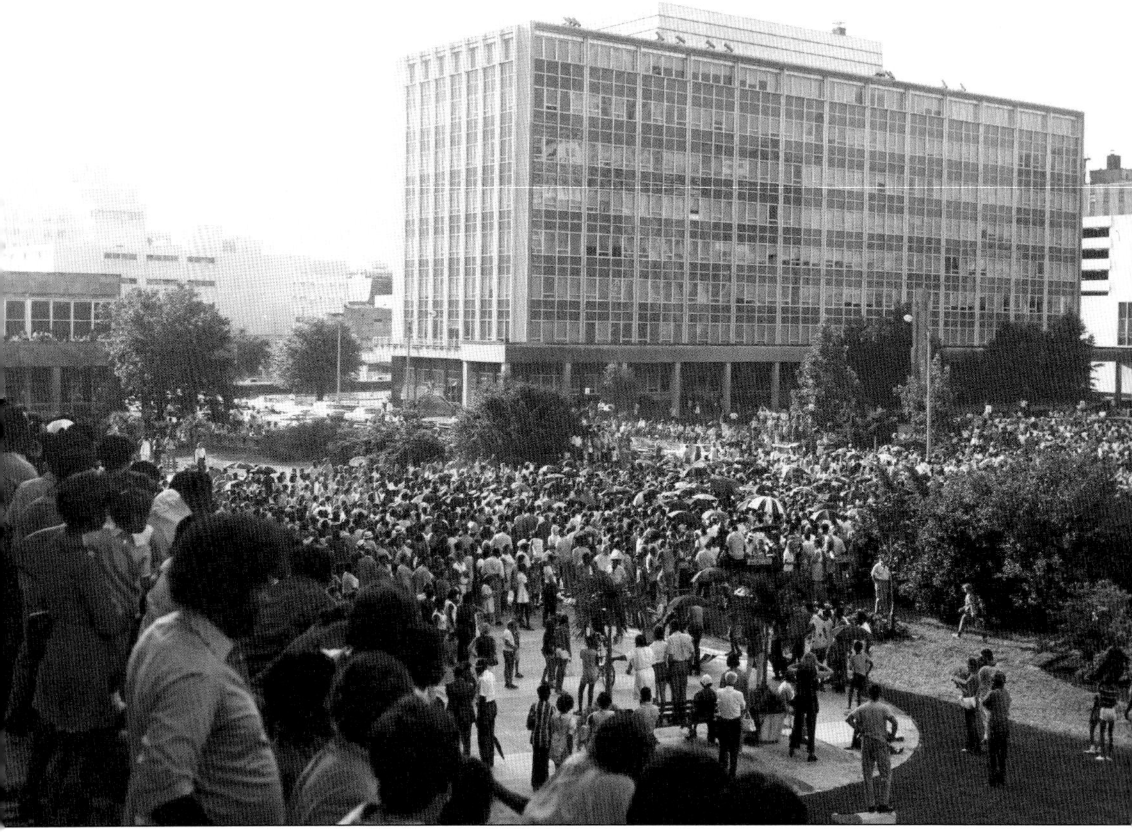

FAREWELL, LOUIS. This gathering honoring Louis Armstrong included what was arguably one of the largest second lines and the longest dirges—both of which are customary in any New Orleans jazz funeral—in the city's history. (Courtesy of the New Orleans Jazz Club/Louisiana State Museum.)

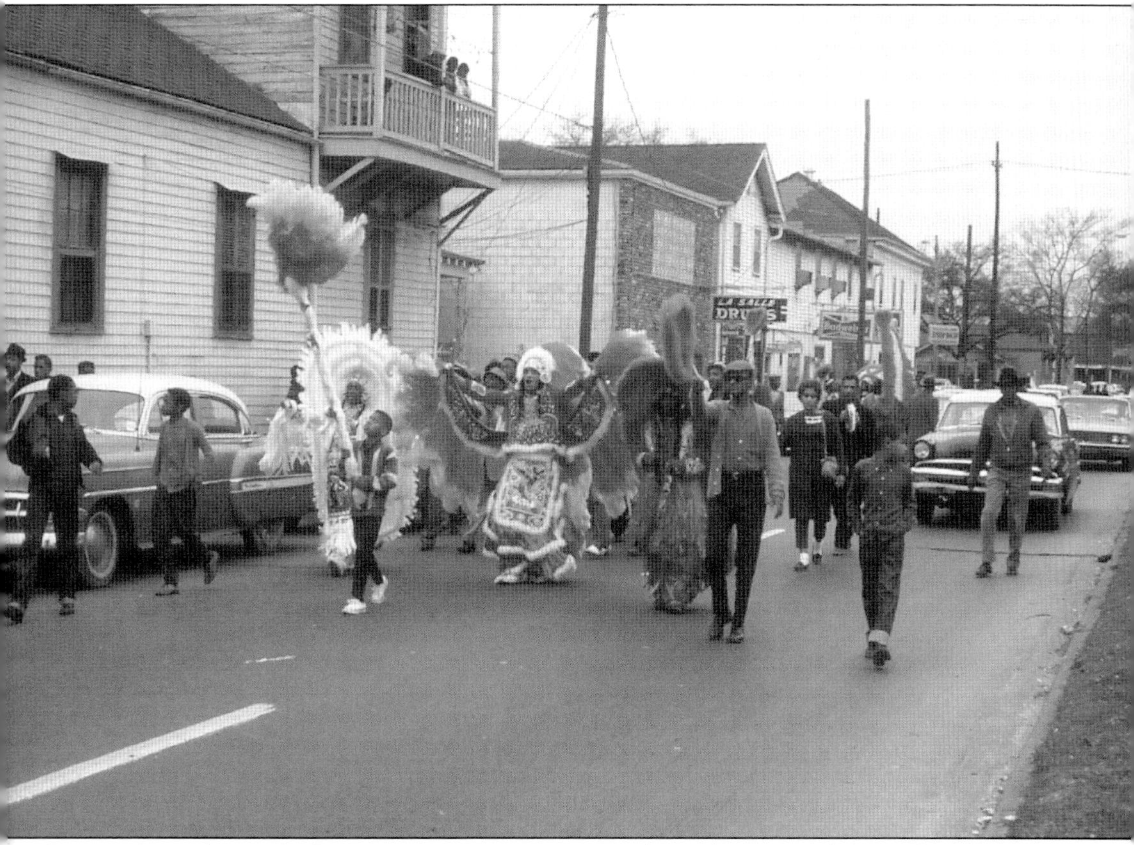

PRIDE. The tradition of African American men in New Orleans dressing in elaborate handmade costumes on Mardi Gras Day remains a favorite occurrence of locals and tourists alike. The outfits are reminiscent of North American Indian costumes and the beadwork of the Yoruba people of West Africa. It is with great pride that these men display their works of art. Shown here is a photograph of the Creole Wild West Mardi Gras Indian Tribe on Mardi Gras Day, taken by A. L. Schlesinger in the late 1950s. The Creole Wild West was formed in the late 1880s. (Courtesy of the Louisiana State Museum.)

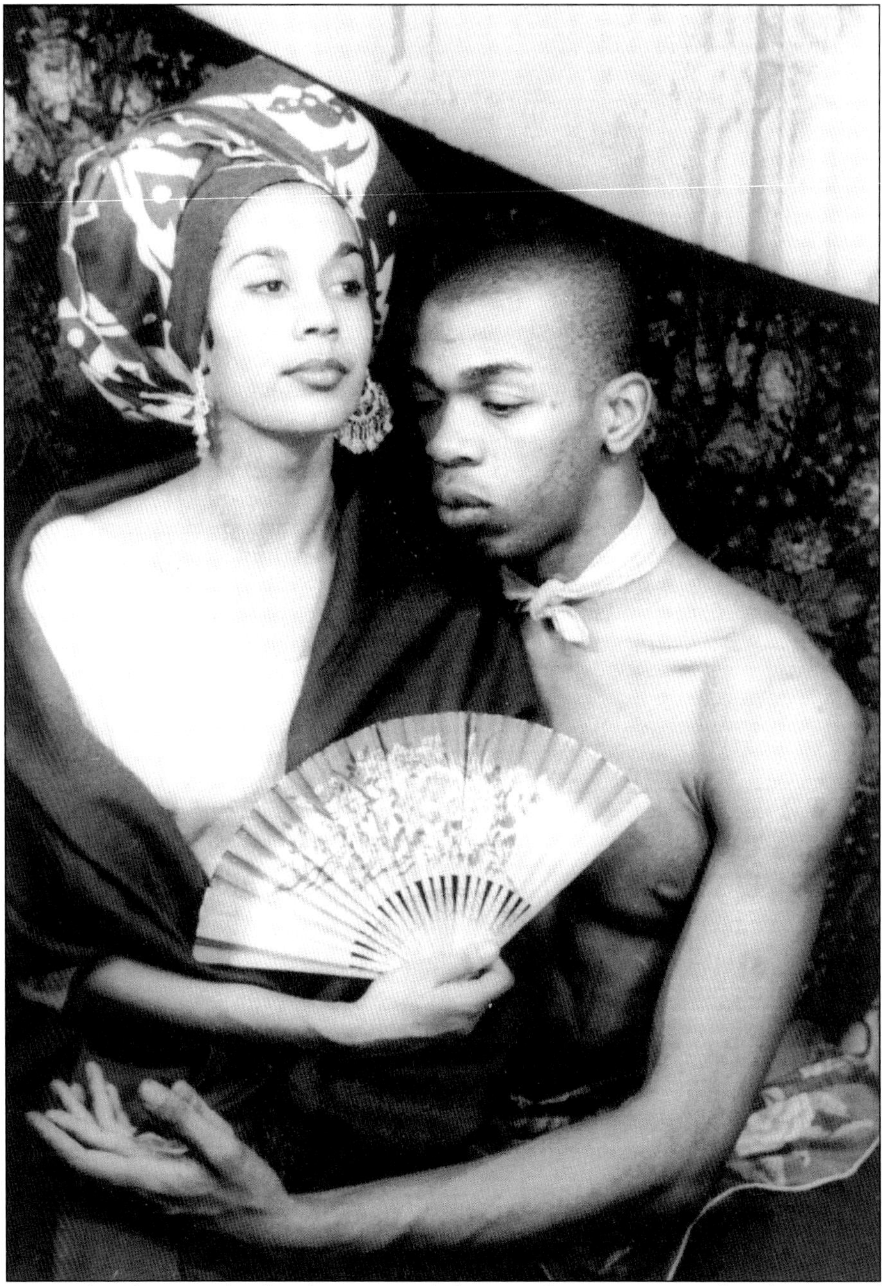

DANSEURS. This photograph taken by writer and photographer Car Van Vetchen (1880–1964) is of New Orleans native Carmen De Lavallade (1931–) and her husband, Geoffrey Holder (1930–). De Lavallade's family left New Orleans for Los Angeles, following a mass exodus of Louisiana natives to California during the 1940s and 1950s. De Lavallade studied dance under the direction of Lester Horton (1906–1953), and it was during this time that she met famed dancer and choreographer Alvin Ailey (1931–1989). De Lavallade met Holder during the production of Truman Capote's (1924–1984) *House of Flowers* in 1955. Capote was also a New Orleans native. Holder is quoted saying about his wife, "Oh God, every day I look at Carmen and I see a painting." (Courtesy of the Library of Congress.)

BIBLIOGRAPHY

Beauchamp-Byrd, Mora. *A Celebration of Faith.* New Orleans: New Orleans African American Museum of Art, Culture, and History (NOAAMACH), 2008.

Bennett, Lerome Jr. *Before the Mayflower: A History of Black America.* New York: Penguin, 1988.

Blassingame, John, *Black New Orleans 1860–1880.* Chicago: University of Chicago Press, 1973.

Cassimere, Raphael. *African Americans In New Orleans before The Civil War.* Unpublished research for the Jean Lafitte National Historical Park and Preserve, 1995.

Davis, Cyprian. *Herriette Delille: Servants of the Poor.* New Orleans: Archdiocese of New Orleans, 2004.

Deggs, Mary Bernard. *No Cross, No Crown: Black Nuns in Nineteenth-Century New Orleans.* Edited by Meacham Gould, Virginia Nolan, and Charles E. Bloomington. Illinois: Indiana University Press, 2001.

Desdune, Rodolphe. *Our History and Our People.* Translated by Sr. Dorothea Olga McCants. 1911 Reprint. Baton Rouge: Louisiana State University, 1973.

Faircloth, Adam. *Race and Democracy: Civil Rights Struggle in Louisiana 1915–1972.* Athens, GA: University of Georgia, *1995.*

Franklin, John Hope. *From Slavery to Freedom: A History of Negro Americans,* Fifth Edition. New York: Knopf, 1980.

Hall Midlo, Gwendolyn, *Africans in Colonial Louisiana.* Baton Rouge: Louisiana State University, 1992.

Hill, Lance. The Deacons for Defense; Armed Resistance and the Civil Rights Movement. Chapel Hill: University of North Carolina, 2004.

Hirsh Arnold R. and Logsdon, Joseph. *Creole New Orleans Race and Americanization.* Baton Rouge: Louisiana State University, 1992.

Medley, W. Kieth. *We As Freemen: Plessy v. Ferguson.* Gretna, LA: Pelican Publishing, 2003.

Rousseve, Charles Barthelemy. *The Negro in Louisiana.* 1937. Reprint, New York: Johnson, 1970.

Rouzan, Laura. *A Rhetorical Analysis of Editorials in* L'Union *and the* New Orleans Tribune. Florida State University: dissertation, 1989.

Wilds, Dufour, and Cowan. *Louisiana Yesterday and Today.* Baton Rouge: Louisiana State University, 1996.